Designing Defensible Classroom Programs for Gifted Secondary School Learners

A Handbook for Teachers

Sonia White

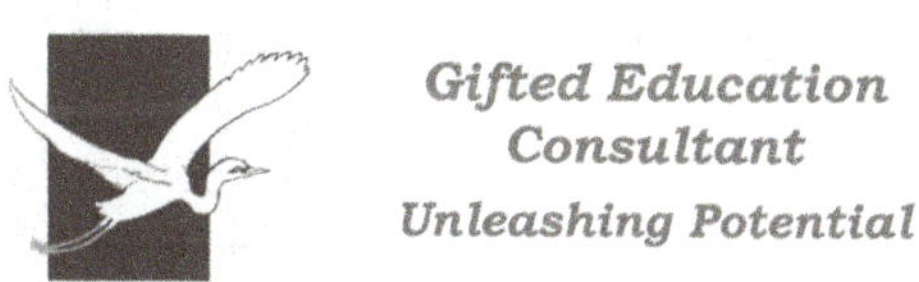

*Gifted Education
Consultant
Unleashing Potential*

Sonia White's Knowing Your Gifted Learner 1
Designing Defensible Classroom Programs for Gifted Secondary Learners
By Sonia White

ISBN 978-0-473-17517-7

Cover Art: *Pohutukawa.* © Sonia White

Pohutukawa trees are native to the New Zealand coast. In centuries past New Zealand's indigenous Māori people regarded the pohutukawa as one of the chiefly trees and individual ones were sacred. Pohutukawa are slow-growing trees which can become as old as 1000 years. They can withstand stormy winds and seaspray because their myriad of aerial roots cling to the cliffs as their wide branches arch outwards. This makes them ideal plants to colonise unstable ground, rock, and lava. Its stunning flowers, tenacity, strength and chiefly status are an apt analogy for qualities to which we hope our gifted learners can aspire.

Acknowledgements

Isaac Newton once said that we stand upon the shoulders of giants when we strive to achieve and whilst writing this book the debt I owe to others has been apparent to me. The field of gifted education is a specialised one, and there are many great names whose expertise and wisdom have fed my quest for knowledge and my passion for serving an oft-forgotten section of our student body.

The texts, charts and checklists, unless otherwise attributed, are all my own work, but the body of knowledge has come over many years from a range of experts whose work I hold in awe. Giants in the field such as Eddie Braggert, Nick Colangelo, Barbara Clark, Mihaly Csikszentmihalyi, Kazimierz Dabrowski, Edward De Bono, Jim Delisle, François Gagne, Miracca Gross, Sandra Kaplan, Mathew Lipman, June Maker, Michael Piechowski, Jane Piirto, Sally Reis, Joe Renzulli, Sylvia Rimm, Karen Rogers, Linda Silverman, Dorothy Sisk, Robert Sternberg, E. Paul Torrance, Don Treffinger, Joyce Van Tassel Baska, and many others will never know what a huge impact they have had upon this teacher from 'downunder' in New Zealand.

On a personal level, I would like to thank Professor Dr Karen Rogers for her generosity in allowing me to reproduce her "Ten Options"; Elaine Le Sueur for being a 'critical friend' and for the use of her adapted Blooms model concept and Tic Tac Toe Strategy; Tony Ryan for his kind permission to reproduce his "Thinker's Keys"; Elliot Aronson for the use of his Expert Jigsaw strategy; and Mariette Poortman, St Mary's College, Auckland for her collaboration on the Graduate Profile example.

As this book is the accumulation of many years' experience in teaching and learning, it is impossible to attribute all of the ideas and strategies that I have been practicing for many years. Many I have developed myself, or have picked up from colleagues along the way and further adapted. Whereever known, original authors have been attributed within the text.

And as for my wonderful family and invaluable dear friends and colleagues who have supported me throughout the writing of this book - you know who you are. Thank you for your faith in me.

Contents

Table of Figures

Introduction

May every student be blessed by a teacher
who inspires them to believe in themselves.
May every gifted student be blessed by a teacher
who challenges them to achieve
that to which they never dreamed they could aspire.

Gifted learners are not always easy to identify, particularly once they are in secondary school. Whilst some are high achieving academics, others become chameleons, and choose the easiest way through a subject that they aren't engaged in, disguising their abilities through work that is just good enough to get by, but far below the level of which they are capable. When students mask their potential it is a challenge for teachers to inspire a passion for learning.

However, a well-designed and well-executed unit of work can coax most reluctant gifted learners out of their safe hiding places and engage these students in stimulating, challenging learning. Most unit plans already have a sound foundation but teachers do not always have planned provision for gifted learners within those units. As a result extension for gifted or high potential students may be incidental, and reliant upon teacher instinct. While sometimes such instinct can be inspired, in the busy lives of teachers on-the-spot inspiration is no substitute for well-planned units.

What is a *'defensible'* classroom program for gifted learners? A program is defensible if it meets the pedagogical requirements that a learning program should meet. That is, gifted students' learning should:

- acknowledge prior knowledge and expertise in the area of talent,
- acknowledge the high potential which gifted learners bring to the classroom, such as speed of learning and capacity for complexity
- have learning goals that are commensurate with learner readiness
- reflect the recommendations of gifted literature and research, and
- be grounded in one or more models of differentiated learning for gifted.

This handbook is grounded in gifted education research and literature, and is the result of almost a decade of my facilitation of in-service teacher professional development as an advisor to schools and almost twenty years as a teacher specialist in gifted education in schools. I believe in the old adage that it is better to "teach a man to fish and feed him for a lifetime". Therefore, rather than supplying endless resources that may fit the needs of one classroom but not another, this handbook aims to give teachers confidence in creating and modifying their unit plans so they can meet the individual learning needs of the students in front of them. Although the internationally-respected New Zealand Curriculum also impacts upon my approach, I have been careful to keep examples general, rather than target the curriculum of any one country. I believe that by asking well-targeted reflective questions, teachers can apply answers appropriate to their own curriculum.

Using This Handbook

The handbook will assist teachers, departments or faculty groups, and school management to focus upon their planning and provisions for gifted learners in the redesign and delivery of their curriculum. It is based upon the premise that teachers and schools will already be doing some things well, and that within any group of teachers there will be a range of pedagogical and domain knowledge, from novice to expert. Therefore there are regular opportunities to measure current practice against best practice for gifted, and for teachers to ask: "What are we doing right?" "What's missing?" and "What can we do better?" Each section includes teacher reflection activities and checklists, so that reflective practice can be both planned and evaluated through a teacher inquiry method (Figure 1 page 4).

All teachers are teachers of gifted. Gifts emerge in a wide variety of talent areas, not only academic areas. Giftedness is a developmental process; secondary schools can be fertile grounds for learners to discover new areas of passion, interest and talent. Providing appropriate learning opportunities for gifted will raise student achievement. Gifted pedagogy has long been the cutting edge of teaching practice. In becoming an experienced practitioners in this field teachers become better teachers for all children.

Why invest so much time and effort into professional learning and pedagogical development?

This handbook has been created to support long term development of gifted pedagogy in a school. Why would or should school management and teachers take a long term approach to improving teaching and learning for a minority group of learners?

There is now a body of research around effective professional growth in teaching and learning. Teacher professional learning is not a one-stop, quick-fix scenario. It takes several years of ongoing professional learning and reflective practice to make a real difference for learners in the classroom. Creating change requires a long term commitment from school management.   Change management involves taking on board new behaviours, new practices, new understandings, and new beliefs. This cannot happen overnight. Schools need not only a vision to work towards, but also a focus upon capacity building[1]. It requires a

---

[1] Fullan, M. (2007).

         Designing Defensible Programs for Gifted Secondary School Learners © Sonia White 2011

cyclical process of new learning, reflection, discussion, innovation, trial, evaluation, and adaptation. It is successful with teachers who are resourceful, risk-taking, resilient, and collaborative.

Gifted Pedagogy brings added value to all classrooms

- Gifted pedagogy is good practice for all teachers. Not only will understanding best practice for gifted learners raise the bar for this group of learners, it will influence the way teachers facilitate learning for *all* students.

- Gifted pedagogy is not about an elite few. There are a far greater number of gifted students than many teachers realise. These often sit within the comfort zone of the main cohort, and underacheive for a variety of reasons. A focus upon identifying potential as well as high achievers, and upon providing an appropriate level of challenge can result in a real increase in student achievement.

- "A rising tide lifts all ships". As previously disengaged or underachieving students lift their sights and begin to achieve at a higher level, other students in the class respond.

- When teachers are well-equipped to provide for diverse learners in their classoom, and match learner readiness with the appropriate level of challenge in their subject area all students benefit with a better 'fit' for their learning.

There are some **key features in teacher professional development** which have often previously been ignored. These are:

Teacher commitment to

➢ trialling new methods, strategies & resources
➢ sharing their practice with colleagues in an environment of trust
➢ using *student voice* in the assessment of new methods, resources & strategies

Professional learning is most effective when:

✓ *it takes place within a professional learning group*
✓ *the group are committed to sharing their practice and supporting each other*
✓ *it is supported by school management with resourcing (time and expertise)*
✓ *there is a climate of mutual trust between the members of the group*
✓ *there is a mutually-held belief that student achievement can be raised*
  AND
✓ *the 'bottom line' is **evidence** that the changes are making a difference to students in the classroom.*

"Effective schools are ones in which principals and teachers focus on student learning outcomes and link this information to improvements in teaching and learning in strategies" (Fullan, 2007).

This process follows a **Teacher Inquiry Method** of professional learning and development described in Figure 1. It works best within a professional learning group that has informed professional leadership and a collective will to 'build knowledge through cumulative, reflective practice'[2].

Teacher Inquiry Process

When developing planning and classroom practice *assess what you already do well, and analyse which elements can be further developed.*

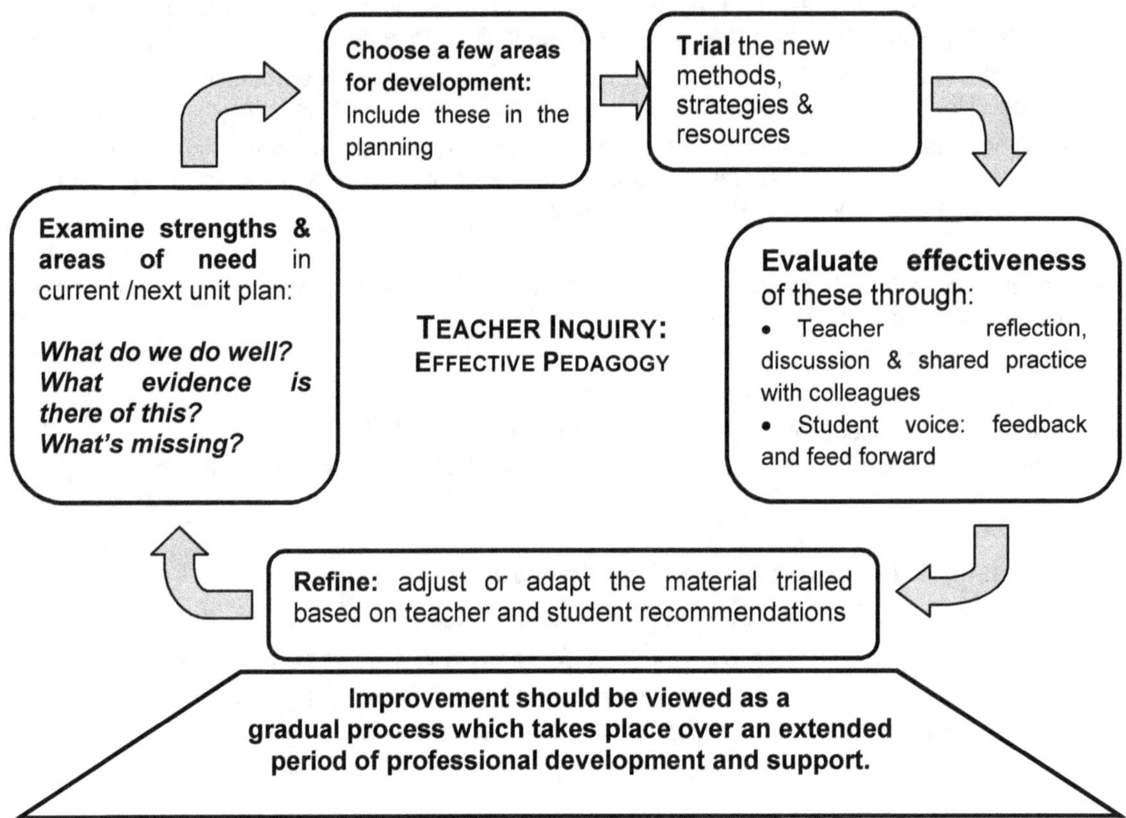

Figure 1 Teacher Inquiry Process

Because of the cyclical process described above, this handbook has pages and concepts that can be returned to again and again, as teachers return from trialling methods and content in their classroom, reflect upon their progress, and consider the next stages in the development of their practice.

---

[2] Fullan, M. (2007).

References and Readings

Fullan, M. (2007). Turnaround schools / Turnaround systems. Auckland, New Zealand: Michael Fullan: Education in Motion.

Fullan, M. (2007). Turnaround schools / Turnaround systems [Electronic Version]. Retrieved 3 October 2010 from http://www.michaelfullan.ca/resource_assets/Turnaround_Schools_Systems.pdf.

Ministry of Education New Zealand. (2007). Effective pedagogy. In *The New Zealand Curriculum: for English-medium teaching and learning in Years 1-13*. Wellington, NZ Learning Media Ltd.

Robinson, V., & Lai, M. K. (2006). *Practitioner research for educators; A guide to improving classrooms and schools*. CA: Corwin Press.

Chapter 1. Gifted Graduate Profiles

"You see things; and you say, "Why?"
I dream things that never were, and I say,
"Why not?"
George Bernard Shaw.

Why create a Graduate Profile?

When we focus upon making a difference for gifted learners, it pays to have a vision of what we are working towards. Time spent on this is worthwhile, as it highlights the end point towards which we are striving, and allows us to ponder upon how we are going to get there. It gives both teachers and students focus. A stated vision becomes a touchstone against which progress can be measured. It remains the constant as your team develop capacity both amongst yourselves as professionals and amongst your students as they grow.

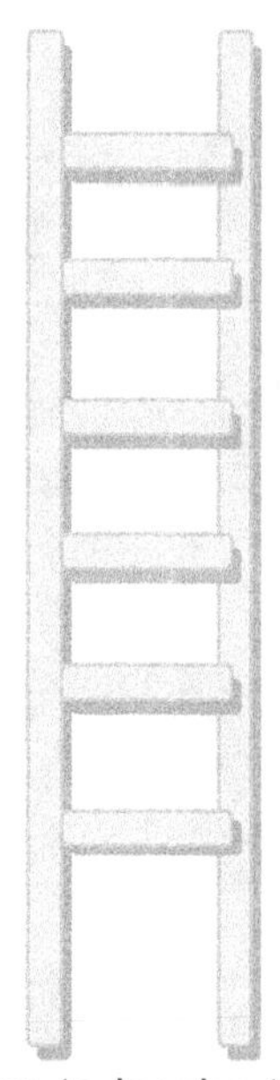

A point of challenge needs to be above a student's current level, but within achievable reach with application and scaffolding. Otherwise growth either remains static or the student is set up for failure.

Your vision for gifted learners becomes your professional learning group's "raison d'être". It underpins what you are doing, and why. An effective way of developing this vision is by creating a Graduate Profile. In doing this you consider the specific qualities that you would hope many students could aspire to, and that some will achieve.

Students are not at the same point in their stage of learning and in their social-emotional development at any specific age. However, if your graduate profile is something all students can achieve by the end of their last year at school, then it has not the depth and breadth to which your gifted students can aspire. It lacks the challenge they deserve.

Naturally, we would hope that all students can develop these characteristics eventually and a Graduate Profile does not diminish students who are not yet at this level of challenge. Rather, it may serve to inspire them. Students are on different rungs of the ladder at different times. They may be more adept in some areas than in others. Indeed, some students gifted in socio-affective areas may not yet have acquired the more academic characteristics. Some teenagers have wisdom beyond their years, and have learned behaviours that others of their chronological age have not yet developed. They may have insight beyond their years and a deep commitment to higher ideals, ethics and moral issues. They may be more deeply concerned with global issues and demonstrate a level of critical thinking and perception that their peers. The top rung on the ladder needs to be high. Like all learning, students need to be able to reach up and grasp the rung of the ladder that will challenge them. It must be within their grasp, not beyond it.

Gifted learners are as diverse and different from each other as they are from others. They will have strengths in some areas, but not in others. With guidance and support they can develop into the well-rounded individuals that your school envisages.

The Graduate Profile should be drafted, shared, adapted, refined, shared again, in a spirit of collaboration and ownership, with your whole school community.

Creating a 'Graduate Profile'

Aim: To establish a range of aspirational characteristics that students can develop by the time they graduate from your school.

What might our gifted graduates "look like"? Key Questions:

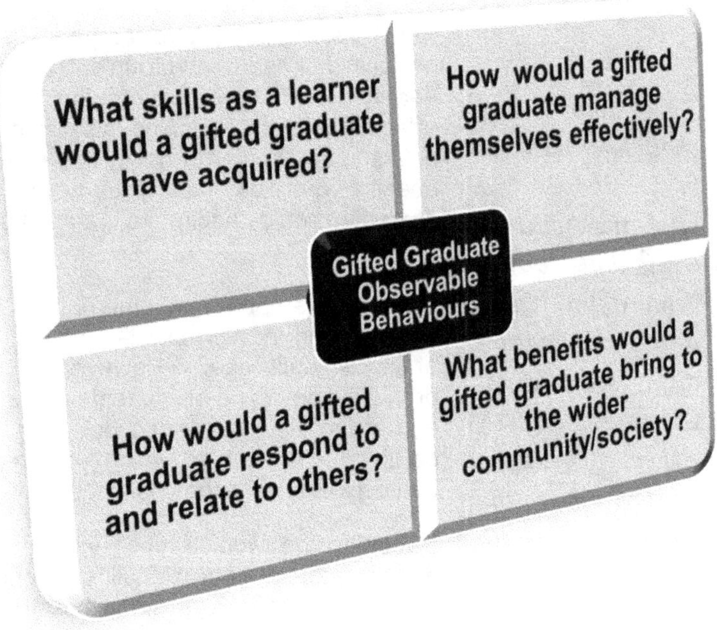

Figure 2 Key Questions for a Gifted Graduate Profile

   Designing Defensible Programs for Gifted Secondary School Learners © Sonia White 2011

The Graduate Student Profile	
Brainstorm a list of skills as a learner you would like to see in your gifted graduates	Gifted graduates can:
Brainstorm a list of self-management skills your gifted graduate should have acquired	Gifted graduates can:
Brainstorm a list of the skills a gifted graduate would demonstrate in responding to and relating to others	Gifted graduates can:
Brainstorm a list of the benefits a gifted graduate would bring to the wider community	Gifted graduates can:

Figure 3 Template for planning a student graduate profile

Note: *Your graduate profile should reflect your community's values. An example is provided overleaf, but your school community can take ownership of your own Graduate Profile by developing one that matches your school's philosophy and culture.*

Skills as a learner	Gifted graduates: • demonstrate intellectual curiosity, are innovative, reflective and can grapple with complex ideas • apply critical, creative and caring thinking at a sophisticated and complex level • reflect upon new knowledge, challenge assumptions and perceptions, question, make links, and create new knowledge and insight • are comfortable with, and fluent in domain specific language and consistently demonstrate this within the context of the domain • adapt readily to evolving communication tools and can utilise these confidently • can lead others to deeper understanding and insight, and can convince or persuade through selecting and applying appropriate communication tools and methods
Self-management skills	Gifted graduates: • know and understand themselves as gifted learners, recognising both strengths and areas of challenge • value excellence; aim high and persevere • have the resilience and the self-belief to be enterprising and resourceful • can self-assess, set and attain realistic personal and academic goals • have the self-confidence and wisdom to discern when to follow or when to take the lead or when to stand alone • has extensive skill sets that contribute to the successful completion of complex tasks and projects
Responding and relating to others	Gifted graduates: • can be sensitive to a diverse range of people in a variety of contexts, and respond with respect • can be tolerant of ambiguity and are flexible in their responses to situations • know when to lead and when to follow; when to compete and when to cooperate • lead effectively from the front or from behind in ways that support and promote others
Benefits to the wider community /society	Gifted graduates: • are driven by deeply held ethical and moral standards and have a confident voice; value equity, fairness, and social justice • are passionate, deeply sincere and strongly motivated to act in ways that will contribute towards making the world a better place • are sensitive to inconsistencies between ideals and behaviours and seek to redress the balance through positive action, alone or with others • are globally aware, and actively involved in making a difference in communities: local, national or global

Figure 4 Example of a Gifted Graduate Student Profile

---

[3] Inspired by: Ministry of Education, New Zealand (2007), (pp 10:13 Values & Key Competencies). Thanks to Mariette Poortman, St Mary's College, Auckland for her collaboration with this.

     Designing Defensible Programs for Gifted Secondary School Learners © Sonia White 2011

Using Your Graduate Profiles

You have a completed a **draft** Graduate Profile. What now?

1. Share your _DRAFT_ Gifted Graduate Profile with:

- other teachers in your department and school
- *your students!*

Have reflective dialogue around the qualities listed.

Ask for criticism.
What would they change?
What would they add?
Remove?

Create your final draft.

Share it with your school community.

2. Refer to the Graduate profile when assessing your program / your department's provisions. (Especially in later chapters of this handbook)

What opportunities are there for these qualities to be developed or further enhanced?

What needs to be added?

Modified?

Further developed?

Use the Graduate profile with students. Because they have had input into it, they will be likely to take ownership of it. Ask them to choose one goal from each area to work on developing. Encourage their development of self-knowledge, self acceptance, and personal goal setting.

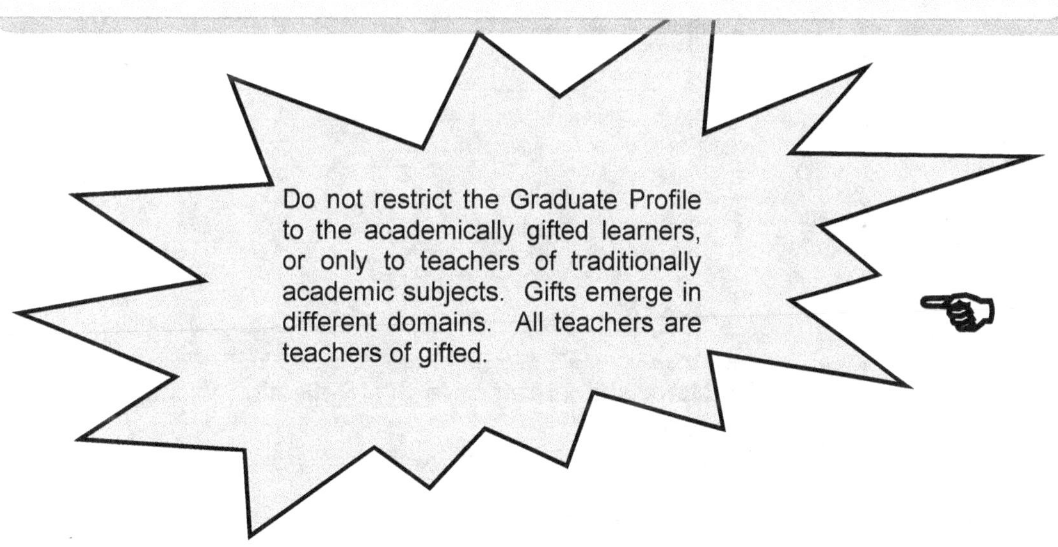

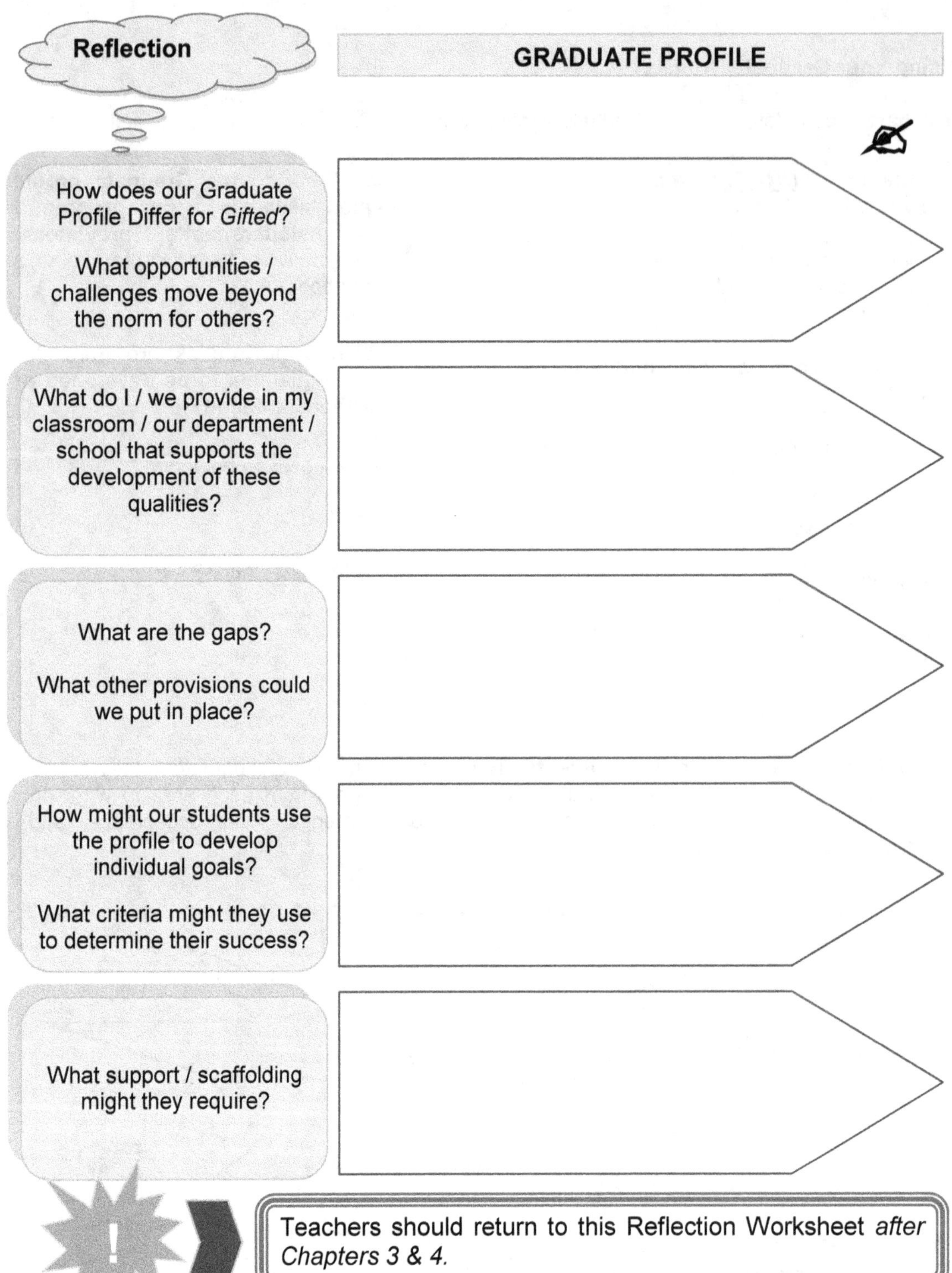

Figure 5 Teacher Reflection: Graduate Profile

References

Ministry of Education New Zealand. (2007). *The New Zealand Curriculum: for English-medium teaching and learning in years 1-13*. Wellington, NZ: Learning Media Ltd.

Chapter 2: Characteristics of Gifted Learners

"Diversity makes for a rich tapestry,
and we must understand that
all the threads of the tapestry are equal in value
no matter what their colour"
~ Maya Angelou.

Gifted learners are diverse in their characteristics, and are unique as individuals. Several areas are particularly important when planning programs to hook a gifted learner into learning.

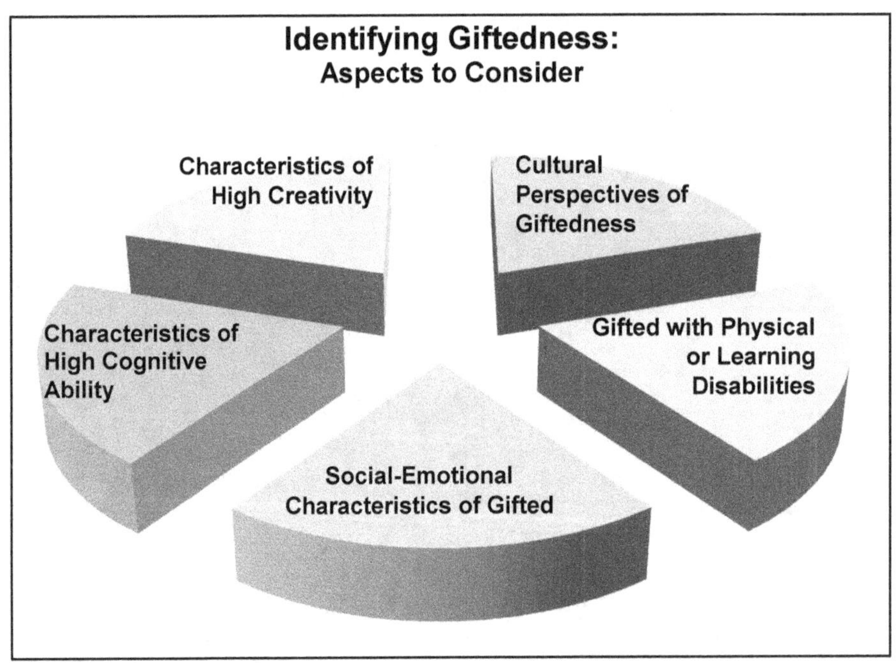

Figure 6 Aspects to consider when identifying giftedness

2. Identifying High Achievers and Hidden Gifted in Your Classroom

Obviously there are standardised tests and educational assessments by psychologists which can be used to ascertain high potential. They are valid in assessing specific areas of ability, but all have limitations. Teachers should not solely rely on school test scores in identifying learner potential. This chapter will explain why.

Too often teachers rely only on finished products and grades to identify gifted learners in their classrooms. Sometimes this works well enough for gifted high achievers, but it does nothing to identify those with high potential who are not yet achieving highly or who choose the disguise their giftedness. Tests and grades are also only useful if gifted students are able to demonstrate knowledge and skills *beyond* the level of their peers – in other words, to demonstrate exactly where their learning readiness level is.

While gifted are diversely different from each other, and are unique, there are specific behavioural characteristics that we can look for. These are not always positive, and neither are they always easily observed.

The classroom conditions need to be right for the positive behaviours to be demonstrated. If, for example, a gifted learner is able to understand abstract ideas and complex concepts, but the classroom program does not require complexity or abstract thinking, then it is highly unlikely a teacher will witness a student's ability to understand at a sophisticated level. Similarly if complexity and abstract thinking is only present at a level at which all students can achieve, then very high ability is unlikely to be demonstrated. Where conditions for learning don't match student ability, negative traits may well emerge in all but the most compliant of gifted learners.

Stephanie Tolan[4] gives a wonderful analogy of cheetahs and gifted learners. A cheetah can run at 70 mph, but *only* when it is chasing antelopes. If a cheetah only has 20 mph rabbits to chase, it will only be observed running at 20 mph. Similarly the gifted student needs the right classroom conditions to demonstrate their potential.

Therefore one of the most valuable identification tools is *informed* teacher observation in a classroom where the right challenges and learning opportunities are being presented.

❯	Use the charts on the following pages to consider who amongst your students may have gifted potential. Then use the teacher reflection tools to consider what strategies you might trial for students exhibiting both the positive and negative behaviours.

❯	Do not use these as a 'one time only' resource. Giftedness is a developmental process – it develops over time, and with new experiences. Revisit the checklists at regular intervals and ponder other possible candidates as they emerge.

---

[4] Tolan, S. S., (1996)

2.1 Cognitive Characteristics

Compared to others of similar age, background, experience and culture, students with **high cognitive ability** may differ from their peers in many of the following ways:

- the pace or speed with which they learn new concepts and master new skills
- ability to understand complex concepts, abstract ideas
- ability to see patterns & relationships, and make links to other areas of learning
- high level of competency in problem solving & *problem finding*
- ability to see and understand the 'big picture' (gestalt thinking)
- real enjoyment of intellectual challenge
- natural enquiring mind - *wants to know*
- learns in 'big gulps' – not necessarily in a step by step (linear) process
- works things out for themselves – often by 'working backwards'
- can be independently enquiring: reshaping information to redefine problems, posing questions, formulating hypotheses, investigating, drawing and defending conclusions

These characteristics will not be observable unless there is opportunity in the classroom to display them. For example, students need:

 opportunities to learn content and skills at a faster pace;

 real intellectual challenge in their daily classroom learning;

 tasks that involve complex and abstract thinking;

 opportunities to understand the 'big picture' before diving into the detail of a topic; and

 opportunities to investigate an area of a topic in-depth, to pose and formulate their own hypotheses, and to consider conflicting evidence and opinions.

On the other hand, when gifted learners are faced with an inappropriate curriculum, **negative characteristics of high cognitive ability** *may be displayed.*

Gifted learners with high cognitive ability may also:
- be easily bored, & resist drill and repetition
- monopolise conversations, dominate class discussions (because of their knowledge)
- show off, brag, be egotistical or impatient with others & evoke peer resentment
- neglect other responsibilities; be non-productive, or do 'just enough'
- be overly critical or dogmatic in social situations & may correct other students and adults

Figure 7 Cognitive Characteristics and Behaviours of Gifted Learners

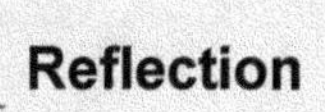

Consider both the negative and positive characteristics!
Seek potential in the negative behaviours, and look for
ways of challenging and engaging that potential.

High Cognitive Ability: Teacher Reflection Tool	
Who?	**Strategy**
Which students in my class demonstrate some of the positive high cognitive characteristics? (List below)	Which strategy or strategies might I consider that I do not already apply?*
How will I know if I'm successful? What evidence will I look for?	
Who?	**Strategy**
Which students in my class demonstrate some of the negative cognitive characteristics? (List below)	Which strategy or strategies might I consider that I do not already apply?*
How will I know if I'm successful? What evidence will I look for?	
*Consider strategies from following Chapters as well as the previous page	

Figure 8 High Cognitive Ability: Teacher Reflection Tool

2.2 Creative Characteristics

Compared to others of similar age, background, experience and culture, a student with high **creative ability** may differ from their peers in many of the following:

- is highly imaginative and intellectually playful
- fantasises; enjoys imagining the absurd without fear of being 'wrong'
- has a keen sense of humour; can laugh at oneself
- has an advanced level of curiosity; is questioning
- can come out of 'left field' with unusual insights
- is not afraid to be different
- is aware of aesthetics
- ability to generate a large number of ideas quickly (fluency)
- ability to generate different types of ideas quickly (flexibility)
- ability to generate original ideas or inventions (originality)
- ability to elaborate on their ideas: add quality detail, give substance to (elaboration)

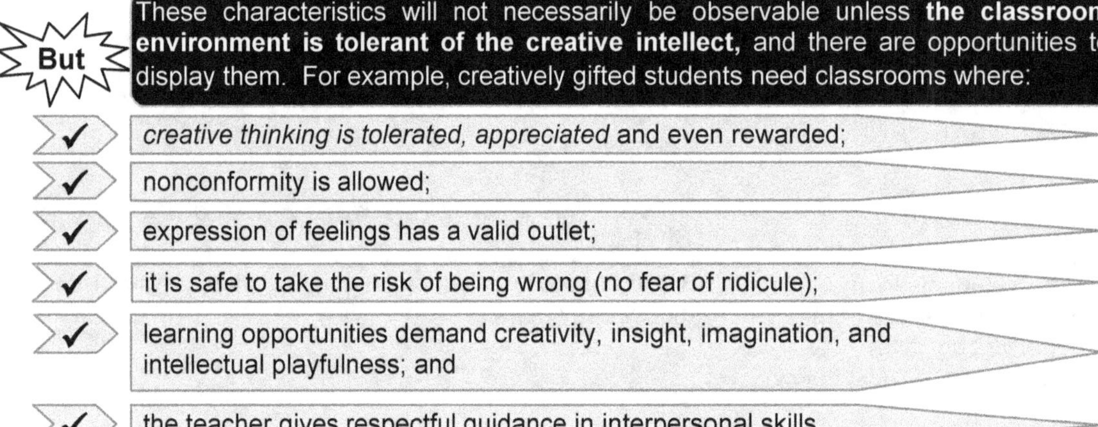

*On the other hand, when creatively gifted learners are faced with an inappropriate curriculum, **negative characteristics of high creativity** may be displayed.*

Gifted learners with high creativity may also:
- be bored, frustrated, challenging of rules, rebellious and defensive
- be highly sensitive, and more vulnerable than others (may drop out).
- have poor self-control, be in conflict with peers, engage in power struggles
- go off on tangents, with little follow-through
- play tricks or make jokes at others' expense; may use humour to control others
- May be constantly inattentive and off-task

Figure 9 Creative Characteristics and Behaviours of Gifted Learners

     Designing Defensible Programs for Gifted Secondary School Learners © Sonia White 2011

High Creative Ability: Teacher Reflection Tool	
Who?	**Strategy**
Which students in my class demonstrate some of the positive high creative characteristics? (List below)	Which strategy or strategies might I consider that I do not already apply?*
How will I know if I'm successful? What evidence will I look for?	
Who?	**Strategy**
Which students in my class demonstrate some of the negative creative characteristics? (List below)	Which strategy or strategies might I consider that I do not already apply?*
How will I know if I'm successful? What evidence will I look for?	
*Consider strategies from following Chapters as well as the previous page	

Figure 10 High Creative Ability: Teacher Reflection Tool

2.3 Social-Emotional Characteristics

Compared to others of similar age, background, experience and culture, a gifted student may differ from their peers in some or many of the following **social-emotional** behaviours. They may:

- be highly idealistic, with strong personal values and standards
- have advanced moral judgement
- be intensely sensitive and have emotional depth
- have a deep appreciation of aesthetics and value abstract qualities
- have a deep concern for humanity and global issues
- be passionately committed to service projects
- be unusually sensitive to the feelings of others
- be deeply reflective
- be intrinsically motivated and strive for high standards
- be self-confident, self-accepting, self-directed, independent
- be adaptable and flexible and can tolerate ambiguity
- show initiative
- inspire others to work towards a common goal
- be persuasive; convince others to follow
- be socially mature

But *These characteristics may not be observable unless* there is opportunity in the classroom and in wider school life to display them. For example, gifted learners need:

✓ authentic learning situations that capitalise on interests and talents

✓ exposure to moral & ethical issues, rights, justice, global issues

✓ assistance in developing tools for autonomous learning

✓ learning experiences that provide a platform for personal growth and self-understanding

✓ opportunities to exercise social responsibility & participate actively in making a difference to others

✓ exposure to career pathways and opportunities in their areas of talent

Gifted learners may also disguise their giftedness or have negative behaviours. For example they may:

- be underachieving, deny talent or prefer the anonymity of "pass" grades
- question authority, be disruptive, non-conforming
- fear failure, procrastinate, and/or underperform because of unhealthy perfectionism
- be impulsive, thrill-seeking (or conversely, be risk-averse)
- lack intrinsic motivation and only perform for the approval of others
- choose activities they can safely succeed in; resist challenge
- be cynical or anti-social, influencing others negatively;
- be ruthlessly self-critical or harshly critical of others (unhealthy perfectionism)

Figure 11 Social - Emotional Characteristics and Behaviours of Gifted

 Designing Defensible Programs for Gifted Secondary School Learners © Sonia White 2011

Consider the social – emotional characteristics of many gifted learners, and how these may best be catered for in your classroom.

Social Emotional Characteristics: Teacher Reflection Tool	
Who?	**Strategy**
Which students in my class demonstrate some of the positive high social emotional characteristics? (List below)	Which strategy or strategies might I consider that I do not already apply?*
How will I know if I'm successful? What evidence will I look for?	
Who?	**Strategy**
Which students in my class demonstrate some of the negative social emotional characteristics? (List below)	Which strategy or strategies might I consider that I do not already apply?*
How will I know if I'm successful? What evidence will I look for?	
*Consider strategies from following Chapters as well as the previous page	

Figure 12 Social-Emotional Characteristics of Gifted: Teacher Reflection Tool

2.4 Other 'Hidden' Gifted Underachievers

As well as those already described whose giftedness may be masked or misinterpreted, there are other groups at risk of non-identification. These include:

2.4.1 Gifted Minority Groups & Lower Socio-Economic Groups
- Those whose culture is not the dominant culture in the country. This includes indigenous peoples such as Native Americans, Aboriginal Peoples, New Zealand Māori, and others.
- Those whose first language is not English (or is not the dominant language of the country). Variously referred to as ESOL, ESL, or EFL students.

Such students are at risk of non-identification because they may not perform highly in standardised testing with a cultural /language bias. Nevertheless, there will be gifted students among this cohort.
- Giftedness is not limited to dominant cultures or defined by wealth.

Figure 13 Identifying Gifted Minority Group and Lower Socio-Economic Group Students

     Designing Defensible Programs for Gifted Secondary School Learners © Sonia White 2011

2.4.2 Cultural Perspectives of Giftedness

All cultures value knowledge and learning. However, cultural perspectives of giftedness vary, and ways in which valued strengths are demonstrated can differ. This section highlights a few of the differences in the hope of inspiring school management to 'dive deeper' into community partnership in identifying and providing for its gifted and talented students from minority groups.

The most powerful motivating factor for minority ethnic group students is when schools and teachers appreciate the cultural perspectives of minority cultures within their student body. Feeling accepted and valued for the richness their cultural background brings a sense of belonging, and benefits the students and to the whole school community[5].

Identifying giftedness from other cultural perspectives is perhaps the most challenging aspect that schools with minority groups face. Cultural perspectives can only be understood from within that culture, so it behoves us as educators to consult with our cultural communities, asking *them* for the answers in defining and identifying giftedness.

Three examples are given here to illustrate the point: Cultural perspectives of 'spiritual' giftedness, leadership and cultural knowledge and skills. These examples are deliberately described in broad brush strokes, because this handbook is intended to have international relevance, and communities really need to have these discussions themselves.

Spirituality

Many cultures view spiritual values as a high priority, yet the ways in which those spiritual values are demonstrated in one culture may be quite different from another culture. It is a mistake to assume that behaviours demonstrating deep spirituality will 'look' the same as, for example, traditional Christian perspectives. Even if the same descriptive words are used, the meaning and interpretation will be culturally different.

---

[5] Bishop, R., Berryman, M., Tiakiwai, S., Richardson, C., (2003).

Depending upon the cultural lens through which they are viewed, leadership qualities can be quite different. Some cultures place high importance upon leading from "out front", while others value the leader who can inspire and lead from 'behind the scenes'. Some cultures value inherited leadership while others value the confidence shown by those who step forward voluntarily to lead. Other cultures would find it inappropriate for an individual to thrust themselves forward for leadership. In these instances, group honour and respect for an individual means the group nominates the leader. Such honour cannot be assumed, only given by others.

The behaviours that are valued for gifted leadership, therefore, will differ according to cultural expectations. Needless to say, all perspectives have validity.

Many minority cultures place high value upon fluency in their language, along with their cultural heritage in all its forms. Students and adults who are outstanding among their cultural peers in these areas are prized and recognised. This is not an area that the school can readily identify, and yet it has huge implications for the potential of the student. Such students, whose second language is the language of the dominant culture, can often remain severely undervalued, or worse, unrecognised. This underscores the value in consulting school cultural communities to identify giftedness in this area.

Finally, teachers should be aware that specific types of culturally prescribed behavior can disguise ability. For example, the student who is taught at home never to question the authority of the teacher is unlikely ever to ask provocative questions or push themselves or their opinions forward. These students are especially at risk of non-identification as they may instinctively shrink into the background rather than 'show disrespect'.

Further reading on this important topic is listed at the end of the chapter.

2.4.3 Gifted with Physical or Learning Disabilities

Gifted students with physical disabilities such as hearing, sight impairment, dyspraxia and other physical disabilities are at high risk of non-identification. Similarly, there are quite a number of gifted students whose learning is frustrated by an unidentified learning disability. Such students may have difficulty getting their work down on paper even though they demonstrate a high level of knowledge verbally. They often perform badly in timed test situations (though they may do well in multiple choice options and better in untimed test situations). The profiles of gifted with learning disabilities (GLD) are diverse, and professional diagnosis is important.

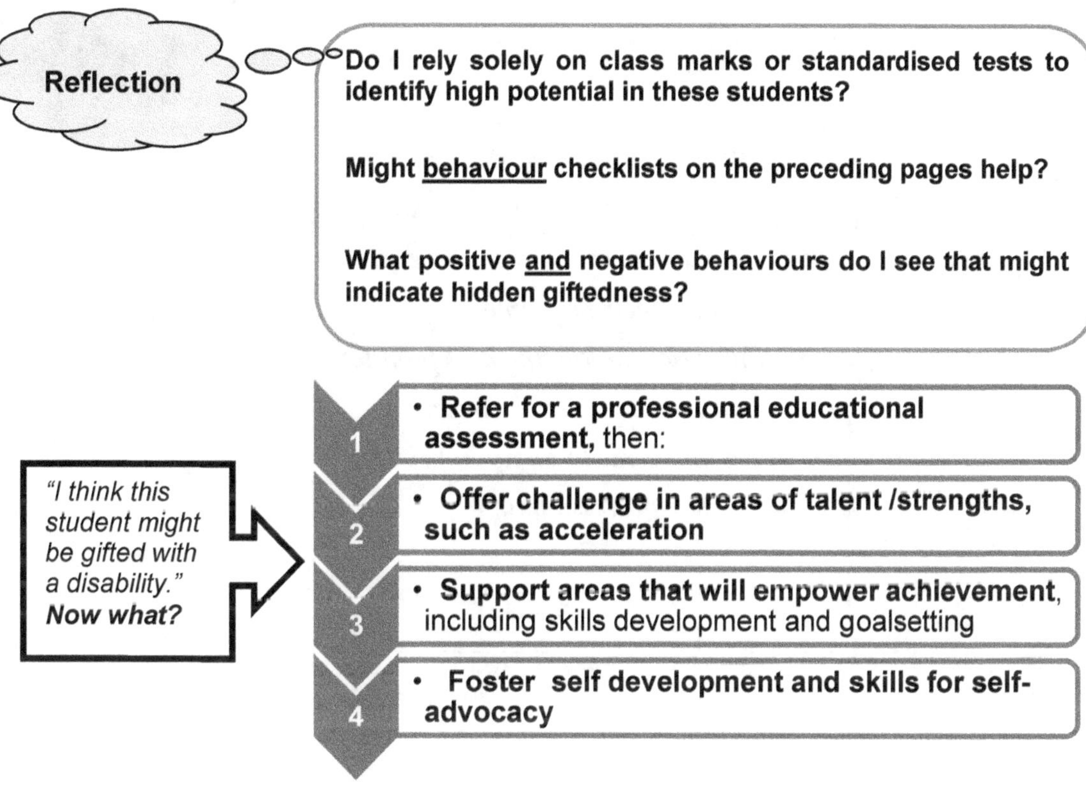

Figure 14 Identifying and Empowering Gifted with Disabilities

There is a wealth of important information surrounding un-identified GLD or 2E (twice exceptional) as they are often called. Significant literature and recommended readings in this area are listed at the end of this chapter.

*Real progress can be made
when teachers notice a discrepancy
between a student's verbal potential
and their performance
in information processing and product,
then act upon their concern
with a referral to an appropriate
professional.*

TEACHER LEARNING MAP:
Characteristics of Gifted Learners

What I know	What I thought I didn't know BUT I do!
What I thought I knew BUT I don't	What I didn't know I didn't know!

What I would now like to know more about

What I deny or refuse to look at:

Fill in first box before beginning the chapter, and the remaining boxes subsequent to reading and discussion.

Figure 15 Teacher Learning Map Template: Characteristics of Gifted Learners

NOTES:

References and Readings

Baum, S., & Owen, S. V. (2004). *To be gifted & learning disabled: Strategies for helping bright students with LD, ADHD and more.* Mansfield Center, CT: Creative Learning Press Inc.

Bevan-Brown, J. (2004). Gifted and talented Maori learners. In D. McAlpine & R. Moltzen (Eds.), *Gifted and talented: New Zealand perspectives* (2nd ed., pp. 171-198). Palmerston North: Kanuka Grove Press.

Bishop, R., Berryman, M., Tiakiwai, S., & Richardson, C. (2003). *Te Kotahitanga: The experiences of Year 9 & 10 Maori Students in mainstream classrooms.* Report to the Ministry of Education. Wellington, NZ: New Zealand Ministry of Education.

Clark, B. (2002). *Growing up gifted: developing the potential of children at home and at school*   (5th ed.). Columbus, OH: Charles E. Merrill Publishing Co.

Csikszentmihályi, M., Rathunde, K., & Whalen, S. (1997). *Talented teenagers: the roots of success and failure.* USA: Cambridge University Press.

Dabrowski, K. (1979). *Theory of levels of emotional development.* Oceanside, NY: Dabor Science Publications.

Davis, G. A., & Rimm, S. B. (2003). *Education of the Gifted and Talented* (5th ed.). Needham Heights, MA: Allyn and Bacon, Inc.

Delisle, J. R., & Galbraith, J. (2002). *When gifted kids don't have all the answers: how to meet their social and emotional needs.* Minneapolis: Free Spirit Publishing Inc.

Department for Education and Children's Services, S. A. (1997). *Thinking, feeling and learning.* South Australia: Department for Education and Children's Services.

Department of Education Western Australia. (2001). Gifted and talented - gifted underachievers. from http://www.eddept.wa.edu.au/centoff/gifttal/giftsund.htm

Dixon, F. A., & Moon, S. M. (Eds.). (2006). *The handbook of secondary gifted education.* Waco, Texas: Prufrock Press.

Fisher, G., & Cummings, R. (1990). *The survival guide for kids with LD.* Australia: Hawker Brownlow Education.

Galbraith, J., & Delisle, J. (1996). *The gifted kid's survival guide: a teen handbook.* Minneapolis: Free Spirit Publishing Inc.

Goleman, D. (1999). *Working with emotional intelligence.* Great Britain: Bloomsbury

Gross, M., Macleod, B., & Pretorius, M. (2001). *Gifted students in secondary schools: differentiating the curriculum* (2nd ed.). Sydney: Gifted Education Research, Resource and information Centre (GERRIC), UNSW.

Heacox, D. (1991). *Up from underachievement.* Australia: Hawker Brownlow Education.

Hebert, T., P. , & Reis, S., M. (1999, Nov). Culturally diverse high-achieving students in an urban high school. *Urban Education, 34,* 428-457.

Hebert, T. P. (2001). "If I had a new notebook, I know things would change": Bright underachieving young men in urban classrooms. *Gifted Child Quarterly, 45*(3), 174-194.

Kaplan, S. N., Henderson, C. E., Henderson, J., & Fleming, D. L. (2002). Socioemotional factors contributing to adjustment among early-entrance college students. *Gifted Child Quarterly, 46*(2), 124-134.

Lovecky, D. (1998). Spiritual sensitivity in gifted children. *Roeper Review, 20*(3), 178.

Lovecky, D. (1992). Exploring social and emotional aspects of giftedness in children. *Roeper Review, 15*(1), 18-25.

McAlpine, D. M., & Reid, N. A. (1996). *Teacher observation scales for children with special abilities*: ERDC, Massey University and NZCER, Wellington.

Macfarlane, A. (Ed.). (2010). *Above the Clouds: Ka rewa ake ki ngā kapua. A collection of readings for identifying and nurturing Māori students of promise* Christchurch: Te Waipounamu Focus Group, University of Canterbury.

McKenzie, J. (2001). Maori children with special abilities: taking a broader perspective. *NZ Principal, June*, 8-10.

Mendaglio, S. (1993). Chapter 6. Counseling gifted learning disabled: individual and group counselling techniques. In L. K. Silverman (Ed.), *Counseling the gifted and talented*. USA: Love Publishing Company.

Miller, N. B., Silverman, L. K., & Falk, R. F. (1994). Emotional development, intellectual ability, and gender. *Journal for the Education of the Gifted, 18*, 20-38.

Moltzen, R., & Macfarlane, A. (2006). Culturally gifted and talented in Aotearoa New Zealand. In Belle Wallace & Gillian Eriksson, *Diversity in gifted education: International perspectives on global issues*. New York: Routledge

Moltzen, R. I. (2004). Characteristics of gifted children. In D. McAlpine & R. Moltzen (Eds.), *Gifted & talented: New Zealand Perspectives* (2nd ed.). Palmerston North, New Zealand: Kanuka Grove Press.

Montgomery, D. (Ed.). (2003). *Gifted & talented children with special educational needs: Double exceptionality*. London: David Fulton Publishers.

Piechowski, M. (1997). Emotional giftedness: the measure of intrapersonal intelligence. In C. Nicholas & G. A. Davis (Eds.), *Handbook of gifted education* (2nd ed., pp. 366-381). USA: Allyn & Bacon.

Piechowski, M. (2006). *"Mellow out" They say. If only I could: Intensities and sensitivities of the young and bright*. Madison WI: Yunasa Books.

Piirto, J. (1999). *Talented children and adults: their development and education* (2nd ed.). Upper Saddle River, New Jersey: Prentice-Hall.

Renzulli, J., Smith, L. H., White, A. J., Callahan, C. M., & Hartman, R. K. (1994). Rating scale for the identification of superior students. Australia: Hawker Brownlow Publication.

Rimm, S. B. (2008). Why Bright Kids Get Poor Grades And What You Can Do About It (3rd ed.). Scottsdale, AZ: Great Potential Press.

Silverman, L. K. (2002). *Upside-down brilliance: The visual-spatial learner*. Denver, Colorado: DeLeon Publishing.

Silverman, L. K. (Ed.). (1993). *Counseling the gifted and talented*. USA: Love Publishing Company.

Sisk, D. A. (2009). *Making great kids greater: easing the burden of being gifted*. Thousand Oaks, CA: Corwin Press Inc.

Sternberg, R. J. (2002). Cultural explorations of human intelligence around the world. . In W. J. Lonner, D. L. Dinnel, S. A. Hayes & D. N. Sattler (Eds.), *Online Readings in Psychology and Culture (Unit 5, Chapter 1),* : Center for Cross-Cultural Research, Western Washington University, Bellingham, Washington USA. Available online from http://www.wwu.edu/~culture.

Tolan, S. S. (1996). Is it a cheetah? [Electronic Version]. Retrieved 23 Feb 2002 from http://www.stephanietolan.com/is_it_a_cheetah.htm.

Treffinger, D. (1995). *Creativity, creative thinking, and critical thinking: in search of definitions*. Saratosa: Center for Creative Learning.

White, S. (2007). The link between perfectionism and overexcitabilities. *Gifted and talented International: The Journal of the World Council for Gifted & Talented Children, 22*(1).

Winner, E. (1996). *Gifted children: myths and realities*. NY: Basic Books.

Chapter 3: Curriculum Delivery & Classroom Practice

On the mountains of truth you can never climb in vain:
either you will reach a point higher up today,
or you will be training your powers so that you will be able
to climb higher tomorrow
- Frederick Nietzsche.

Teachers and school management can sometimes make assumptions about gifted learners based upon their own experiences, historical philosophies and status quo. While this is understandable, when educational philosophy dictates what can and cannot be practiced for specific groups of learners it is important that such ideology is supported by, and defensible against current research. In the case of gifted learners, a good deal of misinformation exists which is neither supported nor advocated by research.

This chapter presents issues faced by gifted learners in the classroom as well as significant metadata analysis by Professor Dr. Karen B. Rogers and her subsequent recommended *"Ten gifted options that produce the greatest effect for gifted learners for the least effort"*. When teachers are familiar with both the common issues faced by gifted learners in their classrooms, and Rogers' recommendations from the research, they are well-placed to make a real difference to the learning of this group of students.

3.1 Gifted Learners Voice: Gifted Research and Literature

When asked, gifted students are very clear about the barriers and enablers they face in the classroom. In this author's own research and in the literature, common themes seem to occur regardless of ethnicity, socio-economic background or gender.

The best way to test this out is to ask your own gifted students! Ask them "What do teachers do that supports your learning?" and "What do teachers sometimes do that impedes your learning?"

What Gifted Learners Say:

What the Literature & Research Says:

Please don't give me twice as many exercises to keep me busy – or make me do all the basic activities that everyone else is doing before I can do the challenging activities

This teaches me to "dumb down" so I'm not punished for finishing quickly.

Provide activities that are challenging, and offer new and more complex skills. Remember: **Gifted learners need work that is** *"Instead of, not on top of!"*

Please allow me to work independently at least part of the time, and not always in groups, (especially when I have to lead those groups all the time)

I become frustrated & de-motivated if I always have to work in mixed ability groups.

Gifted need opportunities to work with other gifted. They also need time to work independently.

Please don't expect me to know everything, and to get everything right because I'm gifted. I haven't lived very long!

It doesn't mean I'm not gifted; it means you have given me something new to learn.

Gifted learners need a classroom environment that encourages curiosity and 'safety' in taking the risk that the suggestions they offer may not be correct.

Please don't expect me to give an answer instantly or explain in a step-by-step manner how I arrived at the answer.

Often we need time to reflect, because we think of all sorts of complexities that might impact on the answer.

Introverted thinkers need time to reflect. 20% of the population are introverted thinkers, 60% of moderately gifted are introverted thinkers and 75% of highly gifted are introverted thinkers (Silverman).

I love it when I'm exposed to new knowledge, but *really* enjoy it when the learning activities around the new learning are challenging and make me think

Doing really simple activities can take the fun and challenge out of learning.

Learning activities need to be differentiated for gifted learners to accommodate their learning needs

Figure 17 Gifted Learner's voice: Curriculum Delivery and Classroom Practice 1

What Gifted Learners Say:

What the Literature & Research Says:

Sometimes the topics we are covering seem shallow and I find it difficult to be interested in them and then I lack the motivation to do the work.

I worry about things that other students often don't care about, like world issues and events.

Gifted learners thrive when they are able to examine the 'big picture', investigate serious, complex issues, and take an active role in deciding where their learning should go.

I like to feel 'safe' in terms of my grades at high school because these are important to me.

Sometimes I won't choose the more difficult options in case it affects my grade.

Lessen the reliance on grades; help students see that tackling more complex issues will benefit them more in the long term.

When I ask how I can improve something, I may mean that I want to go beyond an 'A' because I just want to learn more.

Being told "Don't worry, you will get an A" frustrates me when I want to dive deeper

For this type of gifted learner, learning is not about the grade. It is a passion for learning for its own sake. This needs to be fostered, not frustrated!

I am really embarrassed when teachers refer to my ability in front of other students.

I don't always want other students to know that I'm good at things.

Students will 'dumb down' if they have to. Talk 1 to 1 with the student about their performance. Student privacy is important.

Sometimes teachers tell me I shouldn't ask some things or read certain texts because I'm not yet in the grade where that knowledge or text is taught.

I'm interested in learning the answer. Age has nothing to do with my readiness to learn.

Gifted learners don't learn with a lock-step method. They often learn in 'big gulps'. Question the validity of knowledge 'gate-keeping' by other teachers.

Figure 18 Gifted Learner's voice: Curriculum Delivery and Classroom Practice 2

3.2 Best Practice: The Most Effective Options from the Research

> **What does the research indicate are effective strategies for gifted learners?**
>
> **What can we take from the research to implement in our classrooms, departments or school?**

This section embraces the research of Professor Karen B. Rogers. Rogers conducted a significant, comprehensive metadata analysis of the research into effective strategies for gifted learners. Her analysis established how much effect that a particular adaptation had upon gifted learners, when compared with the expected learning for the year. The studies compared gifted students in particular situations to gifted students in normal classes and not to "normal" students in normal classes. The metadata analysis is a rich source of detailed information, and this handbook focuses upon Rogers' *ten recommended options for gifted learners that produce the greatest effect for the least effort'*.

How to use this section: Teachers, departments and schools can review the effectiveness and evidence of current provisions for their gifted and consider 'what else?' and 'what next?'

1 • **Take your time!** Don't expect to cruise through these in a short time. Each one of these is food for serious departmental and school-wide discussion.

2 • Download and share Professor Roger's original powerpoint which will give you additional background information:
www.giftedpage.org/docs/PAGE%20Morning%20Keynote.ppt

3 • Ask teachers to consider each option for its own value. Use that option to measure what is already done, and how effectively it is being managed.

4 • Consider the degree of impact this option could have upon your students and the degree of difficulty of implementation of each option and transfer those scores to the matrix on page 46

5 • Consider any barriers to implementing the option, and how these barriers might be overcome. Include enabling factors and personnel.

6 • Use the Matrix on page 46 to prioritise areas for development

7 • With what you now know about gifted pedagogy and research, use the SCOB analysis tool on page 47 to assess your school's strengths, challenges, opportunities and barriers. An example has been supplied.

Option One: Daily Challenge in Talent Area(s)

Description	The Effort	The Effect
However it can be managed, gifted learners must be provided with appropriately complex knowledge and skills in their area or areas of demonstrated performance.	**The effort** is in rearranging how high performers are organized so that this can be provided --no additional financial cost or personnel should be necessary.	**The effect** expected should average about 1/3 to 1/2 additional year's growth in the talent area.

Reflection	1. What could **"daily challenge in talent area"** look like in my classroom / our classrooms?		Examples: (Daily) At least 1 key task that matches the ability level of the student; learning goal for the task is at an advanced level; the skill required to fulfil a task is beyond that of the cohort; group work at higher level; cross grouping;

2. How much impact would this have on learning in my classroom /our department?

- ○ Low
- ○ Medium
- ○ High

3. How difficult would this option be to implement in my classroom / department?

- ○ Easy
- ○ Moderate
- ○ Difficult

What are the **barriers** to implementing this?

How might they be overcome?

What are the **enablers**?

Description	The Effort	The Effect
Although this rigor does not have to be daily in every academic area, it must be consistent, articulated across grade & building levels, and consciously delivered. The brighter a student is, the more often this additional challenge will be needed.	**The effort** will be in funding training in differentiation for regular classroom teachers with gifted learners in their classes and in finding/developing and funding the materials & resources for these teachers to use.	**The effect** will be in more positive academic self-esteem, less stress (caused by boredom), more motivation to learn, and higher degrees of higher order thinking, when integrated in the differentiated experiences offered.

Reflection

1. What could **"rigorous challenge"** look like in my classroom / our department?		Examples: Teachers differentiate with high end learning activities for gifted; they personalise learning with individualised learning goals which match the learning needs of the individual student. There is deliberate, department-wide planning for this.

2. How much impact would this have on learning in my classroom /our department?

- ✔
- Low
- Medium
- High

3. How difficult would this option be to implement in my classroom / department?

- ✔
- Easy
- Moderate
- Difficult

What are the **barriers** to implementing this?

How might they be overcome?

What are the **enablers**?

Provocative Thought:
Do we drop something because it is difficult? Or is it a case of 'no pain, no gain?'

Option Three: Opportunities to Work Independently and Be Unique (Rogers, 2010)		
Description	**The Effort**	**The Effect**
Gifted students must be taught the skills (scaffolding) of how to work and learn independently.	**The effort** involves teaching each child how to be successful with an independent investigation, using a model such as Treffinger or SEM-Type 3 or Betts ALM and then providing the supervision and facilitation as the learner "investigates".	**The effect** is in increased motivation to learn, interest in subject area, improved academic resilience (cognitive risk-taking), and self-efficacy.

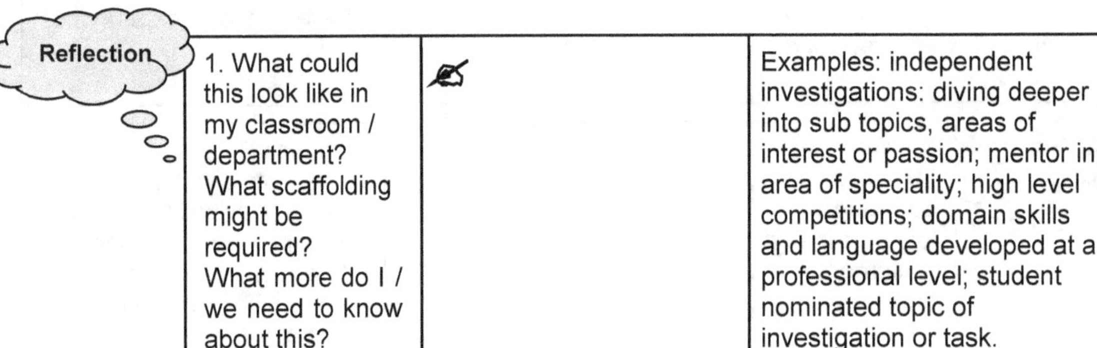

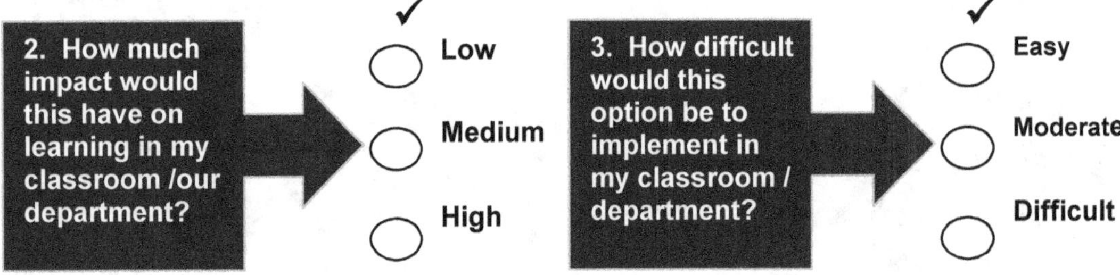

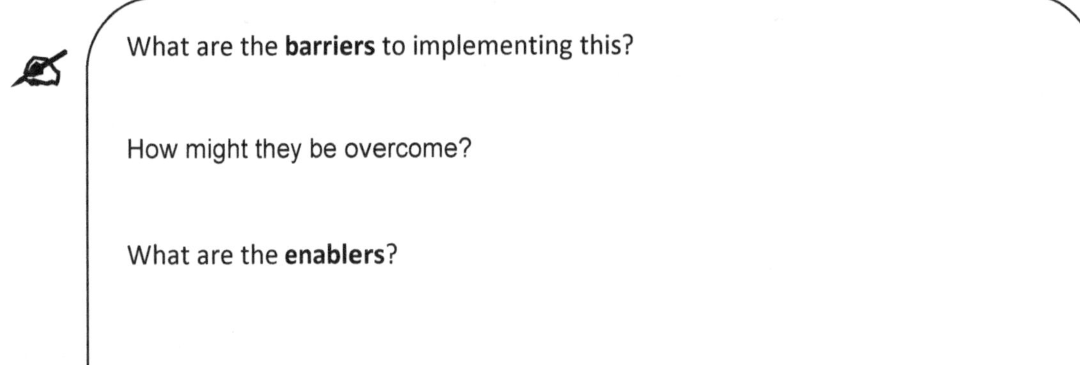

 Designing Defensible Programs for Gifted Secondary School Learners © Sonia White 2011

Option Four: Teaching of Concepts, Issues, Problems, Principles, Generalisations in Whole-to-Part Sequence (Rogers, 2010)		
Description	**The Effort**	**The Effect**
As decontextualists, gifted learners must see the whole "picture" first and then be allowed through analysis to break it down into its parts and relationships. This requires that the whole we start with involves more complex and abstract content such as concepts or problem-based learning.	**The effort** is in training teachers of the gifted to identify the "big ideas" of each content area they teach and helping them find / develop materials and resources to teach in this fashion.	**The effect** will be in greater critical and creative thinking performance, greater motivation to learn, and maximum transfer to other areas of study.

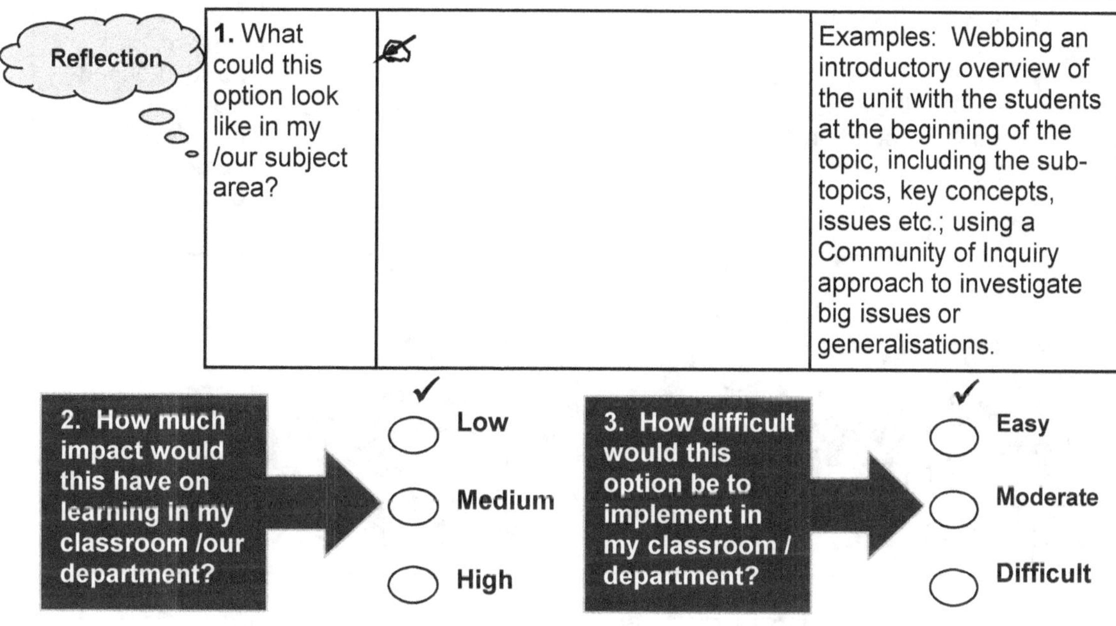

Reflection

1. What could this option look like in my /our subject area?

Examples: Webbing an introductory overview of the unit with the students at the beginning of the topic, including the sub-topics, key concepts, issues etc.; using a Community of Inquiry approach to investigate big issues or generalisations.

2. How much impact would this have on learning in my classroom /our department?

- Low ✓
- Medium
- High

3. How difficult would this option be to implement in my classroom / department?

- Easy ✓
- Moderate
- Difficult

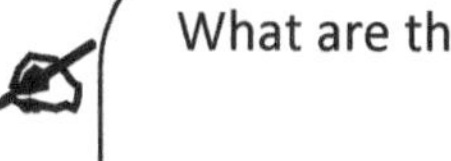

What are the **barriers** to implementing this?

How might they be overcome?

What are the **enablers**?

<table>
<tr><td colspan="3">Option Five: Double or Triple-Time Pacing in Math and Science (Rogers, 2010)</td></tr>
<tr><td>Description</td><td>The Effort</td><td>The Effect</td></tr>
<tr><td>This instructional strategy ensures that mathematically and scientifically gifted learners will retain what they learn with greater accuracy because of their significantly faster learning rate.</td><td>The effort is the training of a single (or all) math and science teachers, especially at the middle and high school levels in how to deliver content at this accelerated pace.</td><td>The effect for students will be between 3/5s and 4/5s of an additional year's growth in the content area.</td></tr>
</table>

Reflection

1. What might this option look like in our Mathematics /Science department?

Examples: Flexible grouping; 'streaming' or ability grouped classes; multi-levelling; curriculum compacting;

2. How much impact would this have on learning in my classroom /our department?

- ✔ Low
- Medium
- High

3. How difficult would this option be to implement in my classroom / department?

- ✔ Easy
- Moderate
- Difficult

What are the **barriers** to implementing this?

How might they be overcome?

What are the **enablers**?

Provocative Thought: Are our beliefs about acceleration founded in myth or research? (See recommended readings: *A Nation Deceived.*)

Option Six: Elimination of Excess Drill and Revision (Rogers, 2010)		
Description	**The Effort**	**The Effect**
Once mastery is demonstrated in a content or topic area, gifted learners should not be made to review or drill on this information more than 2-3 more times, at spaced intervals.	**The effort** consists of training all teachers in ways to eliminate excess drill and review and finding /developing and funding materials and resources that can be substituted for practice time.	**The effect** will be greater accuracy in retained information, greater focus on new learning, and a greater chance that gifted learners will be motivated to continue learning in that area.

Reflection

1. What might **"elimination of excess drill and repetition"** look like in my classroom?		Examples: Flexible grouping: selected students working on alternative activities that are 'instead of' not 'on top of;' setting more advanced learning goals with different success criteria. Match this with "daily challenge in talent area".

2. How much impact would this have on learning in my classroom /our department?

✓
◯ Low
◯ Medium
◯ High

3. How difficult would this option be to implement in my classroom / department?

✓
◯ Easy
◯ Moderate
◯ Difficult

What are the **barriers** to implementing this?

How might they be overcome?

What are the **enablers**?

Provocative Thought: *When once the child has learned that 4 and 2 are 6, a thousand repetitions will give him no new information, and it is a waste of time to keep him in that manner.* – J.M. Greenwood, 1888

Option Seven: Exposure to Content Beyond Grade Level in Specific Area(s) of Talent (Rogers, 2010)		
Description	**The Effort**	**The Effect**
This can be provided through subject acceleration, cross-grading, multi-age or multi-grade classes, dual enrolment, early entrance to school, mentorships, and/or on-line learning.	**The effort** is mostly managerial - making some change in the way or when a gifted learner's education will be delivered.	**The effect** ranges from 1.9 to 5.7 additional grade equivalent months' growth per provision, with substantial improvements in socialisation and self-esteem in many cases.

Reflection

1. Is this something that our department / school considers? Are these provisions reviewed? How defensible are our current provisions in this area? (Examples as above).

2. How much impact would this have on learning in my classroom /our department?

- ○ Low
- ○ Medium
- ○ High

3. How difficult would this option be to implement in my classroom / department?

- ○ Easy
- ○ Moderate
- ○ Difficult

What are the **barriers** to implementing this?

How might they be overcome?

What are the **enablers**?

Provocative Thought: Learner readiness, not age, should be the determining factor for exposure to content and skills learning.

 Designing Defensible Programs for Gifted Secondary School Learners © Sonia White 2011

<table>
<tr><td colspan="3">Option Eight: Shortening the Number of Years Spent in the K-12 System (Rogers, 2010)</td></tr>
<tr><td>Description</td><td>The Effort</td><td>The Effect</td></tr>
<tr><td>This can be provided for those gifted learners performing significantly above grade level in almost every academic subject through grade skipping, grade telescoping, and early admission to college.</td><td>The effort is managerial in nature - someone to coordinate the provision and track the effects on the individual gifted learner or learners.</td><td>The effect will range from 2/5 to a full year's additional growth across all subject areas.
In some cases socialization improves substantially as well.</td></tr>
</table>

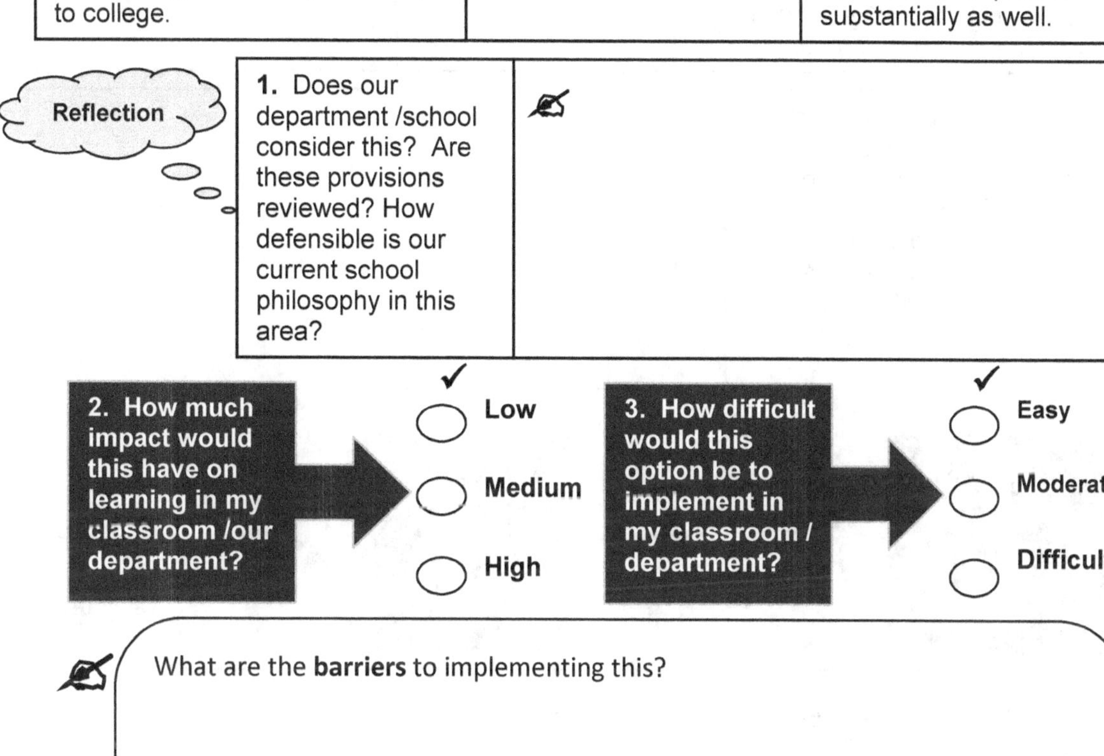

What are the **barriers** to implementing this?

How might they be overcome?

What are the **enablers**?

Provocative Thought: *You don't have the moral right to hold one child back to make another child feel better.* – Stephanie Tolan

Option Nine: Opportunities to Socialise and to Learn With Like Ability Peers (Rogers, 2010)		
Description	**The Effort**	**The Effect**
This can be provided through a number of like ability or like performing grouping options, such as full-time gifted programs, send-out programs, regrouping for specific instruction, within class grouping, like ability cooperative learning, and cluster grouping.	**The effort** is daily implementation of this opportunity for a substantial block of time whether for one academic area or for several.	**The effect** ranges from 2.6 additional grade equivalent months of achievement to 4/5 of an additional year's growth, depending upon the grouping option provided.

Reflection

1. What might this look like in my classroom / our department/ our school? (Examples listed above).

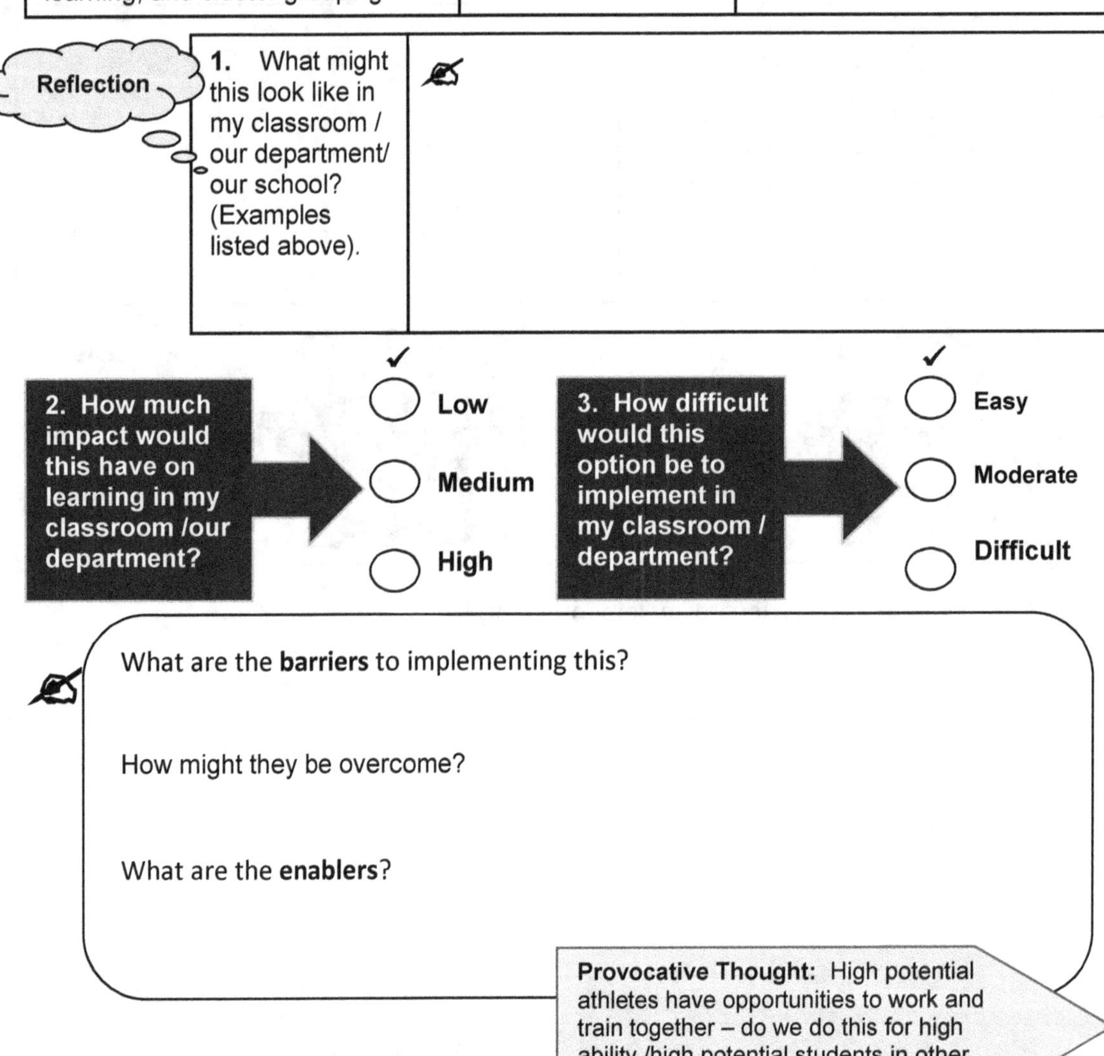

  Designing Defensible Programs for Gifted Secondary School Learners © Sonia White 2011

Option Ten: Opportunities to be Credited for Prior Learning (Rogers, 2010)		
Description	**The Effort**	**The Effect**
This opportunity can be provided through compacting, testing out, or just plain credit for prior learning.	**The effort** required is a coordinator who will determine levels of mastery for the area considered for credit and finding/funding materials and resources to be used with a gifted learner when credit is given.	**The effect** will range from 3/5s to 4/5s of an additional year's growth in the specific academic area credited

Reflection

1. How could **"opportunities to be credited for prior learning"** be acknowledged and implemented in my classroom / our department?

Examples: Literacy & Numeracy levels; end of unit tests prior to unit start; above level-testing; formative assessment tasks (see chapter on assessment).

2. How much impact would this have on learning in my classroom /our department?

- ○ Low ✓
- ○ Medium
- ○ High

3. How difficult would this option be to implement in my classroom / department?

- ○ Easy ✓
- ○ Moderate
- ○ Difficult

What are the **barriers** to implementing this?

How might they be overcome?

What are the **enablers**?

Provocative Thought: *It is not because things are difficult that we do not dare; it is because we do not dare that they are difficult.* – Seneca

3.3 Where to From Here? Planning and Implementing Change

You have considered Roger's ten options on the previous pages, how difficult each option would be to implement, and the degree of impact it will have upon student motivation and learning in your classroom or school. Transfer your evaluations into the appropriate section of the matrix, (i.e. if a task is easy and will have a medium impact, write the number of that task in the corresponding box).

IMPACT MATRIX: Ten Options For Meeting the Learning Needs of Gifted			
How difficult is this option to implement?			
	Easy	**Medium**	**Difficult**
Small			
Medium			
Large			

How much impact will it have?

1. Daily challenge in talent area.
2. Rigorous challenge in all academic areas.
3. Opportunities to work independently and be unique.
4. Teaching of concepts, issues, problems, principles in whole to part sequence.
5. Double or triple time pacing in Maths and Science.
6. Elimination of excess Drill and Revision.
7. Shortening the number of years spent in the school system.
8. Shortening the number of years spent in the school system.
9. Opportunities to socialize and to learn with like ability peers.
10. Opportunities credited for prior learning.

(Professor Dr. Karen Rogers, 2010.)

Highlight your priorities for implementation. Revisit and review.

Figure 19 Impact Matrix: Ten Options For Meeting the Learning Needs of Gifted

Having developed your Graduate Profile for Gifted Learners (Chapter 1), and having examined the research into best practice, use the SCOB Analysis worksheet and Action Plan Template to consider areas of need and plan future areas of development.

S.C.O.B. ANALYSIS of Gifted Education Identification, Assessment and Provisions at ________________ (School Name)

EVALUATION & FEED FORWARD	
STRENGTHS:	**CHALLENGES:**
OPPORTUNITIES:	**BARRIERS:** *(and ways they might be overcome)*

Figure 20 S.C.O.B. Analysis Chart (Strengths, Challenges, Opportunities & Barriers)

<table>
<tr><td>EXAMPLE</td><td>S.C.O.B. ANALYSIS of Gifted Education Identification Assessment and Provisions at Abacus High School</td></tr>
</table>

EVALUATION AND FEED-FORWARD

STRENGTHS:	**CHALLENGES:**
G. & T. group & coordinator position is resourced	Staff changes in advanced learning classes – challenge to fill gaps created by loss of expertise in this area & up skill new staff;
School has advanced learning classes; All classes use an inquiry method	Departure of key staff;
Academic Council; Wings Programme & High performance unit; Multiple Sporting & Arts performance programs available	Timetable is difficult to change;
Leadership opportunities: Arts & Culture Captains, Academic Captains/ Academic Council; Sports Captains, Sports Council; Leadership training programme for Grades 9 -12;	Building gifted pedagogy knowledge amongst all staff and getting 'buy-in' on differentiating in *all* classes for gifted learners;
Class size; a differentiation focus in curriculum delivery;	Tension created by other demands – challenge to make it less onerous so that teachers feel supported;
Specialised classes exist in specialist areas; e.g. Mathematics, Science, English & Physical Education have a timetabled slot for the most highly able;	To make initiatives for G & T learners sustainable;
	To identify underachieving gifted learners;
	To create learning pathways for single subject acceleration given timetable restrictions;
	To address the identified gaps; action plan
OPPORTUNITIES:	**BARRIERS:** *(and ways they might be overcome)*
To widen teacher understanding of the learning needs of gifted learners through teacher professional learning groups	Timetable – *(Where possible, having the timetable meet the learning needs of the students rather than the other way around).* Consider ways of freeing up specific teaching blocks so there is more cross-faculty flexibility.
To increase teacher awareness of the research and best practice, especially with regard to myths about gifted learners and provisions such as acceleration	Staff workload; Assist staff to find ways of working smarter; Consider reallocation of subsidiary staff duties; consider volunteer mentors from outside the school.
To embed of differentiated practice in the classroom in support of gifted learners	Budget Allocation. Put a proposal together which shows how increased funding in this area can result in increased student achievement. Consider professional development budget also: gifted pedagogy makes better teachers for all students.
To use student voice in critically evaluate provisions for gifted learners.	
To review subject acceleration opportunities	

Figure 21 Example of a School's S.C.O.B. Analysis

 Designing Defensible Programs for Gifted Secondary School Learners © Sonia White 2011

Where to from here? An Action Plan Template			
Task What's to be done?	**When / By Whom?**	**Goal** What will be achieved?	**Evidence** of completion /success

Figure 22 Action Plan Template

NOTES:

References and Readings:

Assouline, S. G., N., C., Lupkowski-Shoplik, A., Lipscombe, J., & Forstadt, L. (2003). *Iowa Acceleration Scale Manual: A guide for whole-Grade acceleration K-8.* (2nd ed.). Scottsdale, AZ: Great Potential Press

Colangelo, N., Assouline, S. G., & Gross, M. (2004). *A nation deceived: how schools how hold back America's brightest students (Vol 1).* (The Templeton Nation report on Acceleration): The Connie Belin & Jacqueline N. Blank International Center for Gifted Education and Talent Development, University of Iowa, and Gifted Education Research, Resource and Information Centre (GERRIC), The University of New South Wales. Available free from http://nationdeceived.org/followup.html

Colangelo, N., Assouline, S. G., & Gross, M. (2004). *A nation deceived: how schools how hold back America's brightest students (Vol 2).* (The Templeton Nation report on Acceleration): The Connie Belin & Jacqueline N. Blank International Center for Gifted Education and Talent Development, University of Iowa, and Gifted Education Research, Resource and Information Centre (GERRIC), The University of New South Wales. Available free from http://nationdeceived.org/followup.html

Csikszentmihalyi, M., Rathunde, K., & Whalen, S. (1997). *Talented teenagers: the roots of success and failure.* USA: Cambridge University Press

Delisle, J. R., & Galbraith, J. (2002). *When gifted kids don't have all the answers: how to meet their social and emotional needs.* Minneapolis: Free Spirit Publishing Inc.

Dixon, F. A., & Moon, S. M. (Eds.). (2006). *The handbook of secondary gifted education.* Waco, Texas: Prufrock Press.

Gross, M., & Vliet, H. (Eds.). (2004). *Radical acceleration of highly gifted children: an annotated bibliography of international research on highly gifted children who graduate from high school three or more years early.* Sydney Australia: GERRIC, University of NSW

Robinson, A., Shore, B. M., & Enersen, D. L. (Eds.). (2007). *Best practices in gifted education: an evidence-based guide.* Waco TX: Prufrock Press Inc.

Rogers, K. B. (2010). *An Update on Research in Gifted Education: 10 "Things".* Retrieved 27 January 2011, from giftedpage.org/docs/PAGE%20Morning%20Keynote.ppt

Rogers, K. B. (2006). *Ten gifted options that produce the greatest effect for the least effort.* Paper presented at the Rising Tides. Retrieved 24 June 2006, from http://www.confer.co.nz/gnt/Friday/Spotlight.pdf.

Rogers, K. B. (2002). *Reforming gifted education: Matching the program to the child.* Scottsdale AZ: Great Potential Press Inc.

Sousa, D. A. (2003). *How the gifted brain learns.* Thousand Oaks, CA: Corwin Press Inc.

Chapter 4: Creating DPIs for Gifted Learners

One of the beauties of teaching
is that there is no limit to one's growth as a teacher,
just as there is no knowing beforehand
how much your students can learn -
Herbert Kohl.

Developing curricula for gifted learners should be based upon best evidence and accepted pedagogy. This chapter explores *differentiated, personalised* and *individualised* learning for gifted as a prelude to Chapter 5 which assists teachers to analyse and to develop their unit overviews and unit content against recognised good practice.

The DPI Model for Gifted Learners

Gifted learners differ from one another as much as they do from the rest of the population. There are numerous ways of catering for gifted learners, and schools and teachers are best able to meet the learning and social-emotional needs of their gifted learners when they are well-versed in all of them, so that the individual gifted student, and/or a group of gifted students with similar needs, is catered for in ways that best match the learning needs.

Put simply, the **DPI Model** combines **Differentiated Learning, Personalised Learning** and **Individualised Learning.** It is concerned with providing whichever solutions best meet individual and group learning needs (Figure 23). Gifted learners whose needs extend beyond the classroom may have to have individual provisions set in place; others need to be enriched and extended beyond the year level and/or within the classroom. Differentiating and personalising learning are specific practices which teachers and departments can select from to meet the learning needs of the learners in front of them.

Schools should consider the full range of possible provisions.

They should use the broader brush strokes of differentiated learning in teacher planning and practice,

empower students to take control of their own learning with personalised learning,

and use other, special provisions to meet the extra-ordinary needs of individuals or groups of able students.

 Designing Defensible Programs for Gifted Secondary School Learners © Sonia White 2011

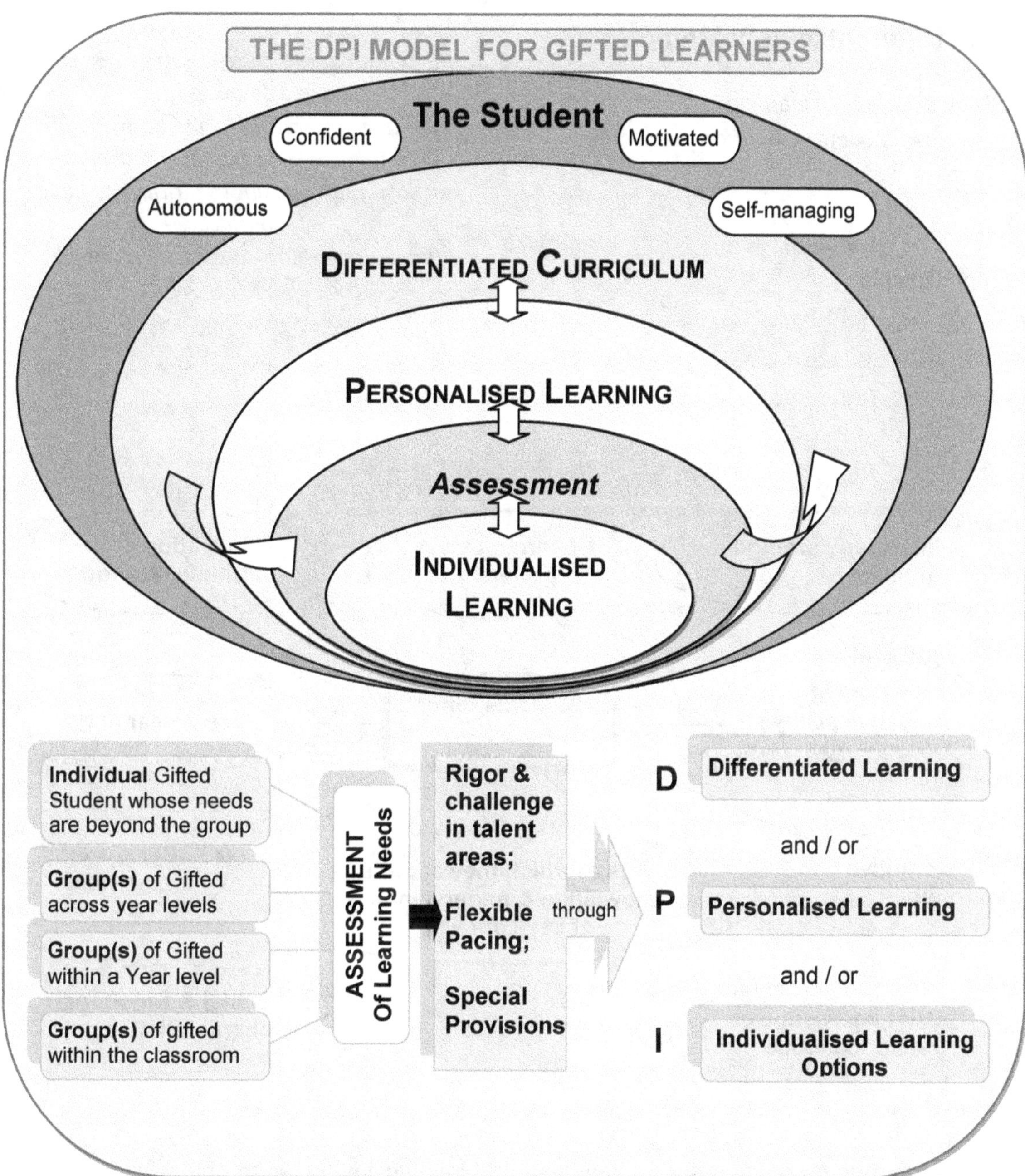

Figure 23 The DPI for Gifted Learners

The following pages in this chapter examine facets of differentiation, personalised learning and individualised learning. Differentiated and personalised learning should occur for all students in all classrooms; individualised learning extends beyond that of the 'normal' classroom and may apply to only one student or a small group of students.

4.1 Differentiating learning

Why differentiate learning?
Because students differ from each other
in many ways.

For example:

> *The surest path to positive self esteem is to*
> *succeed at something*
> *which one perceived would be difficult.*
> *Each time we steal a student's struggle,*
> *we steal the opportunity for them to build*
> *self-confidence.*
> *They must learn to do hard things to feel*
> *good about themselves.*
> *--Sylvia Rimm*

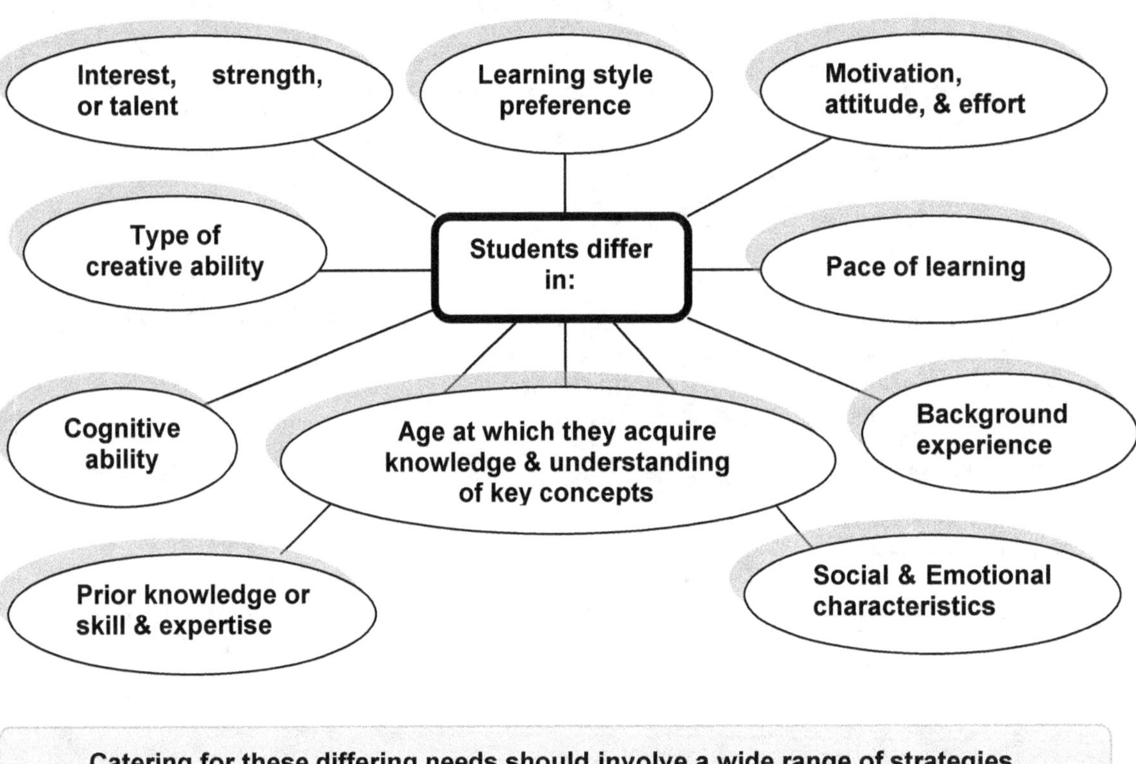

Figure 24 Ways in which students differ

4.1.2 What is differentiated learning?

Differentiated learning is learning that acknowledges and caters to student differences. Students differ from each other in many ways. Gifted learners also differ in many ways, both from other learners and from each other.

TEACHERS can differentiate learning by modifying

- content (what is learned),
- process (how it is learned) and
- product (the evidence of learning). (Figure 25, Page 56)

They differentiate learning through

- using different teaching strategies for different groups of learners
- setting different long term goals for learners
- enriching, extending and accelerating where appropriate
- assessing at the level of learning

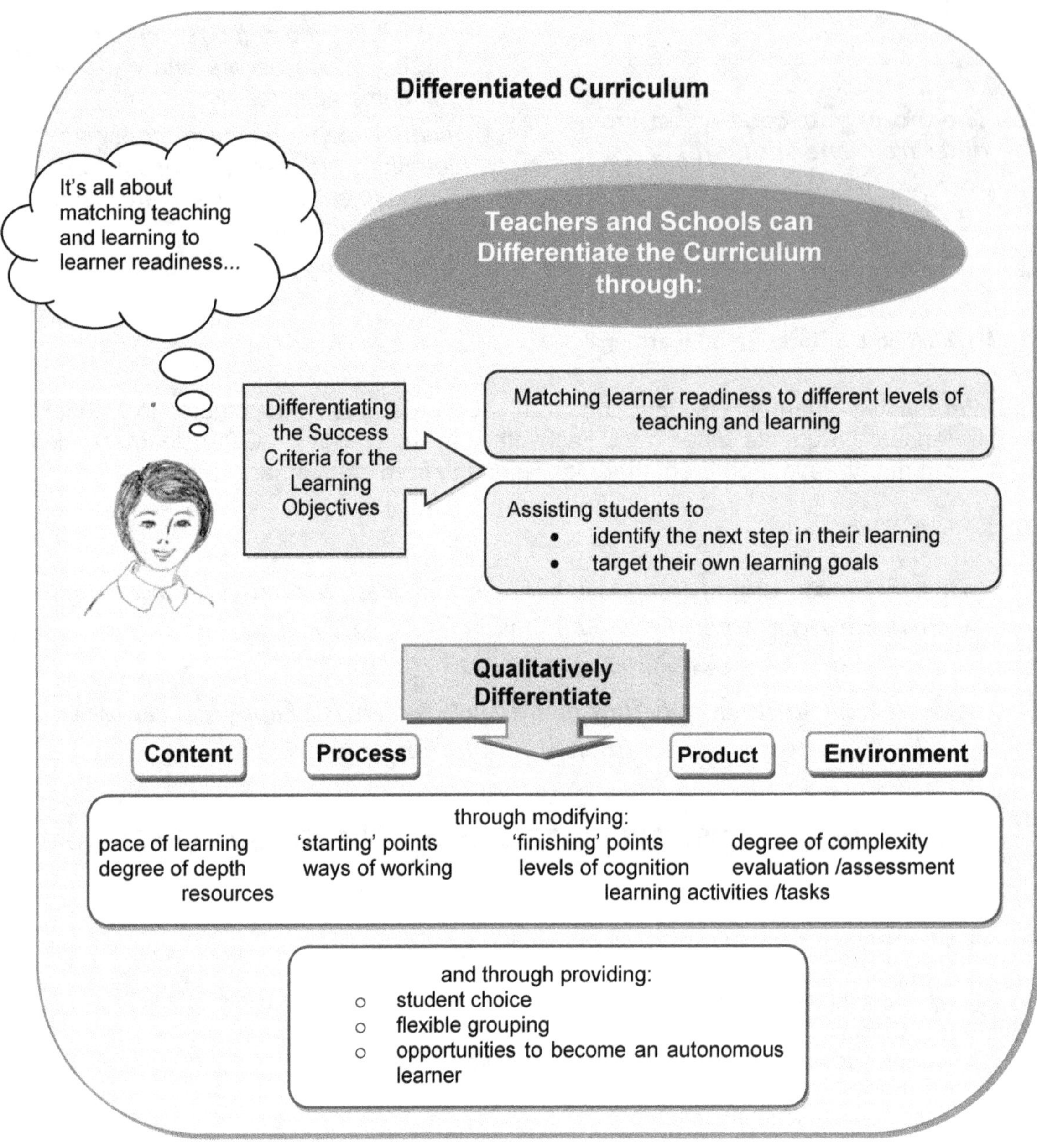

Figure 25 Ways teachers differentiate learning

   Designing Defensible Programs for Gifted Secondary School Learners © Sonia White 2011

Defining Differentiated Learning for Gifted

Differentiating learning for gifted means providing learning experiences that:

- Challenge beyond the level of most students in the class through *more* abstract reasoning and complexity
- Provide flexibility
- Allow for a different pace of learning
- Have different (more challenging) learning outcomes
- Cater for the diverse specific learning characteristics of gifted

NOTE: Differentiation is inextricably linked to student assessment:

- *Acknowledging* prior knowledge / skills already acquired or not yet acquired

- *Knowing* the student learning needs through past performance & pre-testing

In differentiating learning for gifted…

*"…**Quality** changes rather than quantity, and they (gifted learners) must build upon and extend the characteristics (both present and future) that make these children different from other students" – June Maker.*

The 'Could, Would, Should Rule' in Differentiating Learning for Gifted

In determining whether an activity is appropriate for *gifted* learners, teachers can ask:

Could every student do this activity (at this stage of their learning)?

Would every student benefit from doing this activity?

Should every student do this activity (at this stage of their learning)?

If the answer is "yes" to any one of these questions, then the learning activity is not differentiated enough for gifted learners.

(Adapted from A. Harry Passow)

4.1.3 Models for Differentiating Learning for Gifted

There is a range of effective models for differentiating the curriculum for gifted, and schools should choose which model or models they wish to adopt. They may also choose to analyze the components of different models and then design their own model, using a combination of principles and practices from more than one model.

Curriculum Models in Gifted Education

- Maker 'Curriculum Modification' Model (1982);
- Kaplan 'Content-Process-Product Grid ' Model (1986);
- Kohlberg "Moral Reasoning Stages Model' (1971);
- Williams 'Cognitive-Affective Interaction Model' (1970);
- Blooms 'Cognitive Taxonomy Model' (1988);
- Treffinger "Self-directed Learning Model' (1995);
- Van Tassel-Baska 'Integrated Curriculum Model' (2001);
- Betts 'Autonomous Learner Model' (1985);
- Renzulli Enrichment Triad Model (1977) and
- Renzulli and Reis 'School-wide Enrichment Model' (1985)
- Tomlinson, Kaplan, Renzulli, Purcell, Leppien & Burns 'The Parallel Curriculum' Model (2002).

Teachers may read further about these and other models which are referenced at the end of this chapter in 'References and Readings'.

Some models are described in the following chapters, e.g., Blooms 'Cognitive Taxonomy Model' and its subsequent adapted version by Krathwohl & Anderson, and the Williams Model. There are common principles amongst all models which have been included. Emphasis is placed upon adding rigor and complexity to cater for gifted learners. The principles of the Kaplan 'Content-Process-Product' Model, and the Maker Model are also explored in the body of this handbook.

*The **DPI model** embraces the principles of differentiated learning for gifted, personalising learning, and individualising learning with application of all options within and beyond the classroom as befits the learning needs of the gifted individual or groups.*

4.1.4. Differentiating Content, Process & Product.

One of the most effective ways teachers can differentiate learning for gifted is by differentiating Content, Process, and Product (Figure 25, page 56). As described in the Maker and Kaplan Models, these are key areas teacher can modify. The reflection sheet below will assist teachers to decide which of these they have as strengths, and which areas they may choose to develop.

DIFFERENTIATION IN THE CLASSROOM: TEACHER REFLECTION			
Reflection **I Can Modify:**	**Success Criteria:** *(Put a tick for what applies now, use a pencil to double tick when you re-evaluate.)*	Not Yet	I need more work on this / I can do this really well.
Content (what is learned) **through:** • Modifying the point at which learners begin the unit /lesson • Modifying the rate at which they learn • Modifying the point at which they finish the unit /lesson • Allowing student-selected areas of study (topic related or interdisciplinary) • Increasing the complexity in the area of study. **Process** (how it is learned) **through:** • *learning and using higher order thinking skills:* creative thinking, critical thinking, caring thinking, problem solving • Applying abstract thinking skills to student-appropriate content which demand products at a level of sophistication appropriate for the student • Integrating subject specific skills & abstract thinking skills **Product** through: • Allowing multiple forms for communicating learning • Providing opportunity to present information to diverse and appropriate audiences • Involving learners in the assessment of learning			
Highlight the Success Criteria you will be working on. **To be completed by** (date):			
Self Assessment: (Feedback: What I achieved what I have not yet achieved and need to work further on. Feed forward: What I need to do next).			

Figure 26 Differentiation in the classroom: Teacher Reflection Sheet

4.1.5 Differentiating Using Multiple Intelligences and Learning Styles

Quite a number of schools use Gardner's Multiple intelligences and learning styles to meet the individual learning needs of their learners. While these provide worthy ways of ensuring that students can learn in their preferred mode and I recommend a continued focus upon students' learning modes, multiple intelligences and learning styles do not of themselves, offer appropriate learning for the gifted. *It is imperative that higher order thinking be integrated with these approaches otherwise the tasks can become superficial.*

Using Multiple Intelligences or Learning Styles ***without using higher order thinking*** is like 'painting by numbers' or 'joining the dots':

little skill is involved; the process is repetitive, and the product is unoriginal and superficial.

It results in 'Surface Skimming'.

SURFACE SKIMMING

EXAMPLES of Surface skimming

Write a story

Debate a topic

Gather facts about

Do a project on...

Make a game

Make a puppet show

Read about...

Make a graph

Design a...

Fill in the missing details

Create a chart

Listen to music

Write a song

List the attributes of...

Make a collage

Write a poem

Write a book review

Compose a letter

Paint a picture

Make a crossword

Interview a...

Create a role play

All of these activities, whilst interesting, are <u>low level</u> activities
UNLESS
specific instructions accompany them which demand
Higher Order thinking

Figure 27 Surface Skimming

On the other hand, where higher order thinking is integrated with a learning mode activity, and students are offered choice, multiple intelligences and learning modes become appropriately differentiated for gifted learners. Students are challenged to dive deeper into their learning.

DIVING DEEPER
SOME EXAMPLES:

Write a Story:
...that illustrates the disadvantages of... and a potential modification of --
...that justifies the choices made by...
...that shows the decisions that would have to be made when...
... that shows the conflicts that arise when...

Prepare to debate by researching other viewpoints on (X) topic

... examine the facts and look for supporting evidence

...look for contradictory evidence

...Argue convincingly from the other person's point of view

...find "holes" in your own argument

... reverse brainstorm the moot... would your conclusions be the same?

Paint a picture:
...that portrays the feelings expressed by ...
...that illustrates the disadvantages of...
...that illustrates the choices made by...
...that shows the outcome of what might happen if...
... that shows the conflicts faced by...

Explain your picture
And the research that led you to portray it in that fashion

Do a project investigation on:
...the decisions that were made when... and the consequences alternate choices could have brought about by...

...the disadvantages of...

...the choices made by... and decide whether or not you agree

... the conflicts that arise when... and ways in which the conflict could be resolved...

Create a role play:
...that shows the range of emotional responses that arise when... occurs

...that illustrates the disadvantages of... and shows a possible outcome of a decision

...that illustrates the choices made by X... and the factors that may have led them to that point

Gather facts about "X":
... to use as evidence in a mock trial.

... to disprove a well-accepted theory

... Imagine if the reverse had occurred: gather facts that could support this happening and argue why it could be proven legitimate

USE BLOOM'S & WILLIAMS' TAXONOMIES TO DIVE DEEPER INTO THE TOPIC

DIVE DEEPER: Use Learning Styles or Multiple Intelligences, but:
Differentiate the activity by including higher order thinking and by modifying the accompanying instruction!

Link the instruction to the learning outcomes.

Figure 28 Diving Deeper

Reflection

TEACHER LEARNING MAP:
Differentiating Learning

What I know	What I thought I didn't know BUT I do!
What I thought I knew BUT I don't	What I didn't know I didn't know!

What I would now like to know more about

What I deny or refuse to look at:

Fill in first box before beginning the chapter, and the remaining boxes subsequent to reading and discussion

Figure 29 Teacher Learning Map: Differentiated Learning

NOTES:

4.2 What is 'Personalised Learning'?

Personalised learning relates to the **learner**. Its emphasis shifts from teacher to student in a way that empowers the student to understand himself as a learner and take ownership of his learning

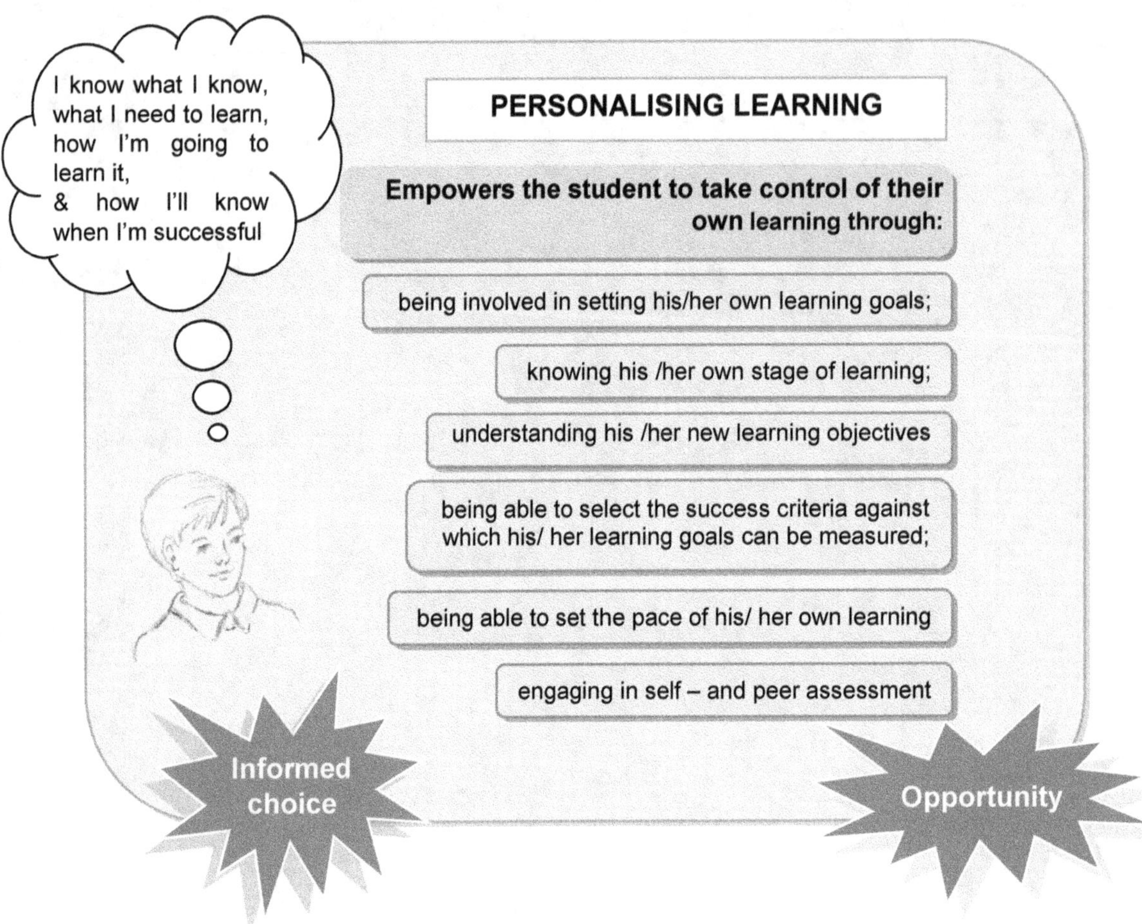

Personalised learning is *not* about individualised learning.

It is about teachers enabling students to learn in meaningful ways, in meaningful chunks, in different student groupings, and in safe and positive environments where people can take risks and learn from them. Personalising learning for gifted takes into account the advanced level at which the student is capable of learning. It is inextricably interdependent upon good formative and summative assessment practice.

     Designing Defensible Programs for Gifted Secondary School Learners © Sonia White 2011

This handbook examines some of the main ingredients for personalising learning. Further readings on formative and summative assessment are included in the References section at the end of this chapter).

4.2.1 How can teachers help students take control of their own learning?

Teachers do *not* lose control of the curriculum through personalising learning. Rather, they place responsibility upon the student to rise to pre-negotiated goals. There are different approaches a teacher may take to do this, but there are key ingredients:

Teacher Practice in Student Assessment	**Teacher sets Learning Goals that**	**Teacher Provides a Learning Environment that**
• is formative & summative • includes the student's own assessment • allows the student to track his /her own success and engage in peer assessment for critical review • is shared with the student so that (s)he can make informed choices about future learning goals	• are shared a) for the unit, and b) for the lesson • allow for reaching beyond the level for those who are ready • have specific success criteria attached that cater for the less able and the most able learners • allow students to make informed choices	• is flexible and allows for student differences • does not force a 'lock-step' method of learning • allows students to negotiate learning tasks and learning goals • encourages students to take charge of their own learning

4.2.2 What is Formative Assessment?

Assessment includes all activities that teachers and students undertake to get information that can be used diagnostically to alter teaching and learning[6].

Summative assessment takes place at the end of a learning cycle, to assess the level of learning that has taken place in specific areas. It often involves a grade or a percentage mark. Ideally, a summative assessment also has feedback and feed forward.

Formative Assessment is assessment that informs both teacher and student *during* the learning process. It is assessment that:

- Examines the current level of knowledge and level of skills that have been reached
- Provides **feedback** (what the student has achieved against set success criteria, and what they have not yet succeeded in achieving)
- Provides **feed forward** (what the next steps in their learning need to be).
- Is circular, i.e. dynamic and ongoing – even summative assessment can be used as a tool for formative assessment.

Far from being an onerous process that involves increased teacher assessment, *formative assessment* becomes much easier when students are given responsibility for self- and peer-assessment. Time spent in training *all* students to do this is well-rewarded when even less able students are able to challenge able students as to whether or not they have achieved their specific success criteria. Remarks such as "you haven't given any evidence to back up that statement" or "your analysis doesn't include other points of view" can be commonly overheard in classrooms where students are comfortable with analysing the degree of success against student-set learning goals.

> *One distinction is to think of formative assessment as "practice." We do not hold students accountable in "grade book fashion" for skills and concepts they have just been introduced to or are learning. We must allow for practice...*
>
> *A good analogy for this is the road test that is required to receive a driver's license. What if, before getting your driver's license, you received a grade every time you sat behind the wheel to practice driving?*
>
> *...In the beginning of learning to drive, how confident or motivated to learn would you feel?*
>
> *...Your final driving test, or summative assessment, would be the accountability measure that establishes whether or not you have the driving skills necessary for a driver's license—not a reflection of all the driving practice that leads to it.*
>
> *The same holds true for classroom instruction, learning, and assessment.*
>
>   - *Garrison, C. & Ehringhaus, M. (2007)*

Students who are not used to formative assessment practice may initially feel that it is the teacher's 'job' to tell them what is wrong, and resist making the effort to self- and peer-assess. But as they realise that the effort applied in doing this can benefit them, they 'buy-in', and are increasingly motivated to achieve.

---

[6] (Black and Wiliam (1998a)

Examples and strategies in summative and formative assessment are developed in chapters 10 and elsewhere. To clarify teacher setting of learning objectives and success criteria, some examples are included in following pages.

4.2.3 Examples of Goal Setting and Student Success Criteria

Designing Success Criteria

It is important to realise there *is not a magic formula*. Subject areas differ as do the requirements of their individual curricula. Success criteria must match the learning objectives or achievement goals of the curriculum being taught. They must also reflect the specific range of abilities within a classroom.

However, in designing success criteria for students to set their learning goals against, it is useful for teachers to:

- ✓ Break each learning outcome or achievement goal into small achievable steps and rephrase them as "I can" statements

- ✓ Make each "I can" statement concrete and specific, so that students can understand them. Avoid phrases like "with increasing sophistication" as this is meaningless to students.

- ✓ Put the learning outcome for each lesson on the board. Discuss the success criteria options with the students, and provide exemplars where possible.

- ✓ Use success criteria for major assessment tasks. Again, provide exemplars where possible. Collect student work / videos of presentations to use as examples of specific success criteria.

- ✓ Have the students 'unpack' what specific success criteria look like. Provide ample opportunity for them to analyse their own, and other's work against specific criteria. This is where many students experience the "a-ha!" moment of understanding how they can improve their work.

- ✓ Model good feedback and feed forward. A mark tells us nothing about how we might improve. Good feedback gives us understanding of what we have mastered, and what is undeveloped or needs further development. Good feed forward tells us where we should be heading next.

- ✓ Have the students provide each other with feedback and feed-forward. Analysis of others' work will help them to analyse their own. Furthermore, it places the responsibility for reflection on learning onto the shoulders of the students.

Te Reo Māori (Māori Language) Unit Catering for Differing Learner Readiness Levels
TOPIC: Te Whānau (the Family, Belonging)

Achievement Objects in listening, reading, viewing reading speaking, writing & presenting:

Entry Level (Level 1)	Level 2	Level 3
1.2 introducing themselves and others and respond to introductions, and 1.4 communicate about personal information such as name, age, nationality and home, and 1.7 use and respond to simple classroom language (including asking for the word to express something in Te Reo Māori).	2.1 Communicate about relationships between people, and 2.5 Communicate about physical characteristics, personality & feelings.	3.1 Communicate, including comparing and contrasting, about habits and routines, and 3.2 Communicate about events and where they take place, and 3.4 Communicate, including comparing and contrasting, about how people travel.

Class description: Main cohort is Level 2, with some students at Level 1, and some at Level 3.

Note: This example gives **only one of 5** differentiated **success criteria** for each level of this unit.

Entry Level (Level 1) Students Can:	Level 2: Students Can:	Level 3: Students Can:
Ask simple questions; imitate pronunciation, intonation, stress and rhythm of Te Reo in Te Reo about Te Whānau. Reproduce letter combinations and punctuation for Te Reo Māori words, phrases and sentences in familiar context in Te Reo about Te Whānau.	Give short prepared talks on familiar topics; describe familiar events, people and things in Te Reo about Te Whānau.	Initiate and sustain short conversations; give short prepared talks on familiar topics; use generally appropriate pronunciation, stress, rhythm, and intonation, in Te Reo about Te Whānau.

Resource: NZ Ministry of Education (2009). *e Aho Arataki Marau mō te Ako i Te Reo Māori - Kura Auraki: Curriculum guidelines for teaching and learning Te Reo Māori in English-medium.* Wellington, NZ: Learning Media Ltd. (pp42:46)

Figure 30 Differentiating Achievement Objectives and Success Criteria in a Language Unit

The above example of a Te Reo Māori Unit Overview which would also incorporate learning activities / contexts at each level, appropriate resources at each level, and formative and summative assessment details.

It is important that success criteria are designed to
- reflect the ability range of the class;
- extend the most able in the class whilst also providing goals for the least able;
- provide student *choice* and different starting places for goals; and to
- reflect your school's curriculum

Therefore teachers should design criteria applicable for *their* students, in their school, in line with their national curriculum. *The few examples given here are illustrative not prescriptive*.

Music – Composition

I can

- create a lyrical phrase
- create a melody or rhythm to accompany my lyrical phrase
- create a graphic notation of the melody or rhythm
- notate the melody or rhythm on a stave
- *include* untuned percussion instruments
- *include* tuned percussion instruments
- *include* strings, brass or woodwind instruments

Response Writing – English Essay

I can:

- Structure an essay with an introduction, body and conclusion
- Write three clear points (**S**tatements) that relate to the set topic.
- Use **E**vidence from the text (facts, quotations) to support my points
- **E**xplain how the evidence proves my point
- Write a perceptive, structured response on the set topic explaining the relevance of the supporting evidence from the text and how it supports my ideas.

Maths - Algebra

I can:
- Find the next term(s) in a pattern
- Write a rule in symbols for a pattern
- Select a rule to match a given pattern
- Substitute into a rule to make a pattern
- Write a rule in symbols for a non-linear pattern
- Solve equations with brackets, fractions or x on both sides
- Solve equations with combinations of brackets, fractions and x on both sides
- Substitute into any formula and find the unknown value
- Rearrange linear formulae

Physical Education

Fielding: Defence

I can
- Place myself in a good position
- Cover space
- Move to where the ball is coming to, i.e. sideways rather than towards the ball
- Respond to call to 'back up'
- Move quickly to the ball
- Use strategies to create pressure situations for opposition
- communicate with team members to work together in order to create pressure on opposition
- Cover a large space effectively from an effective position
- Be perceived as a defender who fields so well that it is too risky to hit to the space I occupy

Film /Photography (Terms)

I can –
- Identify film shots and angles (e.g. CU, high angle)
- Correctly use terminology to describe elements of film (e.g. sound, lighting, costume, editing etc.)
- Discuss the effects of film techniques in the representation of a character
- Discuss the effects of film techniques in the development of a relationship

Figure 31 Examples of Success Criteria

Student Self- Assessment Sheet Subject: ___________ Topic: __________ Grade:___				
Name:__________________________________				
Use an asterisk * at the beginning of the unit. Use a tick √ at the end of the unit.				

Difficulty Level of Activity or Skill	**Unit Content: I know** *(Teacher lists specific areas of content as success criteria)*	I need to do more work on this	I know / can do this quite well	I know /can do this very well
	1			
	2			
	3			
	4			
	5			
	6			
	7			
	8			
	Subject specific skills: I can *(Teacher lists specific areas of skill development as success criteria)*	I need to do more work on this	I know / can do this quite well	I know /can do this very well
	1			
	2			
	3			
	4			
	5			
	6			
	7			
	8			

Setting Goals: (Qualifies for an "Outstanding effort" certificate if satisfactorily completed.) *The most important things above for me to work hard on are the numbers that are circled or highlighted*	**Teacher comment:**
EXTENSION: (Qualifies for an "**Outstanding achievement**" certificate if satisfactorily completed.) A specific area of challenge that I would like to explore instead of repeating the above: *(Teacher lists off-level examples OR student suggests):* 1. 2. 3.	**Student/teacher negotiated variation to unit:** (Student to complete circled numbers above plus…)

Figure 32 A Student Self- Assessment Template

  Designing Defensible Programs for Gifted Secondary School Learners © Sonia White 2011

Student Self & Peer Assessment Template

Student Name: _____________ **Topic:** _________________

Product: (e.g. Seminar, presentation):

LEARNING GOALS: (skills, knowledge)

1. ____
2. ____
3. ____

Success Criteria: I can:	My Feedback (what I did well, what didn't work so well)	My feed forward (what I need to work more on, what I could develop next)
1.		
2.		
3.		
Comments:		

PEER ASSESSMENT: Peer NAME: _____________________

Feedback on your success criteria (what you did well, what didn't work so well)	Feed forward (what you need to work more on, what you could develop next)
Comments:	

Figure 33 Student Self & Peer Assessment Template

4.2.4 Summative Assessment

Summative assessment occurs at the end of a period of learning. Ideally, it can be both a reflective summary of the level of knowledge and skill acquired over the learning period, and informative of next steps in learning.

Traditionally assessment at Secondary school takes one of the following forms:
- Unit tests or summative exams;
- Major assignment or assessment tasks.

As a study prelude to exams, students can revisit prior knowledge assessments.

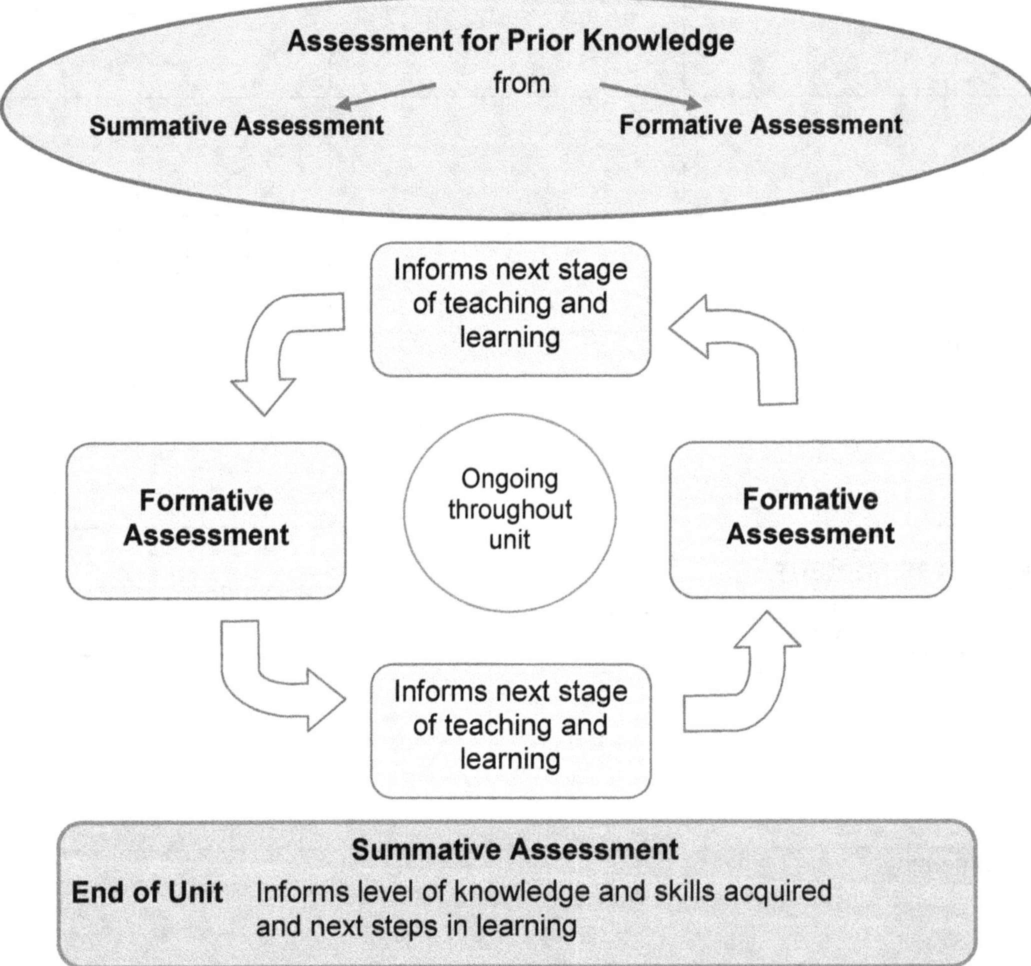

Figure 34 The Cyclical Nature of Formative and Summative Assessment

4.2.5 Testing for Prior Knowledge

If you don't know where you are going,
you will probably end up somewhere else.
- Laurence J. Peter

How do teachers know the prior knowledge and skill level of their students?

When secondary teachers are teaching up to 5 or 6 classes it can seem quite challenging to develop ways of assessing the prior knowledge and skill level of their students. This section offers some suggestions on how this can be done. However it is done, assessment for prior learning *must* be used to inform teaching and learning for the groups of students in those classes.

Provocative Thought:

When learning is only assessed at the *end* of a unit, teachers can take no pride in the achievement of their gifted learners.

There is no evidence that those learners have learned anything new, or gained new skills *unless* the level of knowledge and skills has been assessed prior to the unit, *and* there is *evidence* of a shift in student achievement.

How do students KNOW what they know or don't know?

The answer is a qualified "that depends..." It depends upon how effectively the teacher shares learning goals and achievement with the student. Knowledge about student learning is based around a combination of previous learning experiences, subsequent feedback and feed-forward, and informal and formal assessment practices. At the beginning of a new unit of work, teachers should assess for student prior knowledge. Whilst teachers may be aware of some subject specific skills, students vary in their prior experiences in that subject area. For example, a student who has sat an assessment test in Mathematics at the beginning of the school year may have scored well in some areas, and not in others. Maybe the test was not a diagnostic assessment of proficiency in all areas. A student who is outstanding in algebra may not be outstanding in geometry. Hence prior assessment in different units is important for both teacher and student.

Methods of Assessing Prior Knowledge

The choice of method used to assess prior knowledge will depend on the type of knowledge or skills that need to be assessed. Some options include:

o **Unit pre-tests**; (with the option of using the end-of-unit test) and/or

o **Off-level tests** (for those who ace the pre-test!)

o **Terms and Vocabulary definitions and examples** chart (see Figure 35 p.75)

o **Teacher Observation:** Practical observation of skills in a 'warm-up' or sample activity that incorporates or allows demonstration of increasingly sophisticated skill use. (e.g. physical education, music, drama).

o At the beginning of the unit (or lesson) students attempt the **five most difficult questions** that will reflect high level learning.   This is particularly successful in Mathematics[7].

o Brainstorm a **mind map or web on prior knowledge of subject;** use key words so that the student can show interconnections and depth in specific areas; ask students to write down all the questions they have about the topic. If done in pairs or groups, students can use different colour pens.

o **Learning Map** (Figure 36): What I know; what I thought I didn't know, but I did!; What I thought I knew but I don't!; What I didn't know I didn't know!; What I would now like to know more about. These are good formative self-assessment tools.

o **KN Charts**: 'What I Know and What I need to Know' Charts. Because students don't always know what they need to know, these are useful *after* other strategies. For example, exposure to the 'five most difficult questions' or Terms and Vocabulary definitions and examples charts can give rise to discussion / reflection/ through mind-maps and/or webs which could then culminate in using the learning map or KN Chart.

TIP: Consider telling the students in advance that they are having a pre-test - allow them to 'read ahead' of the unit. Some will be motivated to do so if they know this will mean a successful pre-test will give them more time to dive deeper into more interesting areas of work

---

[7] Winebrenner, (1992).

Key Terms & Vocabulary Test for Prior Knowledge

This is an example, and is *deliberately incomplete*. It focuses upon the **key terms and vocabulary** of the unit. As well as being a fair test of prior knowledge, this method has the added advantage of highlighting for both student and teacher, misunderstandings and gaps in learning.

ENERGY

What can you tell me about	I've heard of this ✓	Give a meaning or a definition if you can	Give an example if you can
energy			
energy transformation			
power			
expansion			
potential energy			
convection			
radiation			
conduction			
energy absorption			
insulatory conductor			

Figure 35 Key Terms and Vocabulary Test for Prior Knowledge

TIP: *The pre-test can be revisited at the end of a unit to demonstrate the shift in student learning. It could be either glued into the student's workbook, or collected by the teacher and held for revisiting at the end-of-unit.*

<table>
<tr><td colspan="2">Student Learning Map   TOPIC: ________________________</td></tr>
<tr><td>What I know</td><td>What I thought I didn't know BUT I do!</td></tr>
<tr><td>What I thought I knew BUT I don't</td><td>What I didn't know I didn't know!</td></tr>
<tr><td colspan="2">What I would now like to know more about</td></tr>
<tr><td colspan="2">What I deny or refuse to look at:</td></tr>
</table>

Figure 36 Student Learning Map Template

 Designing Defensible Programs for Gifted Secondary School Learners © Sonia White 2011

TEACHER LEARNING MAP:
Personalising Learning

What I know	What I thought I didn't know BUT I do!

What I thought I knew BUT I don't	What I didn't know I didn't know!

What I would now like to know more about

What I deny or refuse to look at:

Fill in the first box before beginning this section, and the remaining subsequent to reading and discussion

Figure 37 Teacher Learning Map: Personalising Learning

Formative Assessment: Planning for Change

Which formative assessment practices on the previous pages best suit my/our subject area?

Which do we already do? How effectively do we do this? What evidence do we have that it is successful?

What can I/we begin developing further (in the next month/next unit)?

Who /What /How? What processes need to be put in place? (e.g., set-up, implementation, evaluation).

What area might I/we need more professional development support or advice in?

Feed back: (What worked /what needs further development)

Feed Forward: (What next?)

Figure 38 Formative Assessment: Planning for Change Template

   Designing Defensible Programs for Gifted Secondary School Learners © Sonia White 2011

NOTES:

4.3 Flexible Pacing: They've 'Aced' the Pre-Test! Now What?

This is where individualising learning takes over. When students demonstrate their proficiency on pre-tests (and off-level testing) teachers and departments need to consider a range of options, several of which are described in Chapter 3 and some of which are enlarged upon here. Flexible pacing and curriculum compacting should be considered.

Flexible Pacing ...allows students to move forward in the curriculum at the same time as they master content and skills. For gifted, this generally includes some form of acceleration, either by moving the student up to advanced content or moving the content down to the student.

Rate of Progress Can Vary ...gifted students typically have asynchronous development. Learning experiences will differ between and even within subjects. Flexible pacing allows challenge at a rate that reflects the students' specific learning needs, and alleviates the potential for pressure and frustration.

Ways to implement Flexible Pacing

Continuous progress Students move ahead as they master content and skills. This removes the lock-step learning process.

Compacting the Curriculum Course is covered in less time, e.g., a two year course in 1 year (subject specific).

Advanced level course(s) Students learn *some* subjects at an advanced level. When a student does courses at different year levels, this is called **dual enrolment** or '**multi-levelling**'.

Early Entrance: to Middle or Secondary school, or College, and **Whole Year Grade Skipping** Student is accelerated in all subjects one or two or more years

Examination Credits: Students sit examinations earlier than their age peers. This allows them early entry to College or Advanced Placement Programs.

Remember to offer 'off-level' or beyond -the -level tests to students who ace a pre-test or a year level test.

Figure 39 Flexible Pacing

4.3.1 Curriculum Compacting

Curriculum compacting should be an option for all students in the classroom, not just those labelled "gifted"[8] . Students who have strengths in a particular content area or who have studied a topic that they are interested in on their own time will benefit from having an opportunity to pursue other activities.

Five Basic Steps to Successful Curriculum Compacting

1 Pre-test students at the beginning of a unit

Analyze an upcoming unit to determine the key concepts and skills. Select the best ways to identify students **who have already met the learning objectives**. (e.g., end-of unit tests, above-the-level tests, most difficult 5 questions)

2 Eliminate content that students already know, or skills already mastered

Agree (with student) on content that must still be covered and skills still to be mastered. Use a student contract if you are unsure the student will comply.

3 Replace the skipped content with *meaningful* alternative topics or projects.

Offer student choice, including student generated research questions for diving deeper into the topic, going beyond the level, or even exploring a whole different area

4 Match the Assessment with the learning

Students will quickly become cynical if they are assessed at the end of a unit at a level that does not match the level of their learning. Using higher level success criteria for assessment is critical for successful curriculum compacting.

5 Evaluate effectiveness: use student voice as well as test results.

Teachers are sometimes surprised to hear from students that even when the curriculum has been compacted, the program still lacked challenge. Often gifted learners are able (and *want)* to push themselves further or faster for the challenge. Teachers need to know if the 'instead of' options offer that level of challenge.

---

[8] Renzulli & Reis (1998).

NOTE: Students and parents should be involved in discussion and decision making around choices for flexible pacing.

How can flexible pacing be managed in-class?

Classroom Management

Student Collaborates with teacher to:

Work independently on projects of their own design

Work on an activity beyond the level that the class is not yet ready to learn.

BUT! Sometimes there will be specific areas in which the student is still developing skills.

Student participates in class at certain points during the unit.

OR student completes skill-building activities on his/her own.

With some scaffolding into areas of greater challenge, gifted learners can become less dependent upon their teachers and *more independent, autonomous learners.*

P.S.

Do not be surprised if gifted teens are initially reluctant to work independently: some will be afraid it will lessen their grades. They need to understand their learner readiness level.

The more we allow our learners to take control of their learning, the more motivated they become.

Cultivate a 'difficult is good' environment. Allow students the thrill of achieving something they have had to strive for.

TEACHER LEARNING MAP:
Flexible Pacing

What I know	What I thought I didn't know BUT I do!
What I thought I knew BUT I don't	**What I didn't know I didn't know!**

What I would now like to know more about

What I deny or refuse to look at:

Fill in first box before beginning the section, and the remaining boxes subsequent to reading and discussion

Figure 40 Teacher Learning Map: Flexible Pacing

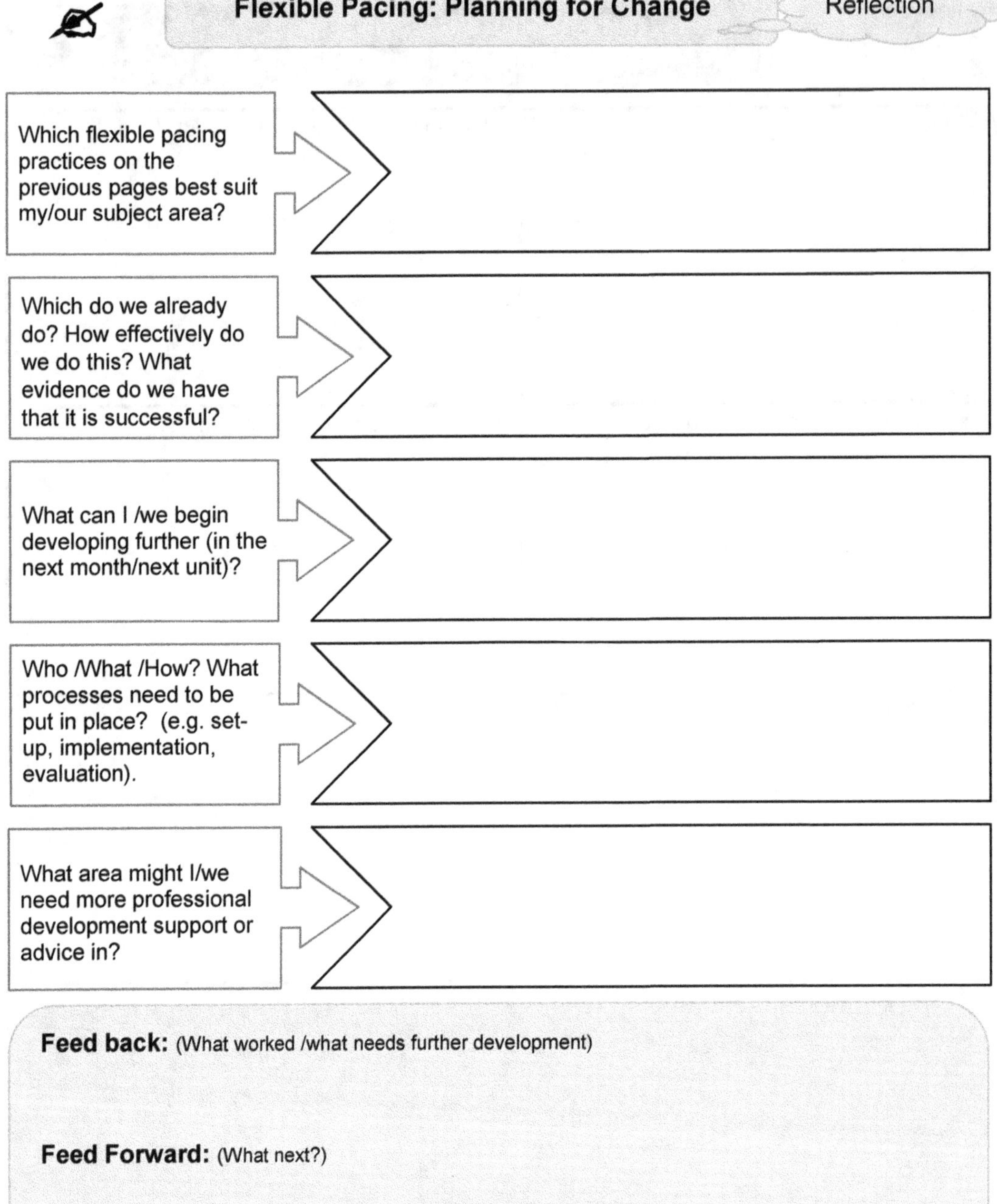

Figure 41 Flexible Pacing: Planning for Change Template

4.4 Individualised Learning for Gifted

Individualised learning can be applied to *all* students. However, individualised learning for gifted learners has specific components.

> **The key components of individualised learning are:**
>
> - **Individual *long term goal setting*** involving student aspirations academically, culturally, and with respect and support for the social-emotional development of the student.
> - **Creating a 'match' with those long term goals within *and beyond* the school framework**, wherever possible.

Individualised learning for gifted flourishes in a school environment where teachers are flexible and are tolerant of ambiguity. Individual long term goal setting requires careful planning and support. It most definitely will involve some form of flexible pacing, and curriculum compacting and will place responsibility for deeper level or advanced level learning firmly upon the shoulders of the student. Learning extends beyond the classroom, and often even beyond the curriculum in ways that best meet the individual student's learning needs. It will be focussed upon the students specific areas of strength and in line with their current long term goals.

There are numerous combinations of possibilities for an individual gifted learner. Secondary schools already have many of these in place. It is worth considering the range of options overleaf to see which may suit some individual gifted learners in your class, department or school. While many of these provisions need to be managed by a Gifted Education Coordinator or other professional in charge of provisions for gifted, it is important that classroom teachers are flexible and accepting of these provisions for gifted. Teachers should feel reassured that their seeking and supporting provisions beyond their classrooms for their gifted learners is a testament to the professionalism they are demonstrating in recognizing diverse student needs.

Teachers should feel reassured that their seeking and supporting provisions beyond their classrooms for gifted learners is a testament to the professionalism they are demonstrating in recognizing diverse student needs.

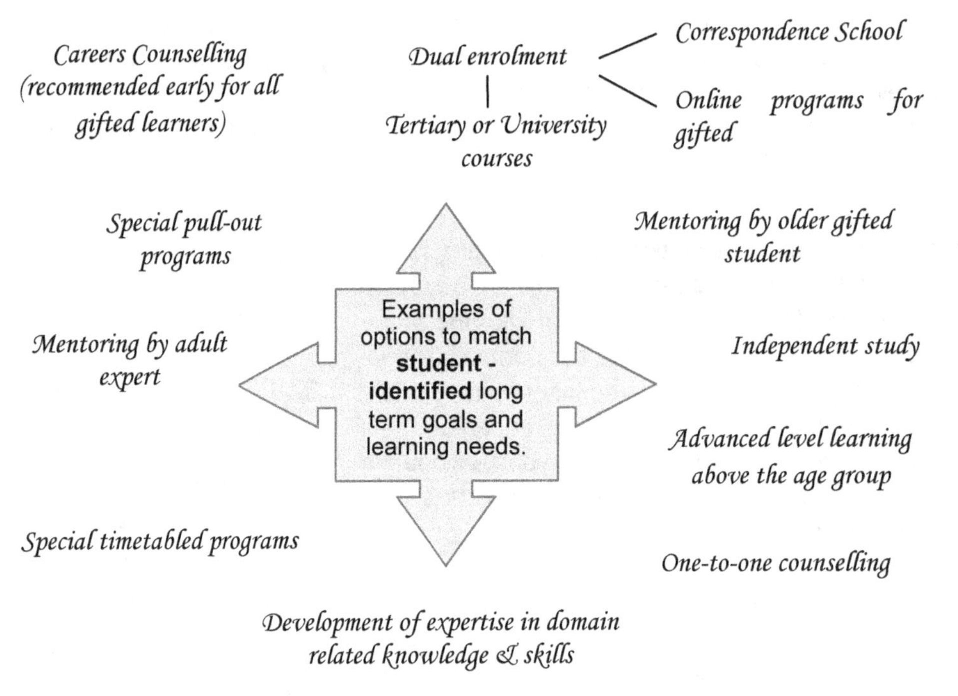

Figure 42 Examples of Options for Individualised Learning

 Designing Defensible Programs for Gifted Secondary School Learners © Sonia White 2011

REFLECTION

Individualised Learning: Planning for Change

Reflection

Which individualised learning practices on the previous pages do we already implement? How effectively do we do this?

Which practices will we implement that we don't already do?

What processes & resource personnel do we have in place to facilitate individualised learning?
Who else do we need?

Which students in my class/ our department/ our school need individualised learning?

What area might I/we need more professional development support or advice in?

Feed back: (What has been done/ what worked /what needs further development)

Feed Forward: (What next?)

Figure 43 Individualised Learning: Planning for Change Tempalte

NOTES:

References and Readings

Black, P., Harrison, C., Lee, C., Marshall, B., & Wiliam, D. (2003). *Assessment for Learning: Putting it into practice.* . Berkshire, England: Open University Press.

Black, P., & Wiliam, D. (1998a). Assessment and classroom learning. . *Assessment in Education, 5*(1), 7-74.

Black, P., & Wiliam, D. (1998b). Inside the black box: Raising standards through classroom assessment. *Phi Delta Kappan, 80*(2), 139-148.

Bloom, B. S. (1956). Taxonomy of educational objectives: the classification of educational goals. Handbook 1: Cognitive domain. New York: Longmans, Green & Co.

Braggett, E. J. (1997). Differentiated programs for secondary schools: units of work for gifted & talented students. Melbourne: Hawker Brownlow.

Cathcart, R. (2010). *Gifted programming made practical.* Invercargill, New Zealand: Essential Resources Educational Publishers Ltd.

Cathcart, R. (2010). *Differentiation made practical* Invercargill, New Zealand: Essential Resources Educational Publishers Ltd.

Gardner, H. (2000). *Intelligence reframed: multiple intelligences for the 21st century.* USA: Simon & Schuster.

Gardner, H. (1993). *Frames of mind: the theory of multiple intelligences* (2nd ed.). New York: Basic Books.

Garrison, C., & Ehringhaus, M. (2007). Formative and summative assessments in the classroom. [Electronic Version] from
http://www.nmsa.org/Publications/WebExclusive/Assessment/tabid/1120/Default.aspx.

Goleman, D. (1999). *Working with emotional intelligence.* Great Britain: Bloomsbury.

Gross, M., Macleod, B., & Pretorius, M. (2001). Gifted students in secondary schools: differentiating the curriculum (2nd ed.). Sydney: Gifted Education Research, Resource and information Centre (GERRIC), UNSW.

Kaplan, S. N. (1986). The grid: A model to construct differentiated curriculum for the gifted. In J. S. Renzulli (Ed.), Systems and models for developing programs for the gifted and talented (pp. 180-193). Mansfield Center, CT: Creative Learning Press.

Kohlberg, L. (1971). Stages of moral development as the basis for moral education. In C. M. Beck, B. S. Crittenden & E. V. Sullivan (Eds.), Moral education: Interdisciplinary approaches (pp. 23-92). New York: Newman Press

Krathwohl, D. R., Bloom, B. S., & Masia, B. B. (1964). Taxonomy of educational objectives: The classification of educational goals. Handbook II: Affective domain. New York: David McKay Co.

Maker, C. J. (1982). Curriculum development for the gifted. Austin, TX: PRO-ED.

Millibrand, D. (2004). *Choice and voice in personalised learning.* Paper presented at the DfES Innovation Unit / DEMOS / OECD Conference, Personalising education: The future of public sector reform.

Ministry of Education, N.Z. (2011). Formative assessment and the Assessment Resource Banks Retrieved Feb 7, 2011, from http://arb.nzcer.org.nz/formative.php

Ministry of Education, N.Z. (2009). e Aho Arataki Marau mō te Ako i Te Reo Māori - Kura Auraki: Curriculum guidelines for teaching and learning Te Reo Māori in English-medium. Wellington, NZ: Learning Media Ltd.

Ministry of Education, N.Z. (2009). *e Aho Arataki Marau mō te Ako i Te Reo Māori - Kura Auraki: Curriculum guidelines for teaching and learning Te Reo Māori in English-medium.* Wellington, NZ: Learning Media Ltd. (pp42:46).

Organisation for Economic Cooperation and Development. (2005). Formative assessment: Improving learning in secondary classrooms. [Electronic Version]. *Policy Brief.* Retrieved February 22nd, 2011 from http://www.oecd.org/dataoecd/19/31/35661078.pdf.

Renzulli, J. S. (1993). *The enrichment triad model: a guide for developing defensible programs for the gifted and talented.* Australia: Hawker Brownlow.

Renzulli, J. S., & Reis, S. M. (1985). *The Schoolwide Enrichment Model: A comprehensive plan for educational excellence.* Mansfield Center, CT: Creative Learning Press.

Riley, T. L. (2004). Curriculum models: the framework for educational programmes. In D. McAlpine & R. Moltzen (Eds.), *Gifted and talented: New Zealand perspectives* (2nd ed., pp. 309-344). Palmerston North, New Zealand: ERDC Press.

Riley, T. L., Bevan-Brown, J., Bicknell, B., Carroll-Lind, J., & Kearney, A. (2004). *The extent, nature and effectiveness of planned approaches in New Zealand schools for identifying and providing for gifted and talented students.*, from http://www.educationcounts.govt.nz/publications/assessment/5451.

Treffinger, D. (1995). *Creativity, creative thinking, and critical thinking: in search of definitions.* Saratosa: Center for Creative Learning.

Tomlinson, C. A., Kaplan, S. M., Renzulli, J. S., Purcell, J., Leppiem, J., & Burns, D. (2002). *The Parallel Curriculum: A design to develop potential and challenge high ability learners.* Thousand Oaks, CA: Corwin Press.

VanTassel-Baska, J. (1993). Comprehensive curriculum planning for gifted learners. Boston, MA: Allyn & Bacon.

VanTassel-Baska, J., & Brown, E. F. (2001). An analysis of gifted education curriculum models. In F. A. Karnes & S. M. Bean (Eds.), *Methods and materials for teaching the gifted.* Texas: Prufrock Press.

VanTassel-Baska, J., & Little, C. A. (Eds.). (2003). Content-based curriculum for high-ability learners. Waco, Texas: Prufrock Press, Inc.

Williams, F. E. (1993). The cognitive-affective interaction model for enriching gifted programs. In J. S. Renzulli (Ed.), *Systems and models for developing programs for the gifted and talented* (pp. 461-484). Highett, Vic.: Hawker Brownlow.

Chapter 5. Curriculum Development

An intelligent plan is the first step to success.
The man who plans
knows where he is going
knows what progress he is making
and
has a pretty good idea when he will arrive.
- Basil S. Walsh.

Analysing the Bones of a Good Unit Overview and Unit Content

How effective is your planning, resourcing and teaching practice in differentiating & personalising learning for gifted?

This section provides teachers and school managers with tools to review units of work. Teachers are invited to consider what they already do well, and to establish gaps in terms of appropriate provisions for gifted. The checklists are critical reflection tools which promote teacher inquiry into their practice for gifted. They draw attention to the principles of good practice for gifted learners. Teachers find these tools effective in reviewing their unit plans and developing and trialling new activities, resources and teaching practice.

There are essential components to a unit plan overview and content development that teachers can consider in checking "what's right?" and "what's missing"?

The following pages help 'unpick' the unit overview and unit content, and demonstrate ways in which the unit can be enhanced to improve learning for gifted.

Note: It is not expected that every unit plan would contain every element described on the following checklists! Curriculum areas will differ in their emphasis upon specific practices, and teachers should be free to explore what works best in their subject, and in their classrooms. However...

Provocative Thought:
...no teacher should claim that higher level thinking, flexible pacing or acceleration is inappropriate in their subject area. This is indefensible.

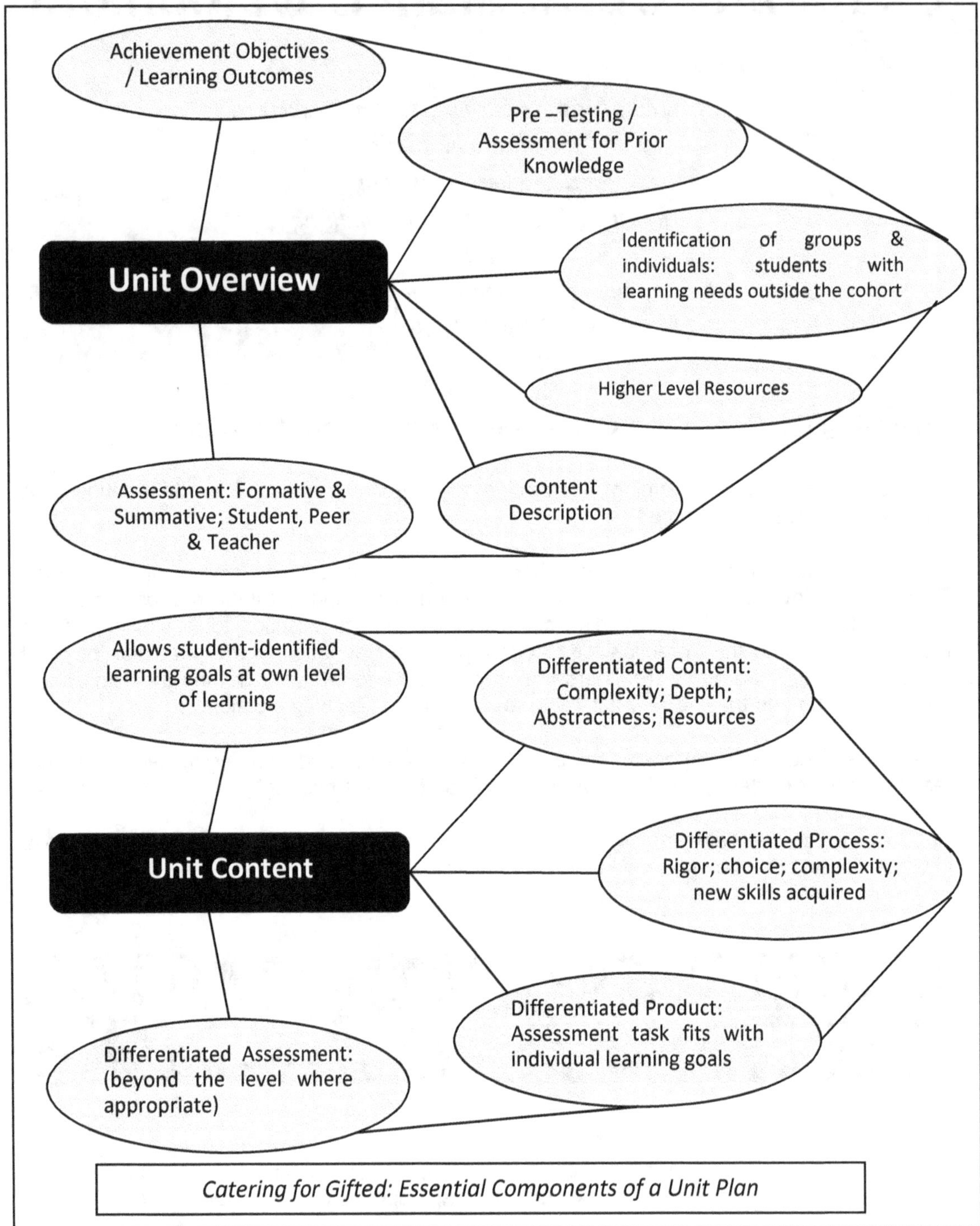

Figure 44 Essential Components of a Unit Plan

5.1 Analysing the Unit Overview

Overview of Unit Plan: Checklist for Teachers

Achievement Objectives /Learning Outcomes: ➡ **Are these listed**? *If not, they need to be.* This should include **subject specific skills** as well as *content.*

Catering for gifted/ students above the level and students below the level:	
Pre-testing & Prior Knowledge	Y/ N
Is assessment of prior knowledge / expertise in skills planned for at the beginning of the unit?	
As a result of this assessment, will prior knowledge be catered for in the unit planning?	
Is there acknowledgement of range of student ability in literacy / numeracy?	
Within the Unit Overview Plan	Y/ N
Are there sections in the overview which cater for learners achieving above or below the cohort?	
Is there space for students identified with needs beyond the cohort to be named?	
Are there explicitly stated learning outcomes for students above the level? (examples pp 68 -70)	
Do the learning outcomes have a focus upon higher order thinking?	
For those above the level, is there a balance between content, higher skills development and higher order thinking?	
Is skill development beyond the level explicitly stated?	
Are there explicitly stated learning outcomes for students below the level? (example page 68)	
Are differentiated resources listed for students above the level?	
Formative & Summative Assessment	Y/ N
Are differentiated success criteria clearly articulated for teacher & students, related to their own specific learning outcomes?	
Is there provision for student self-assessment *prior to, during,* and *at the end* of the unit? *(student formative & summative assessment)*	
Does the assessment reflect the work undertaken? *(Is it differentiated to match student learning goals?)*	

Figure 45 Overview of Unit Plan: Checklist for Teachers

How clear are the achievement objectives (AOs) / or learning outcomes (LOs)?

"At the end of this unit the students will be able to…" (List objectives or outcomes *including specific* subject skills and *thinking skills* acquired. In some subjects it may be easier to express the LOs or AOs through success criteria).

When examining their unit overviews teachers often find that the emphasis is upon increased content rather than higher order thinking, abstractness, depth and complexity.

For gifted learners, content knowledge & understanding are far better assimilated through applying the higher order thinking skills of analysis, synthesis, evaluation, & ethical & moral reasoning. Increased content alone is not defensible.

HIGHLIGHT OR LIST YOUR PRIORITIES

Using the Unit Overview Checklist

This checklist (page 93) is not meant to be intimidating! Rather, it should help you establish priorities that you can work on to improve the unit. With the next unit you develop, you will be able to move into new areas of development. Teachers will have varying levels of expertise in developing unit content suitable for gifted learners, and therefore working as a department team is really beneficial as teachers can support each other as 'critical friends'.

The following process is recommended:

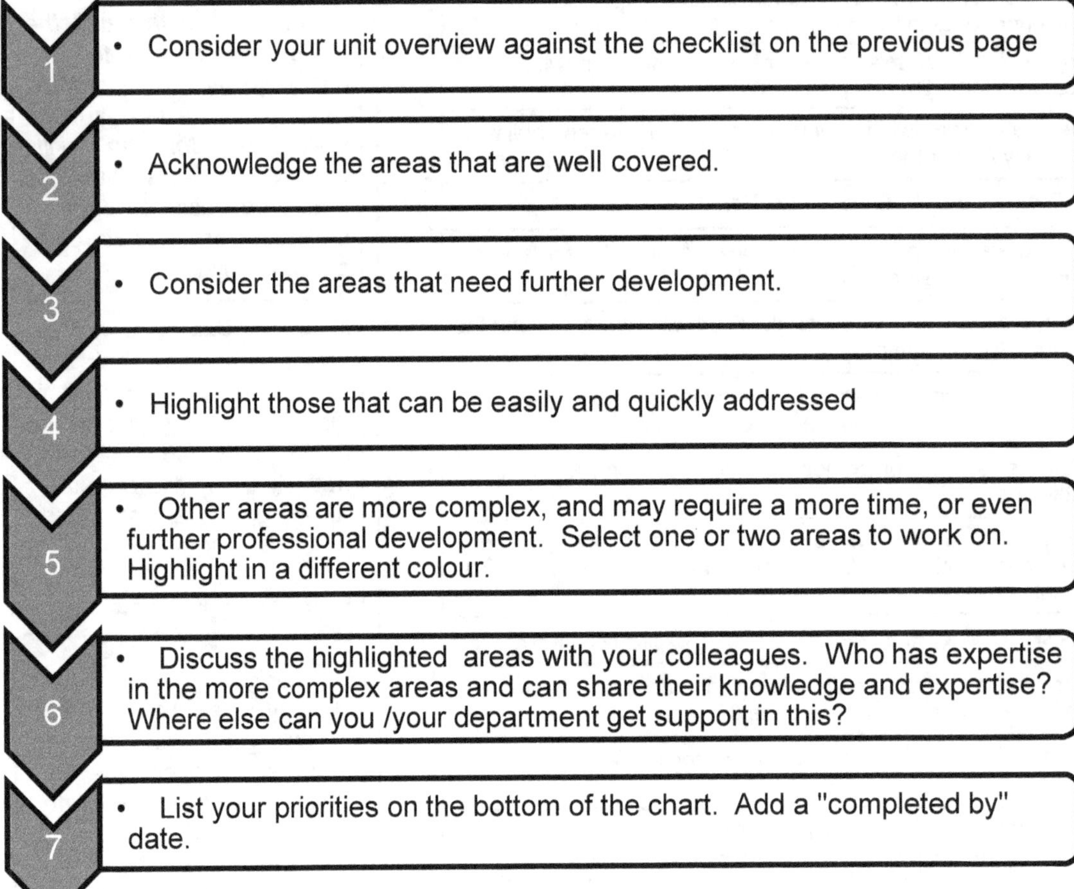

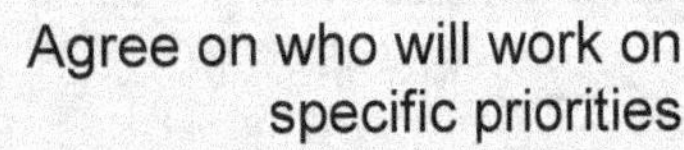

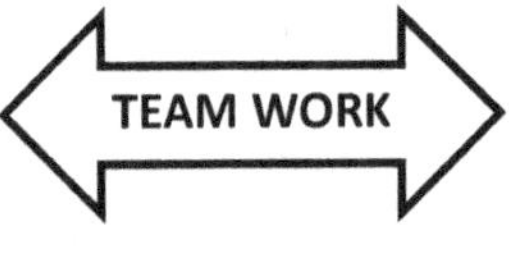

Agree on completion and reviewing, sharing & critiquing dates

5.1.2 Analysing Major Assignments / Assessment tasks

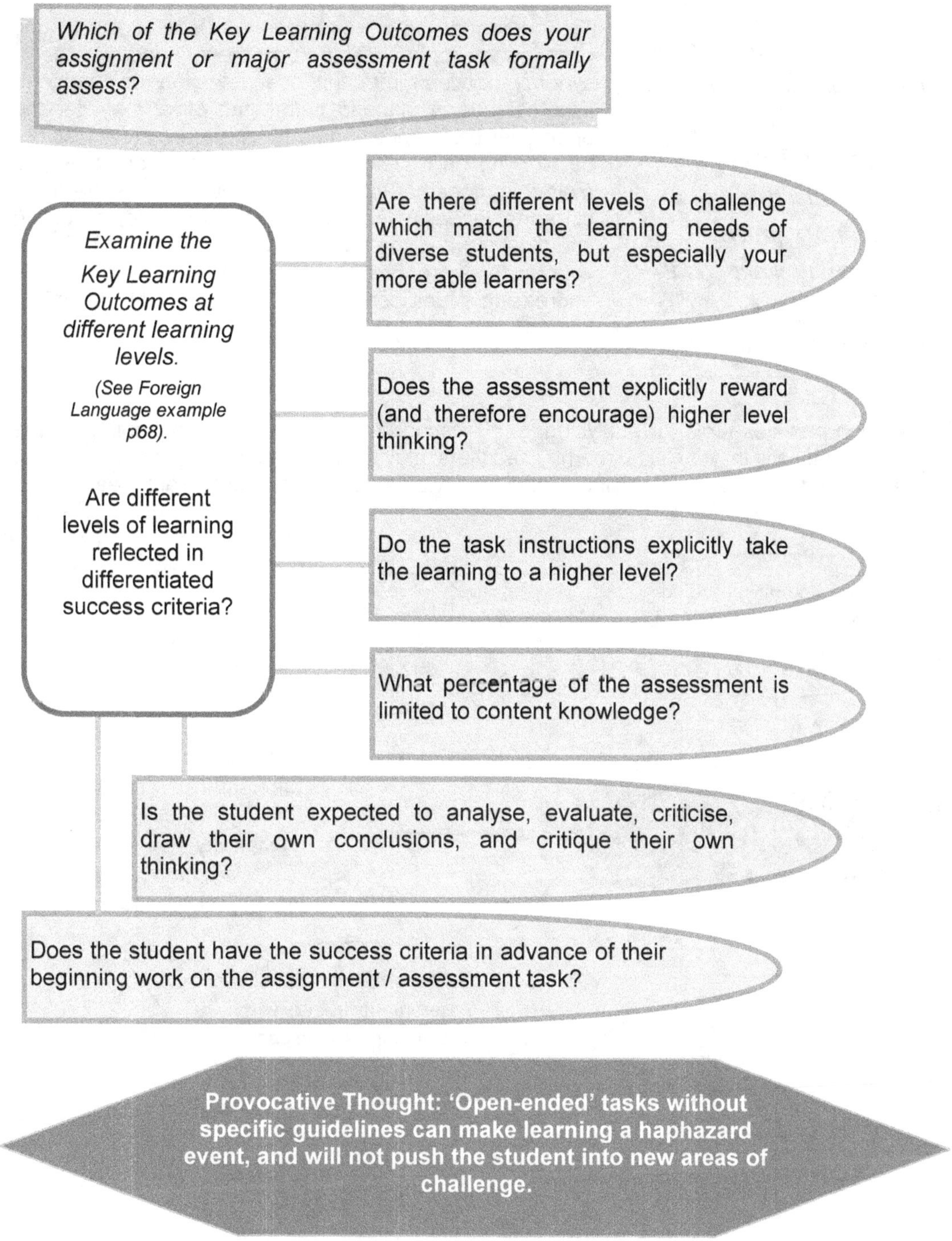

Figure 46 Analysing Major Assignment / Assessment Tasks

5.2 Analysing Unit Content

Change in teaching practice to accommodate defensible practice for gifted takes TIME, and a collective will to improve practice which will make a real difference for more able learners in the classroom.

The content of the unit provides the detail that your unit overview describes. Therefore there needs to be a synergy between the unit overview and unit content. Whether one is planned before the other may depend upon your preference. Some teachers are more inspired by working on developing the content before they pull everything together in a unit overview. Others are more comfortable designing the unit overview before diving into 'fleshing out' the detail of unit contents. Whichever your style, there are certain considerations that need addressing if unit content is to be defensible for gifted learners.

This section provides tools for analysing your existing unit content and its suitability for the more able students in your classroom. Teachers may find one tool more beneficial than another depending upon their individual teaching styles, experience, and subject area.

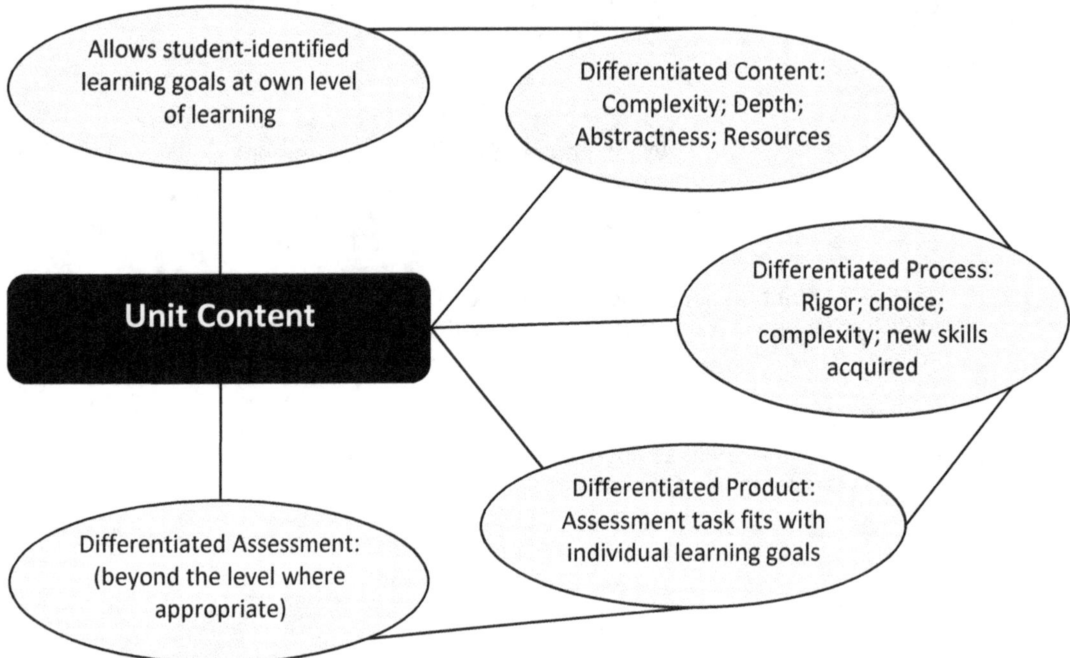

Figure 47 Catering for Gifted: Essential Components of Unit Plan Content

5.2.1 Creating Defensible Unit Content
Rate the learning outcomes: (or the accompanying success criteria)
What percentage of the more able students' learning time is spent upon:
1. Knowledge/understanding, recall (Content)
2. Applying the knowledge (Applying – Blooms Taxonomy)
3. Critical & Creative thinking: Analysis, Creativity, Evaluation (Blooms)
4. Caring thinking: Valuational, Affective, Active, Normative thinking (Lipman's Caring Thinking)
5. Higher level skills development

All students need some learning time spent on critical, creative and caring thinking. Able students should spend most of their time (up to 75% of each lesson and assignment) applying higher order thinking and higher level skills to the content.

Is there a balance between content, higher skills development and higher order thinking?

OR: Is the unit primarily concerned with knowledge, understanding and recall (content based)? (☹)

OR: Does the unit compel step by step learning and a high degree of "practice" or repetition? (☹)

OR: Is the unit flexible enough to allow able students to move with increased pace, and explore certain aspects in depth? (☺)

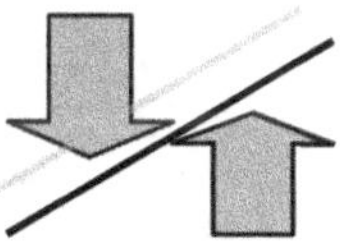

What is the balance? Is there sufficient rigor and challenge for the able learner?
What should there be less of? More of?

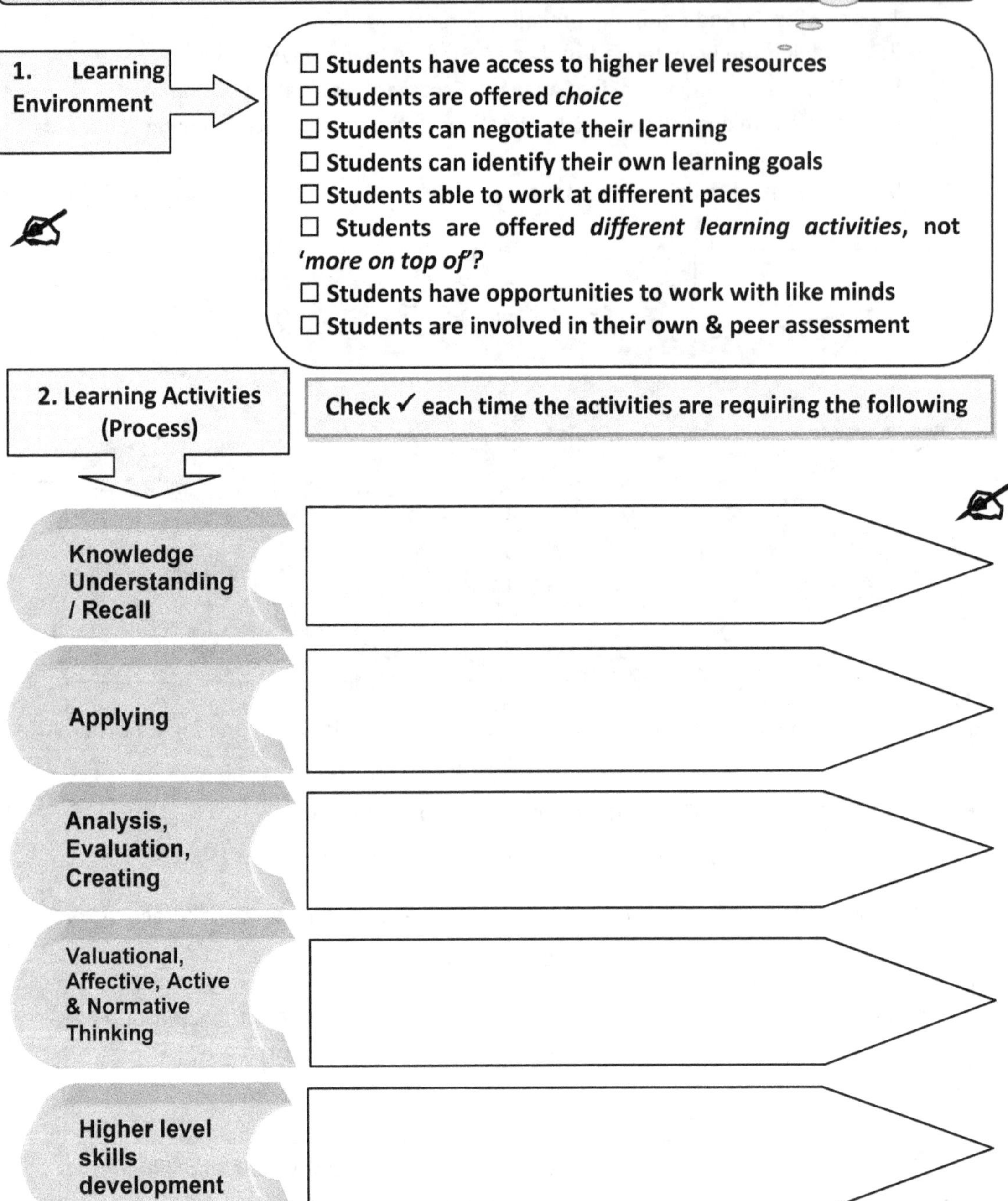

Figure 48 Assessing Learning Environment and unit content: Teacher Checklist

Using the Unit Content Checklist

This checklist is not meant to be intimidating! Rather, it should help you establish priorities that you can work on to improve the unit. With the next unit you develop, you will be able to move into new areas of development. Teachers will have varying levels of expertise in developing unit content, and therefore working as a departmental team is really beneficial as teachers can support each other as 'critical friends'.

The following process is recommended:

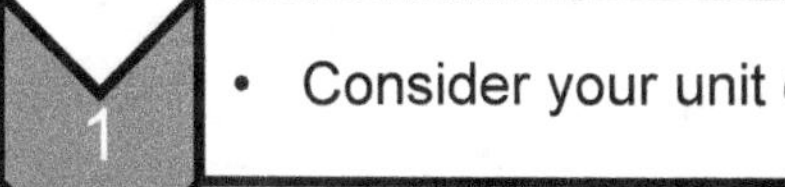

1
- Consider your unit content against the checklist on the previous page

2
- Acknowledge the areas that are well covered. Reduce the amount of 'lower order' thinking for gifted learners where possible.

3
- Consider the areas that need further development.

4
- Highlight those that can be easily, quickly addressed.

5
- Others areas area more complex, and may require a more time, or even further professional development. Select **one or two** areas to work on. Highlight in a different colour.

6
- Discuss the highlighted areas with your colleagues. Who has expertise in the more complex areas and can share their knowledge and expertise? Where else can you /your department get support in this?

7
- List your priorities on the bottom of the chart. Add a "completed by" date, to give yourself a deadline to work to

Agree on who will work on specific priorities

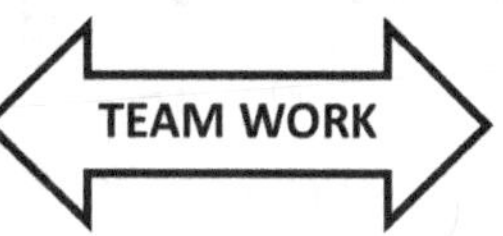

Agree on completion and reviewing, sharing & critiquing dates

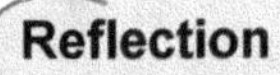

Unit Content, Unit Learning Activities & Classroom Practice

What considerations about **unit content** have caught my attention on pages 96-99**?**	
What adaptations to **unit content** should I make? (Choose 1 or 2 to work on)	
Which **classroom practice**(s) could be easily or quickly accommodated? (Classroom Environment, Page 98 Figure 48)	
Is there a challenge in this area that I could take up to further develop my classroom practice?	
How much rigor and challenge is supplied in the **unit learning activities**? What do I need to change?	
Who else might I ask for support in this?	

Figure 49 Unit content, learning activities and classroom practice: Teacher Reflection Tool

5.3 Further resources: best practice for differentiating learning for gifted

The next two pages contain resources that elaborate on a range of good practices in differentiating learning for gifted.

These encourage critical, reflective thinking and professional growth. It is expected that teachers would choose a few areas for development.

Note: No unit plan could ever contain every element described on these two pages!

     Designing Defensible Programs for Gifted Secondary School Learners © Sonia White 2011

A Unit Differentiated for Gifted Learners:

☐ Follows the principles of a differentiated curriculum model
☐ Identifies the g & t students for whom the differentiated learning is designed
☐ Unit overview includes section showing differentiated learning for g & t students: content and skills development
☐ Incorporates assessment for prior knowledge and skills at the beginning of the unit (formative assessment practice)
☐ Allows for different starting places for g & t students: compacting some content or skills so areas of interest can be explored in more depth
☐ Encourages g & t students with learning difficulties by providing opportunities for product to be expressed in a variety of ways / accommodates different learning styles
☐ Allows and provides for student choice
☐ Includes explicit skill development at a higher level

☐ Develops metacognitive awareness (reflecting on thinking, and on strategies to problem find and to problem solve)
☐ Brings higher order thinking skills to the tasks: especially analysis, synthesis, evaluation and caring thinking
☐ Integrates Thinking skills and problem solving in content, process and product
☐ Promotes and teaches creative thinking skills and solution finding in content, process and product
☐ Deliberately incorporates Caring thinking: valuational thinking, affective (feeling) thinking, active thinking and normative thinking
☐ Allows self-assessment – using pre-arranged higher level success criteria and/or own pre-set goals
☐ Provides **different** work for g & t students, not **more** after all else is finished (is qualitatively differentiated)

Some Strategies (not an exhaustive list): O Thinkers Keys O Six Thinking Hats O Creative problem solving
O Exploring moral dilemmas O Inquiry based learning   O Community of Inquiry O Community Problem Solving
O De Bono's CoRT Thinking O Philosophy for Children   O SCAMPER O CAMPER for the Internet O Socratic questioning
O Analogies O Concept maps, mind maps O Paradoxes O Future Problem Solving O Graphic organisers   O
Directed Thinking O Maker Model O Blooms Taxonomy   O William's Taxonomy O Krathwohl's Taxonomy O
Taylor's Multiple Talent Model   O Lipman's Model of Caring Thinking O Using Bibliotherapy O Using Planning Matrices
to apply Blooms /Williams /Lipman's and/or Multiple Intelligences

Figure 50 Principles of Good Practice & Strategies Used in Differentiating Learning for Gifted 1

CRITICAL THINKING	CREATIVE THINKING	CARING THINKING
✓ *CONTENT – knowledge to be gained*	✓ *CONTENT – knowledge to be gained*	✓ *CONTENT – knowledge to be gained*
• allows for increased pace of learning • provides *real* challenge: abstractness, complexity: • relationships between two or more concepts • takes a thematic approach to some broad-based issues & problems and is cross-curricula • recognises prior learning – allows for: compaction of content & skills, development of *new skills* • Includes content not normally presented for that age group	• does not force a lock-step method of learning • allows for playful exploration of creative ideas • allows exploration in greater depth and choice of interest development • encourages risk-taking through acquisition of creative thinking tools • includes abstraction at a level beyond that of the rest of the class • includes development of domain-related creative skills	• relevant to student interests • exposure to moral & ethical issues, rights, justice, global issues (affective thinking) • allows opportunities to exercise social responsibility: (active thinking) • provides a platform for self-understanding • provides opportunity to express opinions, feelings and make judgements: affective thinking • has student input: choice of study area and depth of investigation
✓ *PROCESS – the thinking processes used to acquire the knowledge*	✓ *PROCESS – the thinking processes used to acquire the knowledge*	✓ *PROCESS – the thinking processes used to acquire the knowledge*
• emphasises autonomous learning • uses a predominance of higher level thinking: analysing, evaluating and synthesis • problem solving, problem finding, and deductive reasoning • complex concepts explored • encourages problem/issue thinking • develops analytical and critical thinking skills	• complex, open-ended activities allow for a variety of creative thinking processes • encourages divergent thinking • creative thinking skills taught and developed • playful exploration of creative ideas • a wide range of original ideas, have been generated and elaborated upon	• encourages self-motivation for learning • develops skills underpinning autonomous learning • allows for aesthetic appreciation (valuational thinking) and judgement • provides group interaction • provides opportunity to consider reality versus the ideal: (normative thinking) • allows greater degree of student negotiation in aspects of their own learning outcomes
✓ *PRODUCT –evidence of learning*	✓ *PRODUCT –evidence of learning*	✓ *PRODUCT –evidence of learning*
• real world issues & problems • evidence that a higher level of skill(s) has been developed • transformation of information learned into a new form (not just a summary /cut & paste facts) • evaluation – student self assessment ; marking from negotiated pre-set or self-set criteria • assessment values student's critical thinking & is targeted at an advanced level	• demonstrates creativity and critical reflection • shifts from fact finding & definitions to problem finding & solution-finding; • allows for creativity and choice in presentation of learning gained • demonstrates elaboration of creative thought into a credible or polished product • assessment values creativity: originality, elaboration, fluency and flexibility	• Flexibility of product is allowed • Real problems and issues from their own experience are addressed (active thinking) • student reflection and evaluation of their own learning (personal growth) • product is shared with authentic audience(s) • Ethical thinking and/or positive action are valued in assessment

Figure 51 Principles of Good Practice & Strategies Used in Differentiating Learning for Gifted 2

5.4 Stock take

Reflection

TEACHER LEARNING MAP: Planning Learning Units for Gifted - Principles and Strategies

What I know	What I thought I didn't know BUT I do!

What I thought I knew BUT I don't	What I didn't know I didn't know!

What I would now like to know more about

What I deny or refuse to look at:

Fill in first box before beginning the chapter, and the remaining boxes subsequent to reading and discussion

Figure 52 Teacher Learning Map: Planning Learning Units for Gifted - Principles and Strategies

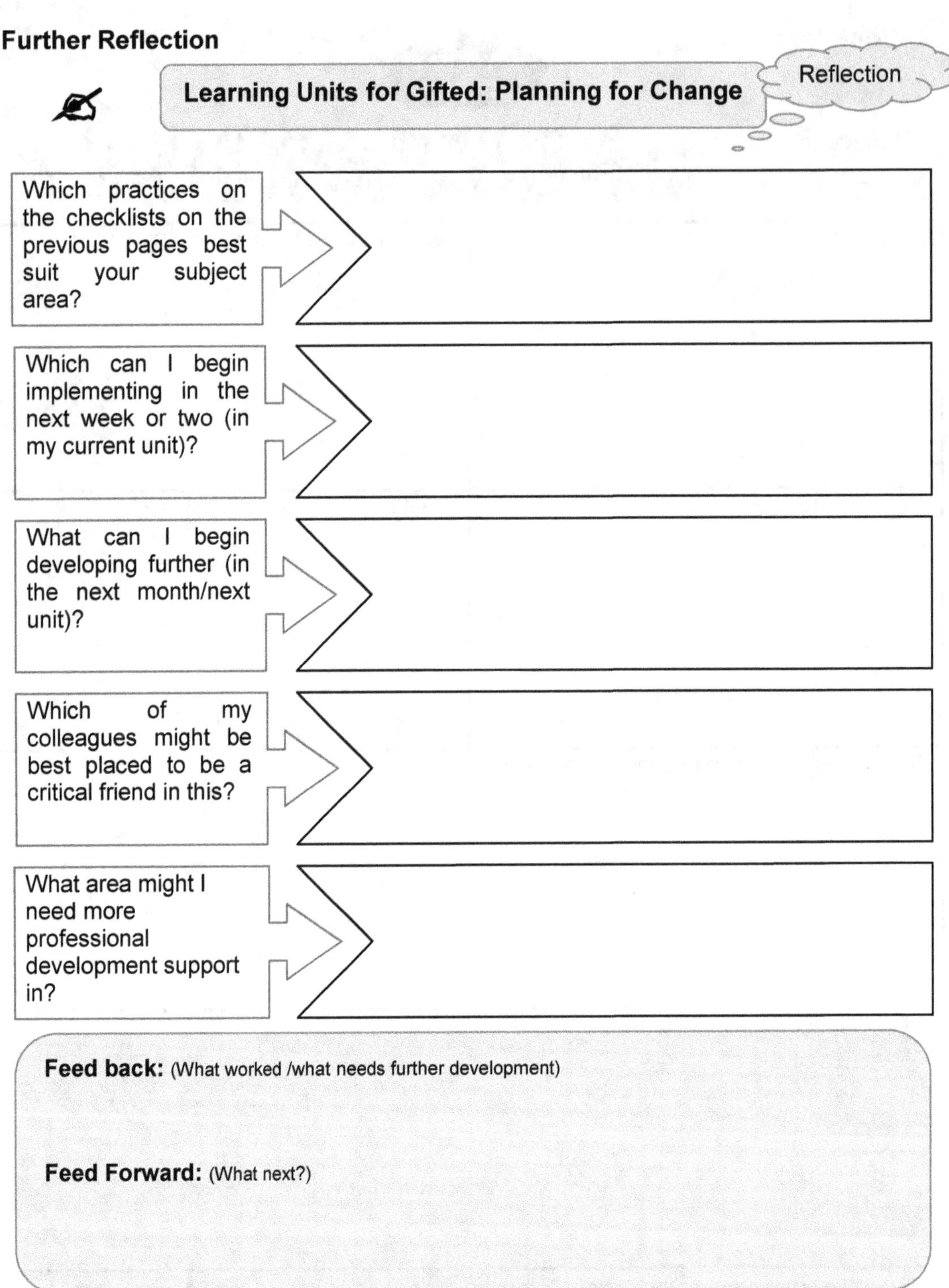

Figure 53 Learning Units for Gifted: Planning for Change Template

NOTES:

Recommended Readings

Black, P., & Wiliam, D. (1998b). Inside the black box: Raising standards through classroom assessment. *Phi Delta Kappan, 80*(2), 139-148.

Bloom, B. S. (1956). Taxonomy of educational objectives: the classification of educational goals. Handbook 1: Cognitive domain. New York: Longmans, Green & Co.

Braggett, E. J. (1997). Differentiated programs for secondary schools: units of work for gifted & talented students. Melbourne: Hawker Brownlow.

Department for Education and Children's Services, S. A., (1997). *Thinking, feeling and learning*. South Australia: Department for Education and Children's Services.

Goleman, D. (1999). *Working with emotional intelligence*. Great Britain: Bloomsbury.

Gross, M., Macleod, B., & Pretorius, M. (2001). Gifted students in secondary schools: differentiating the curriculum (2nd ed.). Sydney: Gifted Education Research, Resource and information Centre (GERRIC), UNSW.

Kaplan, S. N. (1986). The grid: A model to construct differentiated curriculum for the gifted. In J. S. Renzulli (Ed.), Systems and models for developing programs for the gifted and talented (pp. 180-193). Mansfield Center, CT: Creative Learning Press.

Kohlberg, L. (1971). Stages of moral development as the basis for moral education. In C. M. Beck, B. S. Crittenden & E. V. Sullivan (Eds.), Moral education: Interdisciplinary approaches (pp. 23-92). New York: Newman Press

Krathwohl, D. R., Bloom, B. S., & Masia, B. B. (1964). Taxonomy of educational objectives: The classification of educational goals. Handbook II: Affective domain. New York: David McKay Co.

Lipman, M. (1991).*Thinking in education*. Cambridge: Cambridge University Press.

Maker, C. J. (1982). Curriculum development for the gifted. Austin, TX: PRO-ED.

Ministry of Education, N. Z. (2009). e Aho Arataki Marau mō te Ako i Te Reo Māori - Kura Auraki: Curriculum guidelines for teaching and learning Te Reo Māori in English-medium. Wellington, NZ: Learning Media Ltd.

Organisation for Economic Cooperation and Development. (2005). Formative assessment: Improving learning in secondary classrooms. [Electronic Version]. *Policy Brief*. Retrieved February 22nd 2011 from http://www.oecd.org/dataoecd/19/31/35661078.pdf.

Renzulli, J. S. (1993). *The enrichment triad model: a guide for developing defensible programs for the gifted and talented*. Australia: Hawker Brownlow.

Renzulli, J. S., & Reis, S. M. (1985). *The Schoolwide Enrichment Model: A comprehensive plan for educational excellence*. Mansfield Center, CT: Creative Learning Press.

Riley, T. L. (2004). Curriculum models: the framework for educational programmes. In D. McAlpine & R. Moltzen (Eds.), *Gifted and talented: New Zealand perspectives* (2nd ed., pp. 309-344). Palmerston North, New Zealand: ERDC Press.

Treffinger, D. (1995). *Creativity, creative thinking, and critical thinking: in search of definitions.* Saratosa: Center for Creative Learning.

Tomlinson, C. A., Kaplan, S. M., Renzulli, J. S., Purcell, J., Leppiem, J., & Burns, D. (2002). *The Parallel Curriculum: A design to develop potential and challenge high ability learners.* Thousand Oaks, CA: Corwin Press.

VanTassel-Baska, J. (1993). Comprehensive curriculum planning for gifted learners. Boston, MA: Allyn & Bacon.

VanTassel-Baska, J., & Brown, E. F. (2001). An analysis of gifted education curriculum models. In F. A. Karnes & S. M. Bean (Eds.), *Methods and materials for teaching the gifted.* Texas: Prufrock Press.

VanTassel-Baska, J., & Little, C. A. (Eds.). (2003). Content-based curriculum for high-ability learners. Waco, Texas: Prufrock Press, Inc.

Williams, F. E. (1993). The cognitive-affective interaction model for enriching gifted programs.   In J. S. Renzulli, (Ed.), *Systems and models for developing programs for the gifted and talented* (pp. 461-484). Highett, Vic.: Hawker Brownlow.

Chapter 6. Critical & Creative Thinking: Models & Tools

*The significant problems we face today
cannot be solved at the same level of thinking
we were at when we created them. - Albert Einstein*

This chapter explores higher order thinking within the context of learning activities. Because questioning is a pivotal element in the exploration of knowledge and concepts, teachers are encouraged to explore the quality of questioning in their classrooms – both teacher questioning and student questioning.

It is all in the questioning!

"Fat and Skinny" Questions, Higher Order Thinking Questions, Socratic Questions – whichever guise they come under, a thinking classroom focuses upon questions that

- Challenge
- Require reflection, depth and thought before answering, and
- Stimulate investigation

Many of the tools and activities in the following chapters require *time.* Answers expected and given quickly beg for a shallow superficial reply or are often in response to 'lower order' level questions. While quick 'skinny' questions have their place in the classroom as teachers seek to ascertain basic recall and understanding, 'fat' questions inspire and demand far more discerning answers.

> **TIP:** If your more able students answer inquiry questions without offering depth, add further instructions that require they explain further, analyse, evaluate, draw conclusions, give other points of view, or defend their opinions.

It's all in the classroom environment!

Classrooms which are rich in discourse, where teachers encourage opposing viewpoints and thoughtful, respectful questioning of each other's perspectives are not only rich in learning experiences, they are also classes where students are rarely late or off-task.

Cultivate a culture of "difficult is good".

Gifted students confronted with real challenge for the first time may initially resist the challenge. However, when convinced to do so, students gain a huge satisfaction from meeting the challenge. Challenge then provides powerful intrinsic motivation.

CLASS RULES FOR DISCERNING THINKERS!

1. When you are presenting your ideas to other people, **have the intention of seeking help in discovering any weaknesses, errors or potential improvements**, and be grateful when they are pointed out.

2. If you are listening to other people's ideas, **interpret them in the best possible light**. Do not nit-pick or trivially criticise.

3. **Examine the merits of ideas,** not the people who present them. Do not defend someone else's idea because he is your friend. Do not attack someone's ideas because she is your enemy. Do not take an attack on your ideas as an attack on yourself.

4. **Explore the strengths and weaknesses of a variety of ideas,** without regard to how you personally value them, or how popular/unpopular they may be. Defend ideas that you disagree with, as well as those you agree with. For the sake of logical discussion, dispute positions that you agree with, as well as those you disagree with. When someone else presents a position, do not assume that s/he personally agrees with, or values that position.

5. Remember that **critical thinking is <u>not</u> about "beating the other person in an argument" or about "effectively defending your own personal opinions"**. It is about collectively and cooperatively arriving at the truth.

from: Jewell, P. (1996) "Code of the Community of Inquiry".

Discuss these rules with your students. Ask how they might change them. Agree on a 'code of conduct' for class dialogue.

Figure 54 Class Rules For Discerning Thinkers!

Another valuable tool for use with students in developing and maintaining a thinking classroom is Jewell's "Four Rules of Reasoned Discourse".

FOUR RULES OF REASONED DISCOURSE

1.   I don't understand my own point of view unless I understand those opposing it

2.   I don't understand opposing viewpoints until I can state them so well that those who hold them agree with my summary.

3.   Some of the things I believe in firmly are undoubtedly absolutely wrong.

4.   If I am not willing to change my mind, I am not a critical reasoner.

(Jewell, adapted from Erdman, 2001)

6.1 Adding Challenge with Critical and Creative Thinking: Bloom's Taxonomy

Whether it is with questions or with tasks, teachers can challenge and engage more able learners when they ensure that the questions and learning activities the students are focussing on require higher order thinking skills.

There are several models that this can be based around. This section describes Blooms Taxonomy[9] and its later revised version[10]. A *'taxonomy'* is a classification system; in this case it is a classification of various types of thinking, designed for the purposes of improving the teaching of thinking to children.

Bloom divided cognitive thinking into 6 areas, which were later reframed and slightly redescribed by Anderson and Krathwohl. Krathwohl and Anderson's variation renames 'knowledge' as 'remembering', 'comprehension' as 'understanding' and 'synthesis' as 'creating'.

On the next page is an adapted illustration of these six areas of cognitive thinking (Figure 55). These six areas are often displayed inside a triangle to demonstrate a hierarchy. Bloom (1956) developed this for all ages of learners, including adult, and he believed that for those students with less prior knowledge more time should be spent developing the lower order thinking skills and less on the complex thinking skills. However, while true for many students, this doesn't take into account the gifted learner's pace of learning and ability to absorb new learning in 'big gulps'.

---

[9] Bloom, Benjamin S. (1956).
[10] Krathwohl, D. R, Anderson, L. W. (2001).

     Designing Defensible Programs for Gifted Secondary School Learners © Sonia White 2011

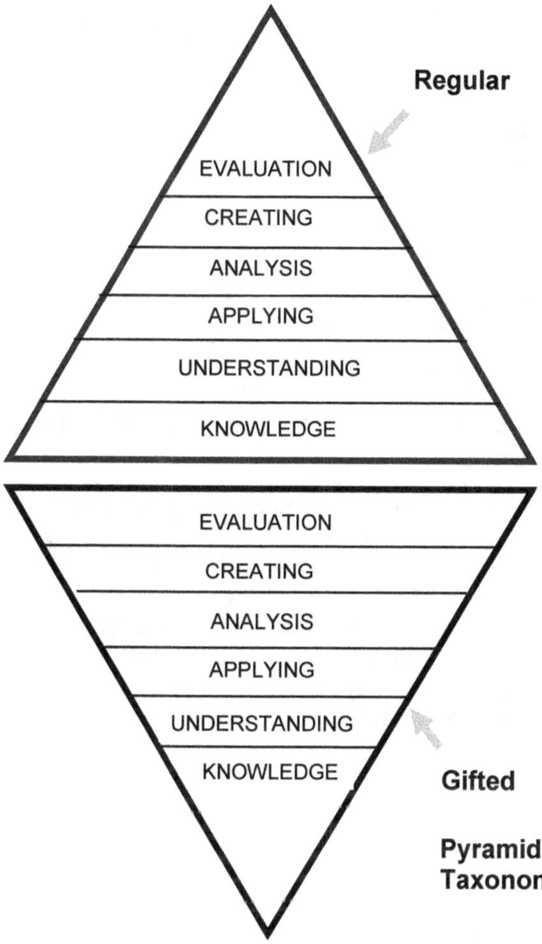

The 'regular' triangle model reflects Bloom's belief that students with less prior knowledge should spend more time on developing lower order thinking skills and less on higher order skills.

However, gifted learners require the opposite, because of their pace of learning, their capacity to learn in 'big gulps', their ability and need to understand the 'big picture'. Some will also have prior knowledge.

A much greater percentage of their learning both in school and at home should involve higher level thinking.

Pyramid Diagram based upon Bloom's Taxonomy (adapted from Davis & Rimm, 1998)

Figure 55 Blooms Taxonomy Pyramid Diagram (adapted from Davis & Rimm)

All students need some learning time spent on critical, creative and caring thinking.
Able students should spend most of their time (up to 75% of each lesson and assignment) applying higher order thinking and higher level skills to the content.

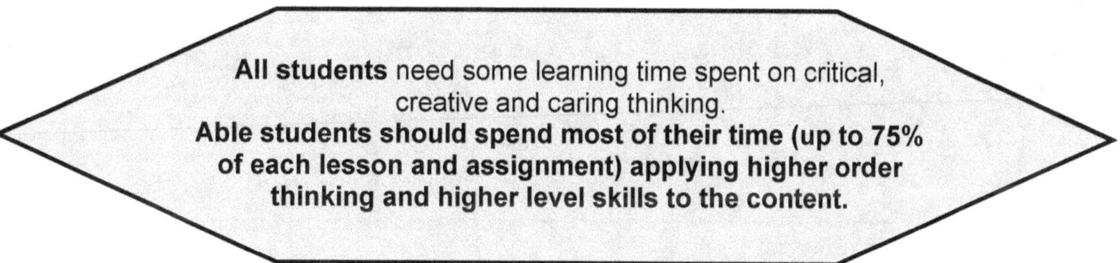

While some argue that there should not be a hierarchy of importance in thinking classifications, teachers should consider four areas in Blooms that are most important for gifted learners[11]:

APPLYING
ANALYSIS
CREATING
EVALUATING

What has happened to 'Knowledge' and 'Understanding'? This is a valid question for teachers who are always concerned about content. They are very aware of the curriculum content they are expected to cover, and this can often lead to a heavy weighting of knowledge recall and understanding in student learning activities and assessment. However, this can be an enormous demotivating factor for gifted learners. These students will report being stimulated whilst absorbing new information, but being frustrated and 'switched off' by followup activities that require little thinking or challenge.

When questions asked are 'lower order', or restricted to information gathering and fact finding and reporting, even when the information is new to the student, there is little challenge in the activity.

When the activity requires complex thinking, students will have to gather information and facts before a comprehensive response can be made. However it is the complexity or abstractness required by higher order thinking that fosters a deeper level of knowledge and understanding of the content. Therefore, knowledge and understanding are implicit in the thinking required to apply, analyse, create or evaluate.

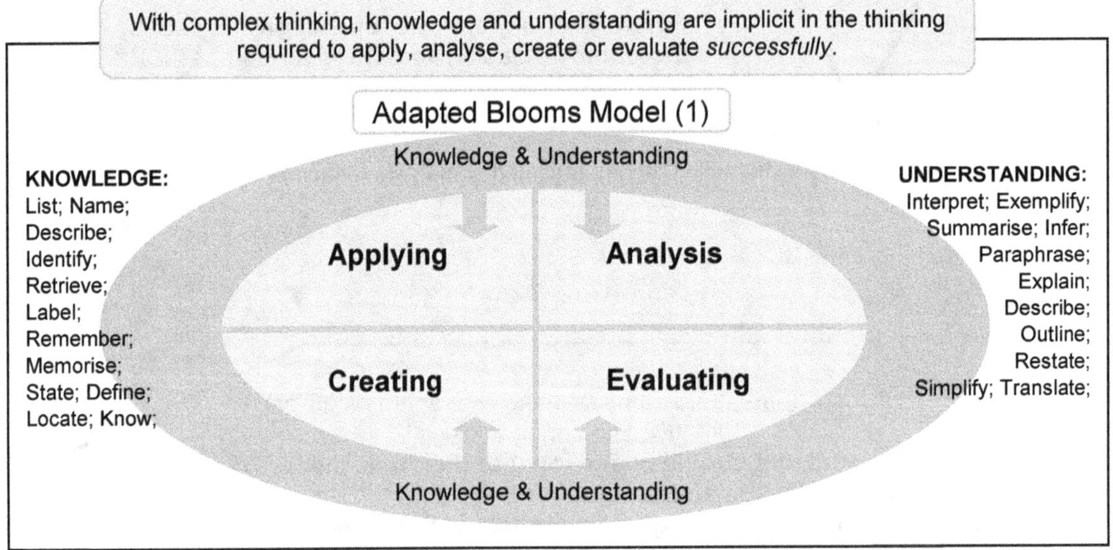

Figure 56 Adapted Blooms Model 1

---

[11] Concept from Le Sueur, E. (2007)

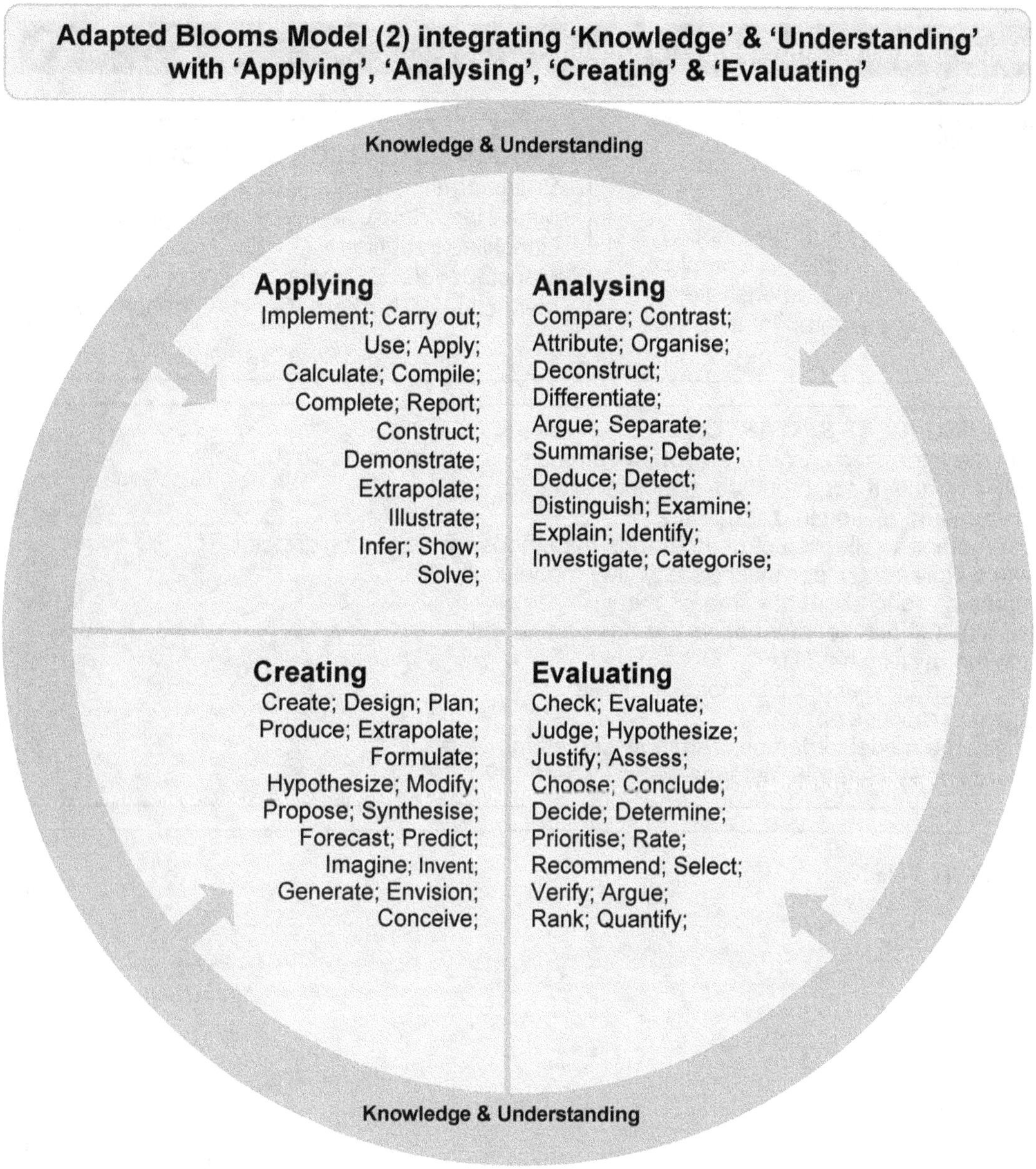

Figure 57 Adapted Blooms Model 2

Using this adaptation, we can focus upon planning higher order thinking learning activities and assessment tasks for *all* learners, but especially for gifted learners. Higher order thinking requires knowledge and understanding of the subject content and skills (at and/or above the level) so designing tasks using Applying, Analyzing, Creating and Evaluating can add more challenge and rigor.

The next four pages provide examples of thinking strategies and tools. Descriptors and examples of the tools described are provided later in the chapter.

THINKING SKILLS

Compare; Contrast; Attribute; Organise; Deconstruct; Differentiate; Argue; Separate; Detect; Summarise; Debate; Distinguish; Examine; Explain; Identify; Deduce; Investigate; Categorise;

THINKING STRATEGIES & TOOLS:

Metaphor; Decision-making Matrix; Fact/Opinion T; 5 Ws; Mind map; KNWL; Good/ Poor Logic; SWOT Analysis; Silent Card Shuffle; 6 Hats; T Charts; Y Chart; 5W & 1 H; Community of Inquiry; **Williams:** Analogy; Skills of search; Attribute Listing; Discrepancy; Examples of Change; Examples of habit; Organized Random Search; Skills of Search; Tolerance for Ambiguity; Adjustment to Development; Study Creative Process; **Thinkers Keys:** Commonalities, Picture, Ridiculous, Attributes, Interpretation, Disadvantages, Different Uses; Prediction, Combination, **De Bono:** Blue hat: CAF; AGO; PMI; OPV;

PLANNING IDEAS & STARTERS

Write a biography of a person analyzing their decisions and choices

What key elements make a successful (play /book/ experiment / poster...)

Analyze (X)... and write a report about your findings

Which events could not have happened? Why?

If --- happened, what might the causes (or result) have been?

Can you explain what must have happened when...?

What were some of the motives behind...?   What was the turning point?

Make a flow chart to illustrate the critical stages of (X)

Construct a graph to illustrate (selected) information

Make a graphic or chart showing the relationships between...

Write a story that illustrates the disadvantages of... and a potential modification of...

How is --- similar to /different from ---? Why did --- changes occur?

Can you distinguish between...? What was the problem with...? How else...?

What evidence do you have to support the argument that...?

Design a questionnaire & gather information. Analyze the results.

Write a commercial to sell your /product / ideas; consider key elements that need to be highlighted.

Devise a play about ...which illustrates key elements of ...

✎ YOUR TURN:

THINKING SKILLS
Check; Evaluate;
Judge; Hypothesize;
Justify; Assess;
Choose; Conclude;
Decide; Determine;
Prioritise; Rate;
Recommend; Select;
Verify; Argue;
Rank; Quantify;

THINKING STRATEGIES & TOOLS:
Criteria development; Ranking strategies; Decision-making Matrix; Evaluative situations; Extent Barometer; Relevant/Irrelevant; Reliable/Unreliable; Y Chart; Community of Inquiry
Thinkers Keys: Disadvantages; What if; Disadvantages; Prediction; **De Bono:** Yellow Hat; Black Hat; Blue Hat; APC; CAP; C&S; FIP; OPV; PMI;
Williams Taxonomy: Discrepancy; Provocative Statements; Examples of Change; Examples of Habit; Organised Random Search; Skills of Search; Adjustment to Development; Evaluate Situations;

PLANNING IDEAS & STARTERS
Is there a better solution to…? Develop criteria to judge the value of --.
What do you think about…?
Write a letter to – evaluating (x) issue or concern and advising the changes needed.
Given (x) situation, how would you have handled…?
Write an evaluation of your work / your progress in (x).
What changes to – would you recommend?
Do you believe (x) is the best idea/plan/ method/ principle/ explanation? Defend your conclusions.   How effective are…?
Conduct a debate / Community of enquiry about an issue
Develop the five most important rules about (x). Convince others.
Prioritize a list of issues /questions/ actions/ methods/ principles.
Discuss differing views. Argue on behalf of an opposing viewpoint.
Find holes in your own argument / plan of action / method/ design.

✍ YOUR TURN:

   Designing Defensible Programs for Gifted Secondary School Learners © Sonia White 2011

CREATING

THINKING SKILLS
Create; Design;
Plan; Produce;
Extrapolate; Formulate;
Hypothesize; Modify;
 Propose; Synthesise;
Forecast; Predict;
Imagine; Invent;
Generate; Envision;
Conceive;

THINKING STRATEGIES & TOOLS:
Creative Problem Solving; SCAMPER;
D.O.V.E.; Metaphor; Y Chart; TWERP
Community of Inquiry
Thinkers Keys: Reverse; What If; BAR; Construction; Different Uses; Prediction; Picture; Ridiculous; Inventions; Alternatives; Question; Variations; Interpretation. **De Bono:** APC; PO – random input; Green Hat; **Williams Taxonomy:** Intuitive Expression; Organised random search; Creative Listening /reading/ writing/; Study Creative Process; Visualisation; Analogy; Paradox; Examples of Change;

PLANNING IDEAS & STARTERS
Design a (x) which will …;   Develop a possible solution to…
If you had access to all the resources, how would you deal with (x)?
Design a CD/DVD/ book/ magazine cover for (x);
What new and unusual uses can you create for…?
Create an original product /song/ video, name it, & plan a marketing campaign.
Write a TV show / play/ puppet show/ role play / song / pantomime showing: the consequences of/ an alternative choice and its outcome/ a reversal of roles…
Research a prominent mathematician /scientist /artist/ writer and show how creativity figured in that individual's success
Devise your own way to…?   How many ways can you…?   Sell an idea;
Write your feelings about (x) situation /event/ dilemma.
What would happen if: a character /ingredient / method / component/ genre / was substituted?
Devise a way to… Invent a … to perform a specific task;
Develop a proposal which would convince others of an unpopular idea.

✍ YOUR TURN:

6.1.1 Differentiating Blooms for Gifted Learners

Even very young children can use higher order thinking, so how can we be sure that the tasks we have set for our able students are appropriate for their level of ability?

A task designed for one group of students may be regarded by another group or individual as facile and lacking in challenge.

Offering the Choice of Challenge

Teachers may wish to consider the following process in initially planning learning activities or assessment tasks:

The 'Could, Would, Should Rule' in Differentiating Learning for Gifted

- **Could** every student do this activity (at this stage of their learning)?
- **Would** every student benefit from doing this activity?
- **Should** every student do this activity (at this stage of their learning)?

If the answer is "yes" to any one of these questions, then the learning activity is not differentiated enough for gifted learners

- Adapted from Harry Passow.

Designing a Differentiated Activity or Assessment task

1. Design the learning activity /assessment task.

2. What are the learning outcomes for this task? Is this task relevant, or is it 'busy work'?

3. What higher order thinking is involved?

4. Would the task meet the 'Could, Would, Should' Rule? If not:

5. What challenge could be added to make this task more suitable for able students?

6. What activities /assessment tasks could this replace so that students selecting this would not have to do extra work 'on top of' and can use the time to give serious thought to the task?

7. What (differentiated) success criteria could be applied to this task?

Consider using the template on the next page when designing new tasks, until you are comfortable automatically analysing the learning and assessment tasks.

| **BLOOMS TAXONOMY Activity /Assessment Task Planner** |
| Curriculum Area: ___________________________   Level: _______ |

Activity:

| **Learning Outcomes:** | **Type of thinking required:** |

Is this activity more challenging than many of the class could manage successfully? (Could, Would Should Rule)

YES   NO

| What activities could this activity <u>replace</u>, so students choosing to do this activity wouldn't have to do extra? *(Quality, not quantity, of work)* | Ideas for alternative (more complex) adaptations: |

What criteria would indicate successful completion of this task?
Students can:

Figure 58 Blooms Taxonomy Activity / Assessment Task Planner

6.1.2 Planning Matrix: Adapted "Tic Tac Toe"[12]

Use Bloom's Taxonomy, William's Taxonomy, Lipman's Caring Thinking, Thinker's Keys or other tools to design activities to fill the grid. (Some such as Williams and Lipman's contain a mix of Blooms. If so, decide which area of Blooms the activity best fits.

TIC TAC TOE (adapted)

Applying	Analysis	Evaluating	Creating
Evaluating	Creating	Applying	Analysis
Creating	Evaluating	Analysis	Applying
Analysis	Applying	Creating	Evaluating

Students can choose any **three** in a row – (Tic tac toe) – across, down, or diagonally from corner to corner. The ability to choose is important. You may leave one whole row blank so that the student can design his/her own activities.

---

[12] Thanks to Elaine Le Sueur for this strategy.

     Designing Defensible Programs for Gifted Secondary School Learners © Sonia White 2011

WAYS OF DESIGNING THE GRID:

1. Make the grid above for only your advanced learners. It could then cover activities for the whole unit. (Remember to allow *choice!*).

2. **Design the grid for all students in the class**. Graduate the difficulty level so that the easiest ones are in the first two columns, and the most challenging are in the last column. Tell your advanced learners they cannot touch the first column, but may start anywhere else.

The Tic-tac-toe chart for using this way would be designed like this:

Easy Level ⇓	Moderate Level ⇓	More Difficult ⇓	Very Challenging ⇓
Applying	Applying	Applying	Applying
Analysis	Analysis	Analysis	Analysis
Evaluating	Evaluating	Evaluating	Evaluating
Creating	Creating	Creating	Creating

If you have a high level activity, it is easy to simplify it. Similarly, you can gradually increase the sophistication of *thinking* required if you start with a simple activity.

e.g.

"A" Level: List some advantages and disadvantages *(analysis & evaluating)* of Hercules's decision.

"B" Level: List the advantages and disadvantages of Hercules's decision and give reasons why you would have made (or not made) the same decision *(analysis & evaluating with elaboration)*.

"C" Level: List the advantages and disadvantages of Hercules's decision. Generate another 2 choices he could have made. Demonstrate and argue which option would have been best *(analysis, evaluating, creating with elaboration)*.

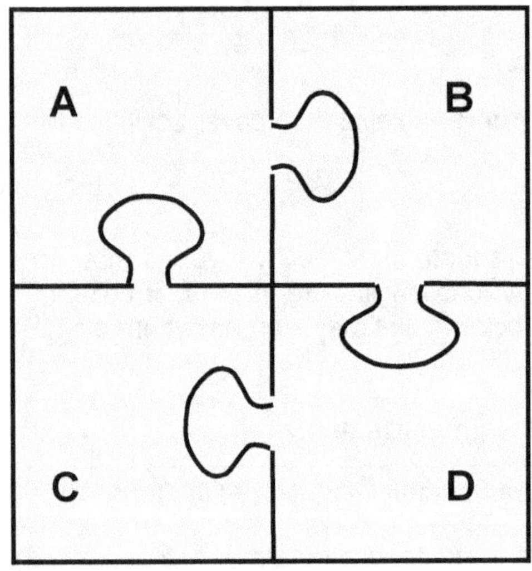

6.1.3 TEAM Expert Jigsaw
(Adapted from Aronson)

Divide your class into 'Jigsaw' groups of 4 or 5.

Each Jigsaw group should have 1 comparatively advanced learner, 1 learner who needs to work at a more basic level, and 2 (maximum 3) mid-range ability students.

GOAL: Each individual will become the 'expert' on specific areas of group tasks.

Individual tasks are set based upon different learning needs, talents and abilities.

---

1. Design the activities for each level: There may be one activity per level, for one lesson, or, for a unit, there may be several activities per level.

A – Basic level challenges, (e.g. may contain mostly fact-finding, and 'applying' instructions. Should contain some analysis, synthesis or creating).

B – Moderate level challenge, (e.g. with a range of fact-finding and applying and moderate amount of analysis, evaluation or synthesis or creating).

C - Moderate level challenge, (e.g. with a range of fact-finding and moderate amount of analysis, evaluation or synthesis or creating - but different activities from B, above).

D – High level challenge, (e.g. all applying, analysis, evaluation and creating) with more complexity and abstract thinking.

(You might like to label these groups by colour, to disguise any sense of hierarchy)

How Expert Jigsaw works:

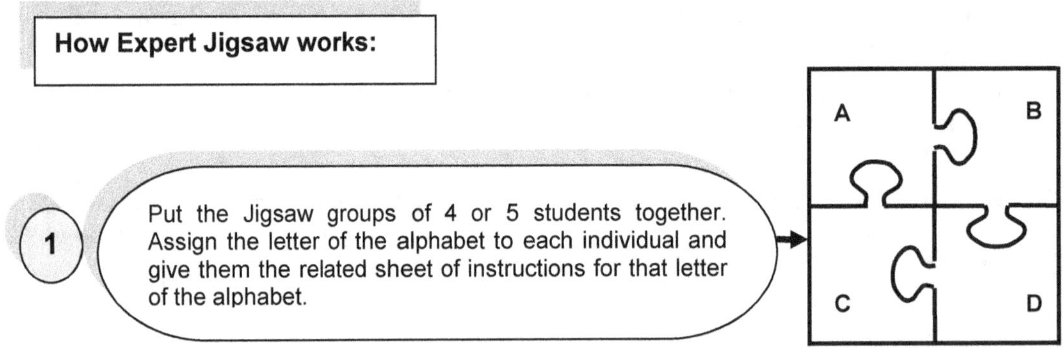

APPLYING

THINKING SKILLS
Implement; Carry out; Use; Apply;
Calculate; Compile; Complete;
Report; Construct; Demonstrate;
Extrapolate; illustrate; Infer; Show;
Solve:

THINKING STRATEGIES & TOOLS
Brainstorming; listing; recording;
Mind Map; Flow Chart; Graphic Organiser;
Checklist; Fact file;
Maps; Models; Exemplars
Instructions; **Thinkers Keys:** Alphabet Key.

PLANNING IDEAS & STARTERS
From the information given, can you develop a set of instructions about…?
Apply a … rule/ theory/ method/ principle …to
Organise information into sequence
Take /gather a collection of photographs to demonstrate a particular point
Make a diorama / paper-mache map/ clay model to illustrate…
Prepare a report about the area of study
Give a talk about the information you have found out.
Fill in the missing details…
Write information about this topic for others
Make a scrapbook about...
Construct a model to demonstrate how something works
Do you know of another instance when / where …?

✎YOUR TURN:

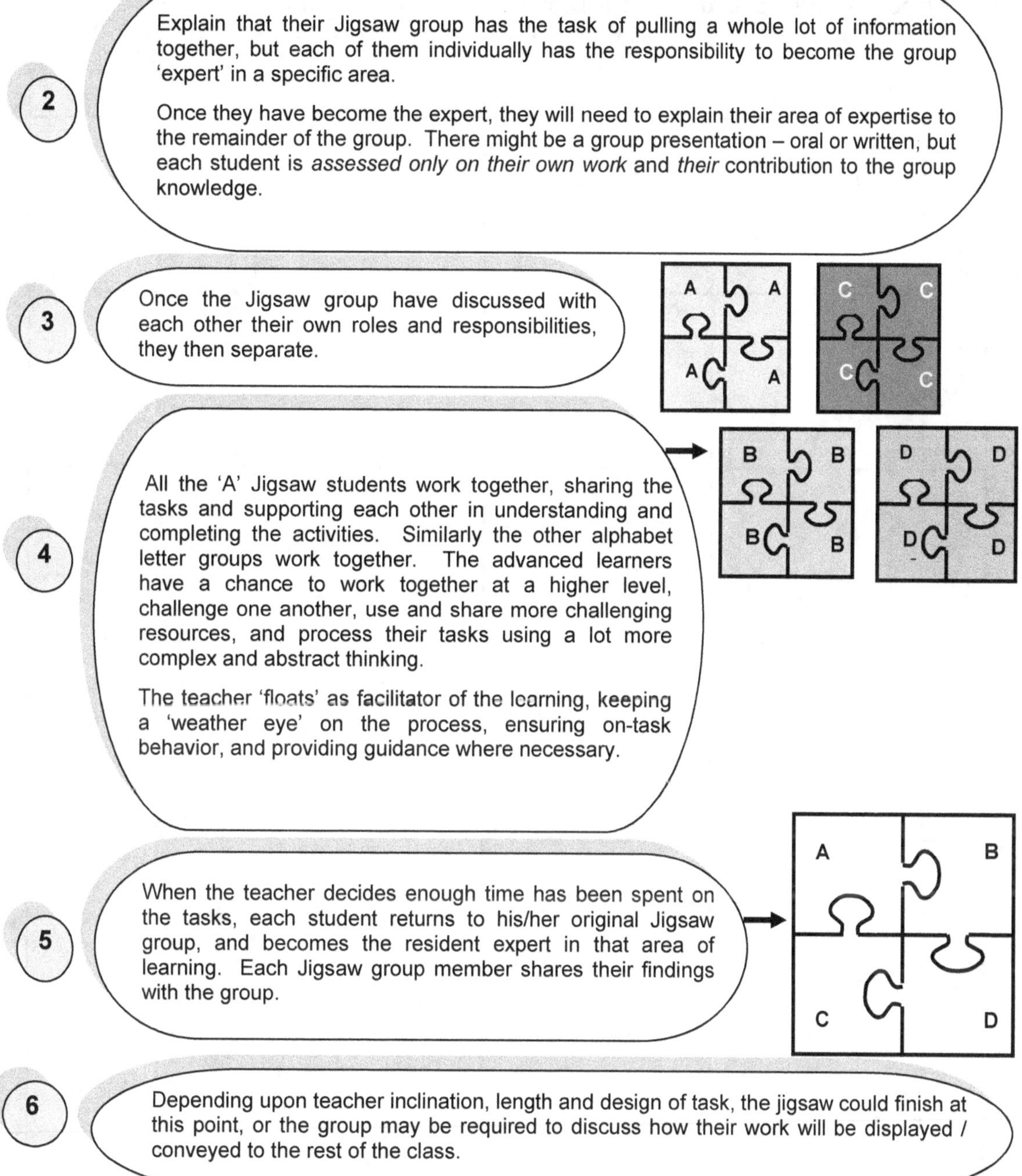

2

Explain that their Jigsaw group has the task of pulling a whole lot of information together, but each of them individually has the responsibility to become the group 'expert' in a specific area.

Once they have become the expert, they will need to explain their area of expertise to the remainder of the group. There might be a group presentation – oral or written, but each student is *assessed only on their own work* and *their* contribution to the group knowledge.

3

Once the Jigsaw group have discussed with each other their own roles and responsibilities, they then separate.

4

All the 'A' Jigsaw students work together, sharing the tasks and supporting each other in understanding and completing the activities. Similarly the other alphabet letter groups work together. The advanced learners have a chance to work together at a higher level, challenge one another, use and share more challenging resources, and process their tasks using a lot more complex and abstract thinking.

The teacher 'floats' as facilitator of the learning, keeping a 'weather eye' on the process, ensuring on-task behavior, and providing guidance where necessary.

5

When the teacher decides enough time has been spent on the tasks, each student returns to his/her original Jigsaw group, and becomes the resident expert in that area of learning. Each Jigsaw group member shares their findings with the group.

6

Depending upon teacher inclination, length and design of task, the jigsaw could finish at this point, or the group may be required to discuss how their work will be displayed / conveyed to the rest of the class.

Adapted From Aronson, E. (1997) Basic Jigsaw 1. Available http://www.jigsaw.org/tips.htm

6.1.4 Differentiated Bloom's Grid
Some teachers may prefer to use the full Bloom's Grid, and differentiate by planning activities for 4 Levels of Learning: e.g. **B**asic, **P**roficient, **A**dvanced, and **E**xpert (above the Level).

	B	P	A	E
Knowledge				
Understanding				
Applying				
Analysis				
Evaluating				
Creating				

Tip: Where Learning Activity grids cover the key elements of a unit, some teachers encourage students to use them as a revision resource prior to examinations.

Figure 59 Differentiated Blooms Taxonomy Grid

   Designing Defensible Programs for Gifted Secondary School Learners © Sonia White 2011

NOTES:

6.2 Creativity

When I examine myself and my methods of thought,
I come to the conclusion that the gift of fantasy
has meant more to me than any talent for abstract, positive thinking. –
Albert Einstein

There are multiple definitions of creativity, and models of creative thinking and creative problem solving which teachers could examine and argue. Some experts refer to the characteristics of the creative individual (Chapter 2), others refer to the process. Current theorists believe that instead of asking "how creative are you?" as we did in the past we should be asking "in what ways are you creative?" No longer is a definition of creativity limited to expression through the arts. Critical and creative thinkers are welcomed in all walks of life.

Teachers should consider how often they deliberately seek to develop creative thinking in their students, as although it is inextricably linked with critical thinking, there are specific aspects of creativity than can be developed in every classroom.

This section is concerned with *creative behaviours* that can be enhanced through various strategies and tools: the *process of creativity*. Further readings on different models of creativity are available at the end of the chapter.

> *I often ask subject teachers if creativity is needed in their specific domain. Not one has ever replied in the negative. And yet sometimes there is the assumption that creativity need only be fostered in certain subjects.*
>
> *What a shame that content and didactic teaching are sometimes seen as the overriding priority when creativity can ignite and enflame a long term passion for learning.*

6.2.1 Creative 'Flow' and Motivation

Why develop creativity? In a word: motivation!

Have you ever become so absorbed in a task that time passes without you noticing? You may have experienced total focus where you were unaware of other extraneous details around you. There was such a feeling of exhilaration, discovery and satisfaction when you stopped that there is a desire to seek out the experience again and again. Csíkszentmihályi called that experience 'flow' and describes individuals as being 'in flow' when they are working in this state.

Csíkszentmihályi describes how human activities often comprise two opposing components, which, in the diagram (Figure 60) are characterized as Challenges and Skills[13]. "So long as the level of challenge facing the person is in rough accord with the level of the person's skill, then they will experience a "sense of discovery", or even a "previously undreamed-of state of consciousness" - that is *flow*."

"But as the person's skill increases, they grow bored. Or when the challenge increases too far beyond the person's skill, frustration sets in. Both boredom and frustration inhibit the flow experience.

"In our studies, we found that every *flow* activity... provides a sense of discovery, a creative feeling of transporting the person into a new reality."

(Mihaly Csíkszentmihályi, *The Psychology of Optimal Experience*, Harper & Row, 1990 p.74)

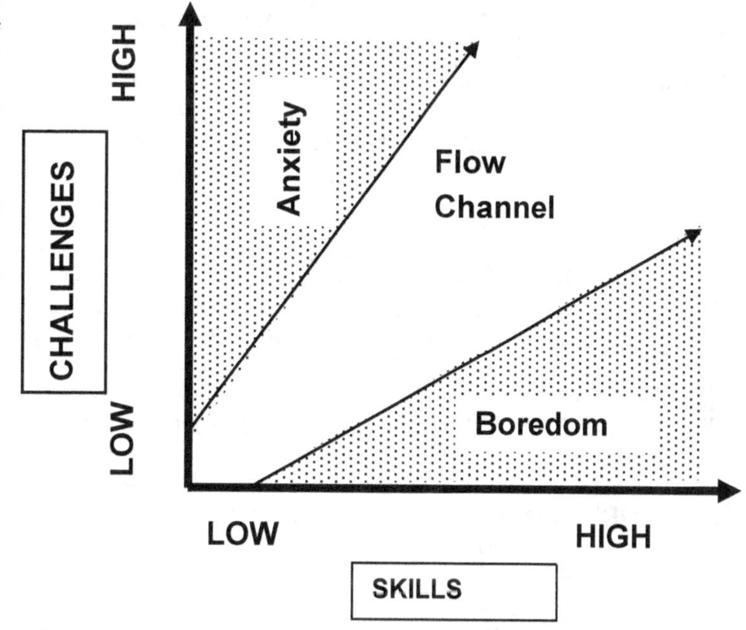

Figure 60 Csíkszentmihályi 's Creative "Flow"

The motivation towards enjoyment provokes one to desire to balance challenge with skill, and so to induce flow".

The research of Csíkszentmihályi and others[14] finds that 'talent development is a process that requires *both expressive and instrumental rewards'* and that most importantly, '*a talent will be developed if it produces optimal* [flow] *experiences'*. This is equally true of arts students as it is of, for example, science students.

'Optimal experiences are important to talent development partly for this reason: Memories of peak moments motivate students to keep improving in the hopes of achieving the same intensity of experience again' - Csíkszentmihályi (1997).

---

[13] Csikszentmihalyi, (1990)

[14] Csikszentmihalyi, M., Rathunde, K., & Whalen, S. (1997).

6.2.2 Creative Behaviours

Fluency
Flexibility
Elaboration
Originality

One way of examining, assessing and further developing creativity is through the four aspects that E. Paul Torrance defined: fluency, flexibility, elaboration, and originality.

Williams has included these in Dimension III of his Taxonomy (see Chapter 8). These four aspects are widely used in programs such as Future Problem Solving to develop creative thinking. Within Dimension III, Williams also decribed the types of affective behaviours that individuals need to pursue creativity:

COGNITIVE BEHAVIOURS

FLUENCY – generation of a quantity of relevant responses

FLEXIBILITY – variety of ideas or a shift in categories and directions of thought

ELABORATION – embellishment or improvement of ideas; addition of details

ORIGINALITY – unusual and /or unique ideas and responses, movement away from the obvious

AFFECTIVE BEHAVIOURS

RISK-TAKING – expose oneself to failure; take a guess; function in unstructured conditions

CURIOSITY – be inquisitive; toy with ideas; follow hunches; be open to puzzlement

COMPLEXITY – delve into intricate problems willingly; seek alternatives; see gaps

IMAGINATION – visualise; build mental images; feel intuitively; reach beyond reality

Figure 61 Williams Taxonomy Dimension III

"The truly creative is always that which cannot be taught. Yet creativity cannot come from the untaught"- Torrance, (1988).

    Designing Defensible Programs for Gifted Secondary School Learners © Sonia White 2011

Some years ago one of my colleagues, a very experienced Head of Department of Graphics and Design was advising that students wishing to further their studies with him should also take Future Problem Solving (FPS) as a subject. I was teaching FPS, which places a lot of emphasis upon student skill development in fluency, flexibility, originality and elaboration. Delighted with his unasked-for endorsement, I asked 'Steve' why he was making the recommendation.

Steve told me that when he had recently arrived at the school he had noticed a class of Year 11 (Grade 12) students who were all particularly bright and talented, but within the class there was a group with skills the others didn't have.

"The design process requires brainstorming solution ideas around the problem," Steve said. "This group of students not only came up with a lot *more* ideas, they also came up with a far better range of ideas rather than slight variations of the same basic idea. As a result they were more original. Furthermore, they were able to critique their ideas, and select the best one to elaborate upon and develop. Their work was completed much more thoroughly, with much more reflection and detail."

Wondering which subject it was that had given these students these skills, Steve took a guess then conducted an experiment. He set a design task and wandered around the room observing the students, and noting down names. At the end of the task he asked the students who took Future Problem Solving to stand. Every name on his list was standing.

"I want my students to have these skills. Hence my recommendation," he said with a smile.

All students can benefit from being taught such skills, which shouldn't be limited to just one or two curriculum areas. They are life skills. Gifted students and adults need to be taught to push those skills to the outer edges of sophistication. They bring strong creative problem solving potential to leadership, and to investigative and workplace situations.

Future Problem Solving[15]

Students who are taught techniques to generate fluency, flexibility, originality and elaboration, and who are given time to practice them will acquire the tools to harness and develop their creativity.

A learning environment that encourages risk-taking, curiosity, complexity, and imagination (Williams' four affective behaviours) is required for the other, cognitive /creative behaviours to flourish. The following pages describe ways of developing these skills.

---

[15] Future Problem Solving Program www.fpspi.org

*Teach **the rules of group brainstorming**:*

1. Say your idea out loud, and write it down yourself.

2. Listen to the ideas of others, but do *not* criticise favourably or unfavourably at this point.

3. 'Hitch-hike' on other's ideas – use them to trigger new ideas

4. Try not to repeat ideas.

5. When you think you have run out of ideas, *keep pushing. That is when original ideas occur.*

(Adapted from the FPSP rules of Brainstorming).

1. Teach **Fluency**

Give students opportunities to practice brainstorming for *quantity* of ideas:

How many...

Different uses for / ways of / signs /items / words / things of (x) colour can you think of ...; different problems might arise when...; different solutions could occur if...;

Be explicit that *number* of ideas is important. Ask them to count... compare groups... stress that practice is important to generate lots of ideas.

2. Teach **Flexibility**

Give students *separate* opportunities to practice brainstorming for *quality* of ideas - different categories of ideas. e.g. not just all vegetables or clothing items that are green, but a diverse range of categories, both concrete and abstract. (e.g. jealousy).

3. Teach **Originality**

Originality of ideas can be measured against the number of times others in the class had the same idea. It is very easily demonstrated with brainstorming. Teach students to try to come up with ideas that no-one else will think of. Compare ideas, so that they will begin to appreciate that the first ideas people come up with are usually quite common, and that brainstorming *longer* will generate more original ideas.

4. Teach **Elaboration**

Give students opportunity to elaborate their best idea. Demand detail – visual detail, process detail and assessment detail; How will it look/ function/ work / be put in place/ solve the problem/ affect others/ affect the environment/ improve the situation? How will they identify and overcome barriers/ know if it is successful... Reward thorough elaboration.

Develop these skills constantly as students use the tools described on the following pages.

Figure 62. Developing Fluency, Flexibility, Originality and Elaboration

6.3 Other Critical and Creative Thinking Strategies

6.3.1 S.C.A.M.P.E.R.

SCAMPER is a powerful tool for inspiring imagination and creativity in students. The principles of the SCAMPER technique were first developed by Alex Osborn. Bob Eberle rearranged them as an acronym in 1991[16] as a tool to increase interest in the creative abilities of children. Since then teachers have used SCAMPER across the curriculum in a myriad of ways, both in developing creative questions for classroom activities, and in empowering students to develop their own creativity. Teaching students the use of SCAMPER in a creative environment fosters curiosity, originality, risk-taking, and elaboration. It enhances fluency and flexibility in thinking, and if teachers demand it, originality and elaboration.

SCAMPER is a mnemonic for

S	*Substitute*	Substitute an object, material, person, quality, place or time, idea
C	*Combine*	Combine substances, objects, materials, ideas, solutions, situations; attributes of different objects;
A	*Adapt*	Adapt to suit: different conditions; other uses; other purposes; other opinions, beliefs;
M	*Modify Magnify Minimize*	Modify parts, frequency of occurrence; Magnify or minimize size, weight or importance;
P	*Put to other uses*	Use for a completely different purpose; use in a different situation in a different way;
E	*Eliminate*	Eliminate a part /person/ factor/ issue/ solution/ quality/ attribute;
R	*Reverse*	Change the sequence /pattern /layout, reverse the process/ cause & effect, do the opposite

SCAMPER tools may be used singly, or in combination. In teaching students how to use the tools, SCAMPER tools are best taught separately. While all students can benefit from using SCAMPER, differentiation for gifted can be achieved by using increased abstractness or complexity.

---

[16] Eberle, B. (1991) SCAMPER – Games for Imagination Development

EXAMPLES

| **S** | ***Substitute*** | Substitute an object, material, person, quality, place or time, idea |

| Substitute the setting of this play with… *A setting in a different country / culture or in a restaurant / circus / school / hairdresser's salon / your choice.* | Substitute the villain in this film /story with… *The Phantom of the Opera /a President / a sportsman / Uncle Fred / your choice* | Substitute: the music tempo in this scene with… An instrument with… Voice with… | Substitute: A character in this novel with a character from another book /nursery rhyme/ film / time period |

| Substitute: symbols; weights; Order of operations; rules; quantities; | Substitute: An attribute of (x) with a different attribute; a kind act with a selfish act; fair with foul; | Substitute: The texture / shade / color; The material /ingredient / quality; Priorities; Choices; |

THINK ABOUT: What might change as a result? How much impact will it have? How might things be different? What might remain the same? Will the impact be positive or negative? For whom?

Your Turn:

| **C** | ***Combine*** | Combine substances, objects, materials, ideas, solutions, situations; attributes of different objects; |

| Combine the attributes of two different things: *texture of a velvet glove with a mallet; the voice of an angel with a villain; the rhythm of one poem with another;* | Combine some of the qualities of: *steel with a table cloth; a pine tree with a nursing home logo; a cash register with a bottle opener; one substance with another;* | Combine: *the philosophy of (X) with the ideas of (Y); the Treaty of Versailles with another treaty; The situation in (X) country with the leadership of Mao Tse Tung / George Bush;* | Combine: *The style of one artist / musician / choreographer / designer with another's; elements of one genre with another's; elements of one method with elements of another* |

THINK ABOUT: What new creation / development / situation occurs? What is its potential for further development? Would the outcome be desirable? Why /why not? What might need changing (M- Modifying)?

Your Turn:

<table>
<tr><td>**A**</td><td>*Adapt*</td><td>Adapt to suit: different conditions; other uses; other purposes; other opinions, beliefs;</td></tr>
</table>

Adapt a product / an item to suit a different: environment; user; climate; time period; place of work; e.g. *Adapt a work desk to suit a paraplegic; adapt a menu to suit a person allergic to one of the main ingredients.*	Adapt a system, method or process to suit a different purpose or situation; e.g. *adapt an emergency survival kit to suit a blind person;*	Adapt to suit other conditions: *Adapt a pushbike so it can be used in the snow; adapt a poem /song / creative piece so that it can be used in a completely different situation*	Adapt a rule so that the opposite is true; adapt a shape / investigation method / formula...

THINK ABOUT: The purpose and end goal; What elements are valuable? What doesn't fit? What are the needs of the consumer /client/ end user? What else changes as a result?

Your Turn: ✍

<table>
<tr><td>**M**</td><td>*Modify Magnify Minimize*</td><td>Modify parts, frequency of occurrence; Magnify or minimize size, weight or importance; distort</td></tr>
</table>

Modify one or more specific parts of: an object / a recipe / a bicycle/ a scene in a film / a character /a mathematical or scientific rule/ a treaty / a process;	Magnify or maximise all or part of something: Place more importance upon a minor character; increase the amount of / the size of the seat on a bicycle;	Minimise the significance of, or the make smaller: The role of a secondary character; the volume of a key instrument; the quantity of an ingredient; an element of a rule	Distort: the words of a famous politician / Shakespearean character; the effects of a statistic; the application of a rule; a specific feature; the shape of a container;

THINK ABOUT: What happens? Is the effect an improvement or a disaster? Does the change add to, or enhance the original? Does it trigger some original ideas? Does it now require further modification?

Your Turn: ✍

<table>
<tr><td>**P**</td><td>**_Put to other uses_**</td><td>Use for a completely different purpose; use in a different situation in a different way;</td></tr>
</table>

In what circumstances can you imagine X poem being used in a media presentation? (e.g., TV ad, documentary) Brainstorm a list of possibilities and choose one to elaborate upon. Describe how the poem would be used, and to what effect. Explain why this poem would be particularly appropriate. Include any adaptations you would make.	Use in a different situation: The process of candidate selection; the law of motion; the local rubbish tip; the role of a Dame; the ghost of Christmas Past (from Dickens); polarity; over-exposure; garden furniture; a tombstone; a Geiger counter;	Find other, unusual uses for: A washing machine; a laptop computer; a GPS system; a dead fish; a feather pillow; a law; an oblique three-dimensional shape; a mathematical rule; a scientific discovery;

THINK ABOUT: Where else? How else? When else (different time / setting)? Can you use part or all of this it item? Should it be modified (M – Modify, minimise, maximise). What added value would the change bring?

Your Turn: 

<table>
<tr><td>**E**</td><td>**_Eliminate_**</td><td>Eliminate a part /person/ factor/ issue/ solution/ quality/ attribute;</td></tr>
</table>

Eliminate: The first step / paragraph / section. Eliminate a character /event / sound effect / instrument / in a book, film or composition.	Eliminate: The numbers from a ruler; the main ingredient; the last chapter; the use of the digit 3; the use of the letter 'e'; the villain's transport;	Eliminate: A clause from a treaty; a key word from an historical statement or quote; what might have been the outcomes of this?	Eliminate: The use of a standard technique / medium / method / rule.

THINK ABOUT: What happens as a result? Is the end result intensified or reduced. Improved or lessened? Is there less structure or more? In this instance, is this a good thing or a bad thing? What possibilities can now occur as a result of this elimination?

Your Turn:

 **R** | *Reverse* | Change the sequence /pattern /layout, reverse the process/ cause & effect, do the opposite

| Reverse the roles of two of the main characters in a play or novel;

Reverse the order of operations;

Reverse the notation in the melody; | Reverse the sequence of events; reverse the order in which something is normally done; | Portray in the negative; (or positive, if that is the reverse). e.g., portray a negatively perceived historical event in a positive light; a villain as his mother may view him; a hero as his worst enemy may view him. | Consider the "nevers" or "impossibles" and how they *could* happen; reverse brainstorm all the things a surgeon / a mathematician / an artist/ a musician / an economist/ would never do; |

THINK ABOUT: How much perceptions might change. The possibilities that might arise if this were the case. New ideas that might need thinking about. What would change? What else might need to be changed?

Your Turn: ✍

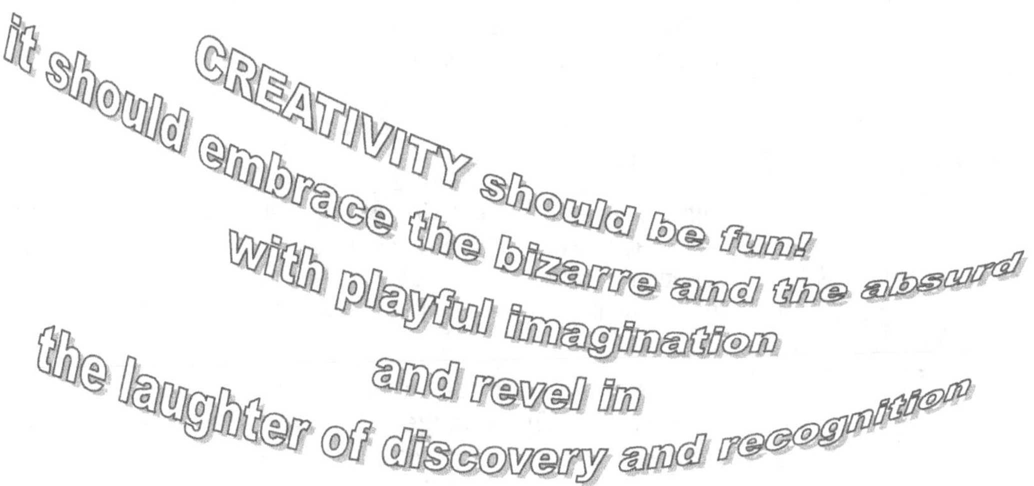

SCAMPER Examples:

Have your teachers work in groups of 3 or 4 to try one or two of these for fun, then plan their own SCAMPER activities that will fit within the context of their current unit. Similarly, you may use this example to introduce SCAMPER to your students.

SCAMPER Example: Theme Cinderella

S	*Substitute*	Substitute the setting of Cinderella with a setting in the Tropics. What would change as a result? Brainstorm as many ideas as possible about the effects of this.
C	*Combine*	Combine the characteristics of... (a well-known character from a comedy show) with those of the Prince. Brainstorm ways he and his actions could be portrayed.
A	*Adapt*	Adapt the magic coach so that Cinderella arrives in a style befitting a 21st century, modern young woman. Brainstorm and creatively use as many modern features as you can.
M	*Modify Magnify Minimize*	Distort the vision that Cinderella sees when her fairy godmother arrives. How might this whole scene unfold differently, yet still finish with Cinderella departing in the coach? Think through the detail and describe.
P	*Put to other uses*	In the fairy tale the fairy godmother chose a pumpkin and mice to become coach and 'horses'. Choose other things that could be found in the environment in which you have set your version of Cinderella. Create an original coach and 'horses'.
E	*Eliminate*	Eliminate the Prince's Ball where Cinderella finally meets him. How else could they meet? Brainstorm a list of possible situations which still allow Cinderella to flee and lose something the Prince can trace her with. Develop one idea in detail.
R	*Reverse*	Reverse the gender roles of one / some of the characters. What changes in the story? Brainstorm a list of possibilities and follow-though with the detail and consequences of one of your ideas.

SCAMPER Tool Adapted from Eberle (1991).

Enjoy the creative process!

Figure 63 SCAMPER example: Theme Cinderella

 Designing Defensible Programs for Gifted Secondary School Learners © Sonia White 2011

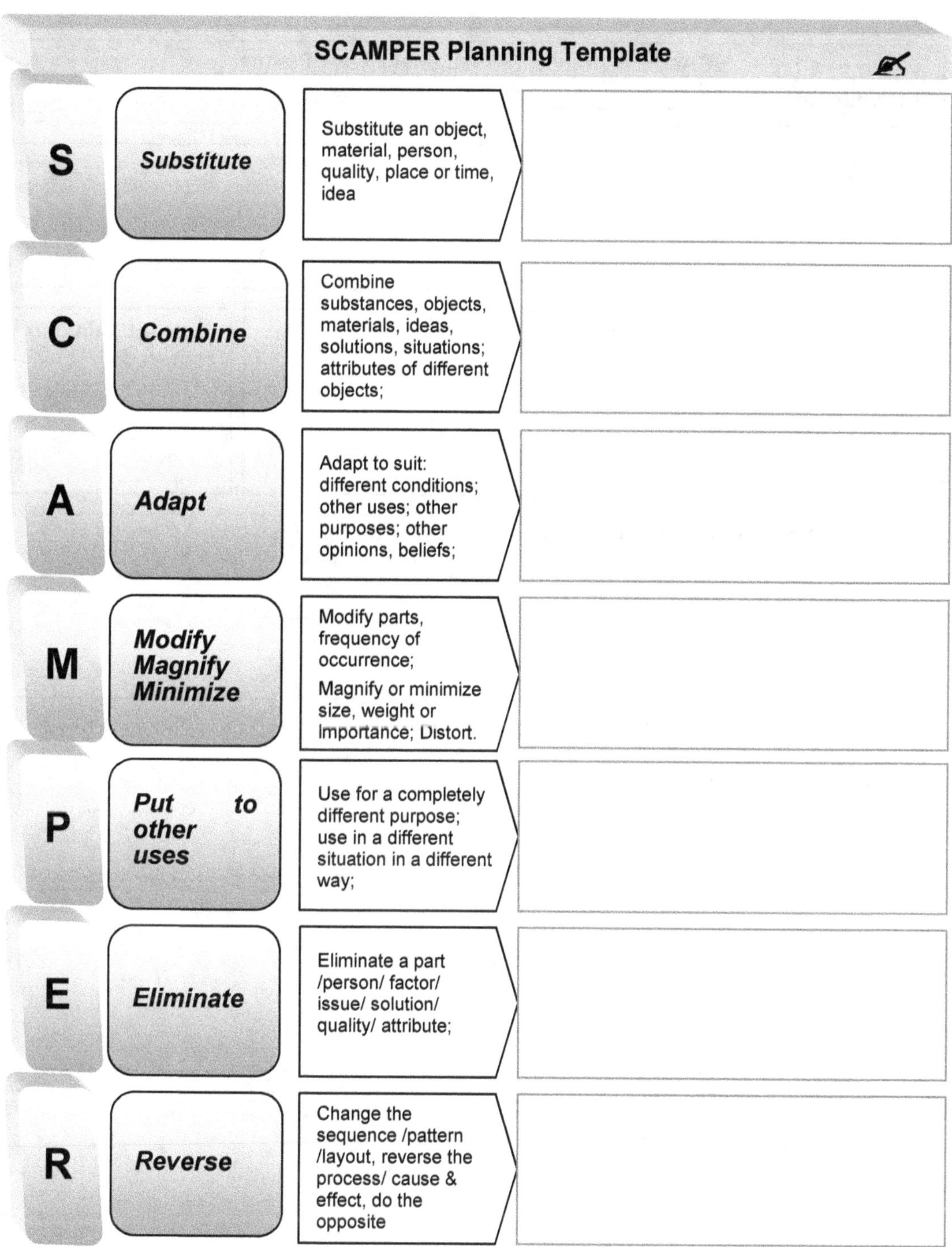

(Adapted from Eberle (1991)

Figure 64 SCAMPER Planning Template

SCAMPER Activity /Assessment Task Planner

Curriculum Area: ________________________   **Level:** _____

Activity:

Learning Outcomes:

Type of thinking required:

Is this activity more challenging than many of the class could manage successfully? (Could, Would Should Rule)

YES

NO

What activities could this activity <u>replace</u>, so students choosing to do this activity wouldn't have to do extra? *(Quality, not quantity, of work)*

Ideas for alternative (more complex) adaptations:

What criteria would indicate successful completion of this task?
Students can:

Figure 65 SCAMPER Activity /Assessment Planner

6.3.2 Tony Ryan's Thinkers Keys

Tony Ryan[17] developed twenty different activities to motivate and engage students in creative and critical thinking. These tools provide great triggers for teachers in designing analytical, evaluative and creative thinking activities. A brief description of each is included here with kind permission from Tony Ryan. Other examples can be found in his resources on www.thinkerskeys.com and other texts in the readings and resources listed at the end of this chapter.

Using Thinkers Keys with Gifted Learners

Once they are taught how to use them, *all learners,* even the very young can use Thinkers Keys. so it is important that teachers expect sophisticated, reflective responses with depth and complexity from able students so that the Key activities do not become trivial time-fillers. Teachers can 'raise the bar' by requiring increasingly complex thinking in fluency, flexibility, originality and elaboration. For more able learners, the questions and instructions that accompany the 'Key' should reflect this expectation.

Reverse 	Reverse list. Use words like 'never', 'cannot' and 'would not' to create the reverse effect. *e.g. List things/ actions /decisions / that you would never see / X person would never take.*
'What If' 	What if...? Any question imaginable, serious or fun. After brainstorming possibilities students can use critical thinking graphic organisers to consider outcomes
Alphabet 	Alphabet list of words relevant to the area of study; could be used for mix and match 'terms and definitions' or even new words for futures thinking.
B.A.R. 	Acronym for Bigger, Add, Replace. Use for improving the design of an item, a set of rules or systems, methods; list the attributes of the item under investigation and use BAR to trigger ideas for change.
Construction 	Use everyday materials (e.g. clean recyclables) in a creative problem solving task that requires construction.
Disadvantages 	Examining the disadvantages of an idea, practice, or object, then finding ways of eliminating or minimising those disadvantages
Different Uses	Brainstorming a wide range of different ways of using everyday objects. Good for training fluency and flexibility in thinking.

---

[17] Ryan, (1990)

Prediction		Predict possible outcomes or reasons for an event / picture / scenario. Use critical thinking to develop logical, defensible reasons.
Picture		Use a simple diagram or picture which has no relevance at all to the area of study. Ask the students to find multiple ways that it can be linked to the area of study / sub-topic / key term.
Ridiculous		Make a ridiculous statement that runs in the face of common practice or would be virtually impossible to implement and have the students attempt to substantiate it.
Commonality		Use an item / term from the area of study and another item outside the area of study and ask the students to find points of commonality. Similarly, use two disparate items for the study.
Inventions		Develop inventions / new concepts / original writing, music, art, designs/ that are constructed in an unusual manner or with an unusual material
Alternatives		Take a usual method within the area of study and ask students to complete a task using that method, but with using the usual tools or implements.
Question		Start with the answer. List 5 questions that can ONLY have that as an answer. Get students to test them out on each other.
Forced Relationship		Design or redesign something using ideas from examining the attributes of several dissimilar objects.
Combination		List the attributes of two unmatched objects (at least one from the area of study) then combine some of the attributes to create a new or better product.
Interpretation	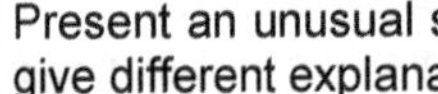	Present an unusual scenario (oral, written or visual) and ask students to give different explanations for that situation.
Brick Wall		Make a statement or describe a negative situation that is generally accepted as being the norm, then get students to 'break down the wall' by finding other ways of developing a desirable outcome.
Variations		Find many different ways of overcoming a problem.
Brainstorming		Brainstorming: Lists; webs; mind maps – identifying items /problems and challenges/ solutions / details for elaboration of an idea or concept.

 Designing Defensible Programs for Gifted Secondary School Learners © Sonia White 2011

Examples of Thinkers Keys

Try some of these Keys amongst your group of teachers. Have them consider what type of thinking is required as they trial the activity, then ask them to consider how that Key might be used in their current classroom topic.

Brainstorm a list of rules a creative thinker should never follow. Choose the best 5 and justify them.

(⊷ Reverse Key)

In what ways are a gifted artist and a gifted scientist the same? Explain and defend your ideas.
(⊷ Commonality Key)

Predict which 3 characteristics or qualities might be most highly valued in gifted adults in 20 years time. Justify your answer.

(⊷ Prediction Key)

A gifted child has destroyed a piece of work he has been labouring over for a long time. Give reasons why this may have occurred and suggestions for managing this. (⊷ Interpretation Key).

List all the different ways you could identify giftedness and talent. Prioritise them in order of preference.

(⊷ Variations Key)

"Parents should not be involved in the identification of gifted and talented students"
Give statements which reflect the opinions that may be held by different sections of the community. (Divide the sheet into sections: teachers parents / caregivers students education 'officials' and "other"). (⊷ Ridiculous Key)

Consider the provisions your school has for its gifted learners. Use the ⊷ BAR Key to generate ideas for improvement. Create 4 criteria to assess these ideas against, and then select the best idea.

Students are often assessed according to content knowledge. Generate a range of alternatives that could be used. Argue in support of your favourite option.
(⊷ Alternatives Key)

What if gifted learners chose their own timetable? What would be the positives and negatives to this concept? What positive aspects could you develop further and what ways could you find around the barriers?

(⊷ What if Key and ⊷ The Brick Wall Key)

In what ways do the objects in this picture Symbolise gifted and talented students in your school?

Brainstorm at least 3 different interpretations for each symbol. Choose the one you like the best.

Draw an analogy or metaphor from this and elaborate upon it.

(Picture Key )

TIP 1: Use only the Thinkers Keys that fit well with your topic. Don't force-fit every Key into your topic, or expect students to do every one. Use the Keys to offer CHOICE rather than only use them as required tasks.

TIP 2: Teach the Thinkers Keys to your students. Have them design their own activities, and then negotiate with you. Add rigor or structure to their Thinkers Key activity if necessary.

Differentiate Thinkers Keys for more able learners!

Even very young learners can, and do, respond to Thinkers Keys activities, and at all students can be engaged by them. Avoid trivial activities without specific learning outcomes.

Often it is the follow-up questions and instructions that accompany the initial key question that adds a level of sophistication for the more able learners in your classroom.

**USE THE PLANNER ON THE NEXT PAGE
AS A TOOL FOR DIFFERENTIATING TASKS
FOR DIFFERENT LEARNERS IN YOUR CLASSROOM**

THINKERS KEYS Activity /Assessment Task Planner

Curriculum Area: _____________________________ **Level:** ______

Activity:

Learning Outcomes:	**Type of thinking required:**

Is this activity more challenging than many of the class could manage successfully? (Could, Would, Should Rule!)

YES	NO

What activities could this activity <u>replace</u>, so students choosing to do this activity wouldn't have to do extra? *(Quality, not quantity, of work)*	Ideas for alternative (more complex) adaptations:

What criteria would indicate successful completion of this task?

Students can:

Figure 66 Thinkers Keys Activity / Assessment Task PlannerTemplate 1

Thinkers Keys Planning Template	
Reverse Key	Picture Kev
'What If' Key	Prediction Key
Construction Key	Interpretation Key
Disadvantages Key	Ridiculous Key
Brick Wall Key	Commonality Key
Question Key	Inventions Key
Alternatives Key	B.A.R. Key
Combination Key	Forced Relationship Key
Different Uses Key	Variations Key
Alphabet Key	Brainstorming Key

Figure 67 Thinkers Keys Blank Planning Template (From Tony Ryan's Thinkers Keys).

6.3.3 Socratic Questions

Various questioning models have been developed in recent years. Socratic questioning teaches students to probe more deeply into what they think they know, and understand what they do not know about complex ideas. It helps them to explore problems and issues, expose assumptions and consider logic.

Once students are familiar with Socratic questions, they can engage in *Socratic Dialogue.*

The Difference between Dialogue and Discussion

<u>Dialogue</u>: involves collaboration to enlarge our understandings and to create new understandings that none of us had when we came into the dialogue. The object is not so much to arrive at a consensus as to discover new possibilities of understanding in collaboration with others.

"In dialogue we attempt to call forth the best the other person has to offer and put forth the best we can imagine. Dialogue requires thoughtful listening and responding. It is a time when participants co-produce meaning" – Peterson, R. (1992)

<u>Discussion:</u> is different from dialogue. In discussion 'the object is to win, that is, to have one's own views accepted by the group as the valid understanding of an experience. It can be exploratory, but contributions rarely build synergistically upon each other. They are more likely to be responsive or reactive than generative. While dialogues explore ways to open up new knowledge, discussions explore the meanings that are already present in the group.

"In a discussion, decisions are made [while] in a dialogue, complex issues are explored" – Peter Senge, (1990).

From Comstock & Fox (1995)

One method of holding Socratic Dialogue is described overleaf. Teachers should familiarise themselves and the students with the Socratic Question cards[18] on pages 147 & 148.

Students may be given one card each to focus upon as they learn the technique, or they may choose a card that allows them to ask the type of question they'd like to ask. Similarly the students could have copies of the questions in their workbooks, and large wall charts with the Socratic questions can be on display.

---

[18] Adapted from R. Paul (1993).

Have topics for discussion ready on a current event or controversial topic: e.g.

'Euthanasia has no respect for human dignity'

'Human life is more important than animal life'

'Capital punishment is a better option than life imprisonment'

'War is sometimes unavoidable'

'Dictators should be forcibly removed'

'A lie is wrong under any circumstance'

'A good friend should forgive anything'

'Freedom of speech is an inalienable right'

'A person should not be allowed to starve themselves to death in protest'

1. Have different readings ready on the topic, with diverse opinions expressed. Dialogue is richer when students are not just plucking thoughts out of the air.

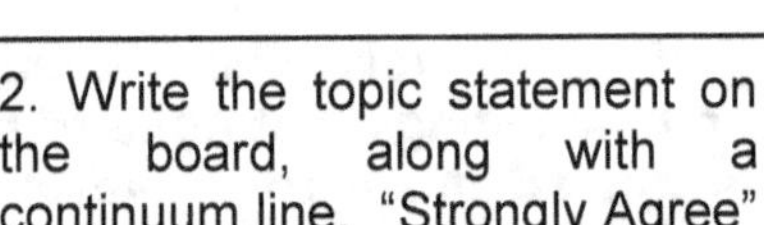

2. Write the topic statement on the board, along with a continuum line. "Strongly Agree" – "Strongly Disagree" (p149).

Ask students to place their names on the continuum. Alternatively, ask them to stand in a line of continuum indicating their opinion.

3. Give out Socratic questions cards. Ask students to ask Socratic questions when it is appropriate.

4. Discuss the topic statement. Students may change their place on the continuum whenever they wish. Remind the students to try to phrase their questions of others in the Socratic Questioning style.

The students should understand they are *not* debating the statement and be clear about the difference between dialogue and discussion (p145). Encourage them to value other viewpoints, even if they do not agree.

Use the 'Class Rules for Discerning Thinkers' and the "Four Rules of Reasoned Discourse' (pp 109, 110).

TIP: Use "Discrepancies" from Williams Taxonomy with Socratic Dialogue.

Figure 68 Conducting Socratic Dialogue in the Classroom

Socratic Questions

QUESTIONS OF CLARIFICATION

- Please explain what you mean by ...?
- Could you give me an example?
- Do you mean that...?
- How does ... relate to ...?
- Could you put that another way?
- What do you think is the main issue here?
- How does this relate to our discussion topic (problem, issue)?
- Janna, would you summarise what Pita said? ... Pita, would you agree that is what you meant?

Adapted from R. Paul (1993)

Socratic Questions

QUESTIONS THAT PROBE ASSUMPTIONS

- What assumptions are being made by the writer / speaker?
- What are you assuming in this instance?
- What could we assume instead?
- All of your reasoning depends upon the idea that ... Why have you based your reasoning upon ... rather than...?
- You seem to be assuming ...   How would you justify taking this for granted?
- Is it always the case? Why do you think the assumption holds here?

Adapted from R. Paul (1993)

Socratic Questions

QUESTIONS THAT PROBE REASONS AND EVIDENCE

- How do you know this is the case?
- What evidence supports that?
- Do you have any good evidence for that?
- Is there reason to doubt that evidence?
- Are your reasons for believing this adequate?
- How could we go about finding out whether that is true?
- What other information do we need to know?

Adapted from R. Paul (1993)

QUESTIONS ABOUT VIEWPOINTS OR PERSPECTIVES

- Why have you chosen this perspective rather than ... perspective?
- Could anyone else see this another way? Who? Why?
- What would someone who disagrees with this perspective say?
- How could you answer the objection that ... would make if they were here?
- What is an alternative viewpoint?
- Maria and Tony hold seemingly opposing views on this. How are their views alike?

Adapted from R. Paul (1993)

QUESTIONS THAT PROBE IMPLICATIONS AND CONSEQUENCES

- What is the writer / speaker implying?
- What would be the result in our accepting / believing this?
- What are you implying by that statement?
- When you say .... Are you implying ....?
- If that happened, what else could happen as a result? Why?
- Would that necessarily happen or only probably happen?
- If ... and ... are the case, then what else must also be true?

Adapted from R. Paul (1993)

QUESTIONS ABOUT THE QUESTIONS

- How can we find out?
- How could someone settle this question?
- Is this the same issue as ...?
- What does this question assume?
- Does this question have a bias?
- Why is this question important?
- Does this question ask us to evaluate something?
- Do we all agree that this is the question?
- To answer this question, what questions would we have to answer first?

Adapted from R. Paul (1993)

Statement or Topic: (news item, article, concept)

Place a mark, with your name above or below, on the line of continuum to indicate how much or how little you agree with the statement / item / article / concept.

Totally
Disagree

Neutral
Position

Totally
Agree

Revisit this line of continuum as the dialogue progresses. Review your position whenever you wish.

There IS no 'right' position!

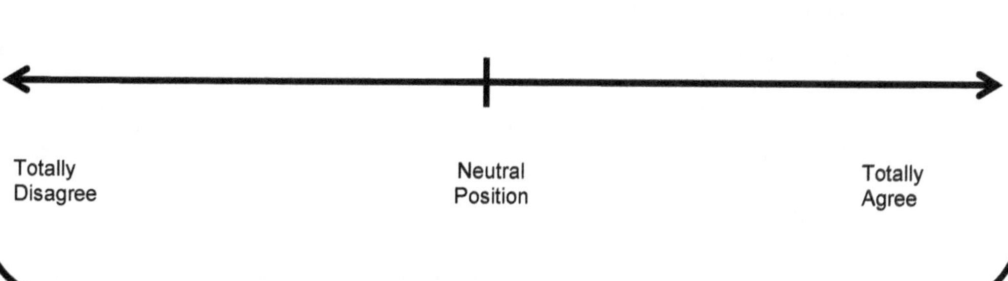

Critical & Creative Thinking: Planning for Change

Which practices in this chapter best suit my / our subject area?	
What can I / we begin developing further (in the next month/next unit)?	
Which of my colleagues might be best placed to be a critical friend in this?	
What area might I need more professional development support in?	

Feed back: (What worked / what needs further development)

Feed Forward: (What next?)

 Designing Defensible Programs for Gifted Secondary School Learners © Sonia White 2011

References Readings and Resources

Amabile, T.M., (1990). Chapter 4 'Within you, without you: the social psychology of creativity and beyond'. In *Theories of creativity.* Papers presented at a conference held at Pitzer College in Claremont, California, 11-13 November, 1988, edited by Mark Runco and R.S. Albert, pages 61-91.

Bloom, Benjamin S. (1956). *Taxonomy of Educational Objectives.* Boston MA: Allyn and Bacon, Copyright (c) 1984 by Pearson Education.

Comstock, D., & Fox, S. (1995). Computer conferencing in a learning community: opportunities and obstacles. [Electronic Version].
Retrieved 14.3.2007 from http://www.seattleantioch.edu/VirtualAntioch/DRAFT7HT.HTM

Csikszentmihályi, M., Rathunde, K., & Whalen, S. (1997). *Talented teenagers: the roots of success and failure.* USA: Cambridge University Press.

Csikszentmihályi, M. (1990). Chapter 9. The domain of creativity. In *Theories of creativity.* Papers presented at a conference held at Pizer College in Claremont, California, 11-13 November, 1988. Edited by Mark Runco and R. S. Albert, pp190-212.

Csikszentmihályi, M., (1990). *The psychology of Optimal Experience.* New York: Harper & Row.

Eberle, B. (1991). *SCAMPER - games for imagination development.* Victoria: Hawker Brownlow Education.

Eberle, B. (2004). *SCAMPER.* Saratosa: Creative Learning Inc.

Eberle, B. (2004). *SCAMPER on.* Saratosa: Creative Learning Inc.

Future Problem Solving Program International. www.fpspi.org

Gallagher, J.J. and Gallagher, A.A., (1994). Chapter 10 'Creativity: its identification and stimulation'. In *Teaching the gifted child.* 4th edition. Allyn & Bacon, pages 317-349.

Gnezda-Smith, N. (1994, December). 'The internal forces of creativity: when hearts start to flutter'. *Roeper Review*, volume 17, number 2, pages 138-143.

Jewell, P., (1996), *Thinking Strategies – Creative, Critical & Caring,* in Munandar, U. & Semiawan, C.(eds.) 'Optimising Excellence in Human resource Development'. Indonesia: UIP

Jewell, P. (2001). *Four Precepts of Reasoned Discourse - adapted from Erdman.* Unpublished manuscript, Adelaide.

Krathwohl, D. R, Anderson, L. W. (2001). A Taxonomy for Learning, Teaching, and Assessing: A Revision of Bloom's Taxonomy of Educational Objectives. Longman, Inc.

Le Sueur, E., and Boswell, R., (2010). *Provocative Questions: expanding horizons for thinking.* Nelson, New Zealand: Thinkshop Thinking Resources Ltd.

Le Sueur, E. (2007). *H.O.T. Units: Higher Order thinking units: Plug them Right into your classroom!* (Vol. 3 Years 9-10). Nelson, New Zealand: Thinkshop Thinking Resources Ltd.

Le Sueur, E. (2006). *H.O.T. Units: Higher order thinking units for gifted readers: Using sophisticated picture books.* Nelson, New Zealand: Thinkshop Thinking Resources Ltd.

Khatena, Joe (1995). 'Creative imagination and imagery'. *Gifted education international*, volume 10, number 3, pages 123-130.

Paul, R. (1993). *Critical thinking: how to prepare students for a rapidly changing world.* Santa Rosa, California: Foundation for Critical Thinking.

Peterson, R. (1992). *Life in a crowded place: making a learning community* Portsmouth, NH: Heinemann.

Piirto, J. (1994). Extract from *Talented children and adults.* Merrill Publishing Company, (171-178).

Pohl, M. (2000). *Teaching complex thinking: critical, creative, caring.* Victoria: Hawker Brownlow Education.

Pohl, M. (2002). *Infusing thinking into the middle years: a resource book for schools.* Victoria, Australia: Hawker Brownlow.

Renzulli, Joseph S. (1992, fall). A general theory for the development of creative productivity through the pursuit of ideal acts of learning. *Gifted child quarterly,* volume 36, number 4, pages 170-182.

Ryan, T. (1990). *Thinkers keys for kids.* Queensland: Logan West School Support Centre.

Ryan, T. (n.d.). *Thinkers keys cards*: Headfirst Publishing.

Ryan, Tony. Website: www.tonyryan.com.au (Thinkers Keys and other resources)

Senge, P. (1990). *The fifth discipline: the art and practice of the learning organization.* New York: Doubleday.

Sternberg, R. J. (2004). WICS: A model of organizational leadership *The Educational Forum, 68*(2), 108-114.

Sternberg, R. J. (2000). Patterns of Giftedness - A Triarchic Analysis *Roeper Review* (June), 231-235.

Sternberg, R. J. (1997). *Successful Intelligence - How practical and creative intelligence determine success in life.* New York: Penguin Putnam.

Sternberg, R.J., and Lubert, T.I., (1991). 'An investment theory of creativity and its development'. *Human Development,* volume 34, pages 1-34.

Sternberg, R.J., (1988). Chapter 5 'A three-faceted model of creativity'. In *The nature of creativity.* Cambridge: University Press, pages 125-147.

Torrance, E.P., (1988). Chapter 2 'The nature of creativity as manifest in its testing'. In *The nature of creativity.* Edited by Robert Sternberg. Cambridge: Cambridge University Press, pages 43-75.

Treffinger, D., Young, G., Nassab, C., & Wittig, C. (2004). *Enhancing and expanding gifted programs: The levels of service approach.* Saratosa, FL: Center for Creative Learning Inc.

Treffinger, D. (1995). *Creativity, creative thinking, and critical thinking: in search of definitions.* Saratosa: Center for Creative Learning.

Weiten, Wayne, (1998) Chapter 9. 'Intelligence and psychological testing'. In *Psychology: themes and variations /Wayne Weiten.* 4th edition. California: Brooks/Cole Publishing Company.

Williams, F. E. (1993). The cognitive-affective interaction model for enriching gifted programs. In J. S. Renzulli, (Ed.), *Systems and models for developing programs for the gifted and talented* (pp. 461-484). Highett, Vic.: Hawker Brownlow.

Chapter 7. Caring Thinking

Thought is the blossom;
language the bud;
action the fruit behind it.
> *- Ralph Waldo Emerson*

The social-emotional characteristics of gifted learners, when carefully nurtured, can empower students to take charge of their learning, and become self-directed, motivated innovators of social change.

Gifted learners have characteristics that can *and should* benefit society. They:

- can have high sensitivity & intense emotional response;
- can be deeply perceptive;
- may be driven by a deep sense of right and wrong;
- may be perfectionist, and/or highly idealistic;
- are often deeply concerned by community and/or world issues
- are quick to *identify* problems, and can generate and implement solutions

Because of these characteristics, gifted learners *need* a curriculum that develops 'caring thinking' alongside other higher-order thinking.

7.1 Affective Thinking is...

...the sense the individual makes of the world around him in relation to what he feels is valuable, ethically or morally right; what he feels is appropriate remedial or supportive action, and what he envisions as the ideal, what he prioritises as important, worth caring about (Lipman).

Mathew Lipman coined the term Caring Thinking and argued that it is the third prerequisite to higher-order thinking (the other two being critical and creative thinking). Whilst Bloom's taxonomy identifies three aspects of higher-order thinking (the analytical, the synthetic or creative, and the evaluative), none of these directly address affective thinking. If we only focus on critical and creative thinking much of the thinking that is taught includes affective thinking by accident rather than by design.

A vague inclusion of aspects of affective thinking is not good enough!

*One might nominate critical thinking as the truth-seeking aspect
and creative thinking as the meaning-seeking aspect.
But what aspect of high-order thinking is especially concerned
with the dimensions of values?*
-   Lipman, (1995).

While there are other models of affective thinking, this handbook focuses upon Lipman's Caring Thinking because it integrates well with critical and creative thinking. In matters of importance this model demands consideration of what *is* and what *ought to be* in relation to what we care about, and what we *ought* to care about. It brings heart and soul into analytical and evaluative thinking, and allows creativity to flourish and be valued and nurtured.

Why is affective thinking important?

Gifted and talented students are in all classrooms; some are gifted affective thinkers; others aren't, but need to be. Many will bear the responsibility of shaping their nation's future, and therefore both implicit and explicit teaching of high level thinking skills is fundamental to the development of all gifted students. All students need affective thinking tools. Moral and ethical personal growth *is* a developmental process, and 'caring thinking' is valued by all cultures in our communities. More than any other model, Lipman's Caring Thinking can promote global awareness and support authentic learning.

*Our actions follow directly upon our emotions.
One hates, one behaves destructively, one loves, one behaves amicably.
Consequently, if we can temper the antisocial emotions,
we are likely to be able to temper the antisocial conduct
Lipman, (1998).*

7.2 Lipman's Caring Thinking: Getting to the *HEART* of Thinking

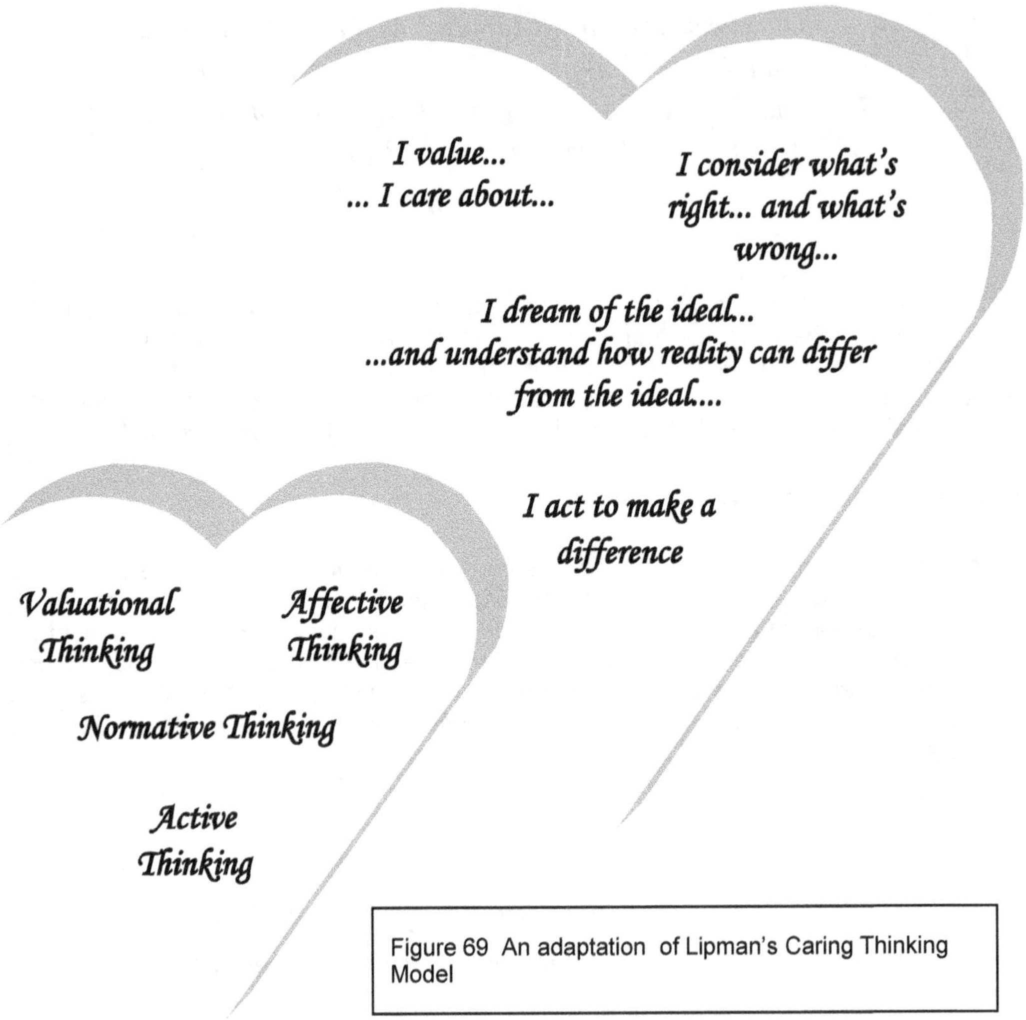

Figure 69 An adaptation of Lipman's Caring Thinking Model

Mathew Lipman's model of Caring Thinking uses valuational, affective, active, and normative thinking.

The following pages elaborate upon each of these four components, which, although they are usually integrated within an inquiry process, have been individually 'unpacked' so that teachers and students can better understand them. In developing valuational, affective, normative and active thinking in the classroom, each can, of course, be focussed upon individually. Strategies marked with an *asterisk are from Williams Taxonomy which is described in Chapter 8.

Characteristics of Gifted Caring Thinkers

Adapted from Brunt (2000)

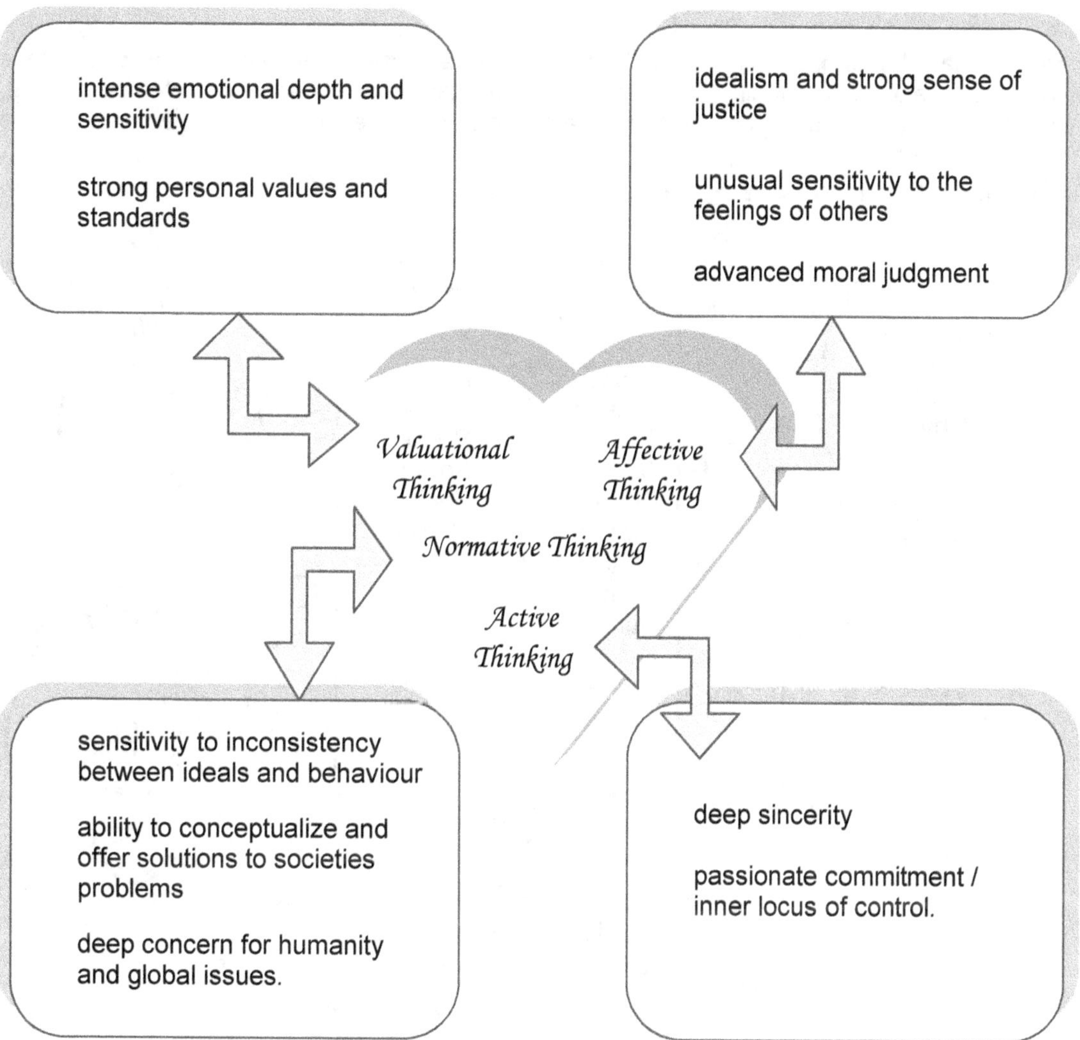

Figure 70 Characteristics of Gifted Caring Thinkers

Valuational Thinking is thinking about *what we value, prize, admire and appreciate.* (It is *not* about evaluating or judging). It is about what matters to us, what we *ought* to care about, and it is about appraising how much we care about, or value this. Things we value can be concrete or abstract.

Valuational thinking asks Big Questions such as:

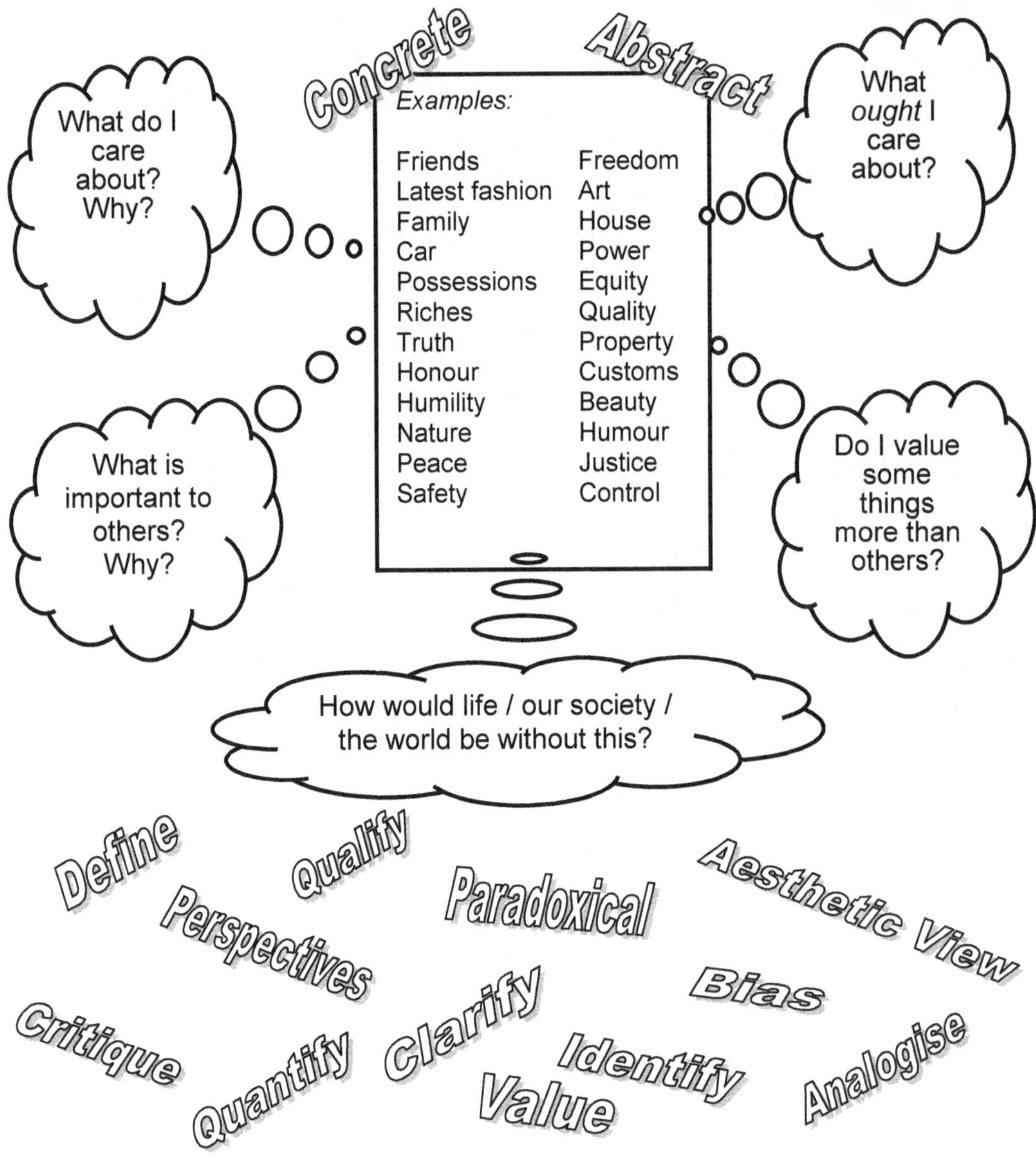

    Designing Defensible Programs for Gifted Secondary School Learners © Sonia White 2011

VALUATIONAL THINKING (what we value, prize, admire & appreciate; concrete & abstract)

THINKING SKILLS	THINKING STRATEGIES
Value	Values clarification
Prize	Metaphor
Perspectives	Debating skills
Qualify	Analogies*;
Quantify	Tolerance for Ambiguities*
Debate	Cultural perspectives
Aesthetic	Religious perspectives
View	Philosophical enquiry
Questioning	Moral dilemmas
Paradoxical	Literary critiquing
Define	Provocative questions*
Clarify	Paradoxes*
Bias	Visualisation*
Visualise	Kohlberg's Theory Moral Development
Infer	Creative writing & reading*
Critique	
Identify	
Analogise	

PLANNING IDEAS & STARTERS

So what? (Why is this important?)

Discuss the value of...?

Qualify / quantify the value of... (concrete or abstract)

What would someone who disagreed with this idea think / say?

Develop a metaphor that explains how you feel about...

Explain how (X) is a / is like a (metaphor or analogy).

What is the cultural bias of this idea?

Investigate the advantages and disadvantages of ... and decide upon the most important factors that should be considered...

Write an analogy that demonstrates the value of...

EXAMPLES

Create a role play / drama / short story / music /picture / sculpture based around the conflict which occurs when an individual's values are challenged by others or tested by events.

Make a chart that highlights the different cultural values of land and land ownership between e.g. Aboriginal /Maori / Indigenous Peoples and European settlers

Analyse the decisions made by a major character in this novel. Summarise the decisions on a flow chart and indicate how these decisions demonstrate the key values of the character. How do these values create conflict in this story?

Create a collage using symbols and /or pictures which depicts differing cultural perspectives of freedom. Present and explain your choices and your research behind each depiction.

Research and generate a list of types of Freedoms. Develop 5 criteria for judging the importance of these freedoms and rate them against the criteria. Place those that you rate most highly in some form of hierarchy for display and be prepared to defend your selection.

✍ What might Valuational Thinking look like in your subject area?

Affective Thinking is responding to how we feel about things we value. This happens when we experience strong emotional & cognitive response to offences or wrongdoing. Affective thinking is about developing our values and ethics as we appraise what is appropriate and inappropriate behaviour.

Affective Thinking asks Big Questions such as:

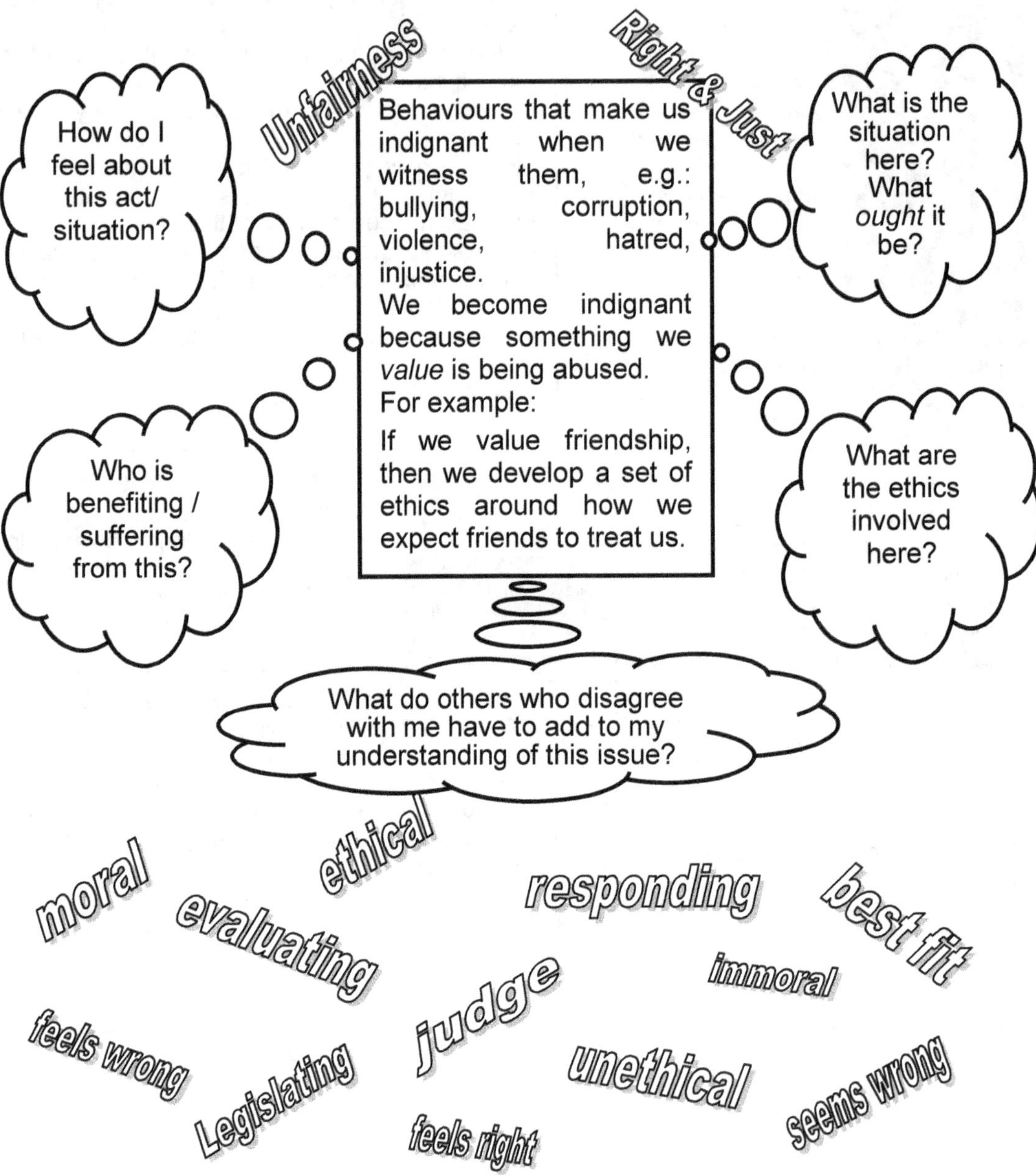

AFFECTIVE THINKING (responding to how we feel; developing values & ethics)

THINKING SKILLS	THINKING STRATEGIES	PLANNING IDEAS & STARTERS
Feels right/ wrong Judge Evaluate Responding Legislating Prioritising Objecting Paradoxical 'Best fit' Moral / immoral Ethical / unethical Conclude Verify Integrate	Black, Yellow, Red Hat Social/ moral issues Moral dilemmas Current events CAF; PMI; OPV; Philosophy; Paradoxes*; Tolerance for Ambiguities* Evaluative situations* Poetry / creative writing in response to issues; Authentic learning (real issues); Environmental studies Role play/ drama to reflect emotional responses to issues* Provocative questions* Discrepancies* Intuitive expression*	How do you feel about…? (moral situation)? Why? Explain. Defend your position. What is morally defensible here? Against what measures? What would someone who disagreed with this idea think and feel? Give an alternative course of action / consequence / punishment which would be fairer … Who benefits /suffers from this? Generate ethical ways of resolving the conflict of this situation Write a story that justifies the choices made by… / that shows the decisions that would have to be made when…/ that shows the conflicts that arise when… Research other points of view on X topic; Argue convincingly from another person's viewpoint; Gather a range of differing views on this topic and analyse the biases.

EXAMPLES

If a different culture had discovered and claimed your country, how might life be different now? Make a T chart showing the main differences. What existing things would you miss? What might be improved? Why do you think this?

"To be truly free one must first bear the weight of responsibility". Discuss the validity of this paradox from the point of view of: a) the parent of a teenager who has just gained their driver's license. b) a victim of a drink/drive accident c) a teenager tired of rules and regulations. Do all viewpoints hold validity? Do some have inconsistencies? Explain.

Imagine if, in the story of Goldilocks & the Three Bears if Goldilocks was substituted by Jerry Springer, The US President, or Mrs Doubtfire? What decisions or issues might change? Write a brief outline then create a cartoon/ role play /puppet show around this idea. Choose a personality of your own to substitute for Goldilocks if you wish.

What possible outcomes may occur if your country or State changes its existing law on the Death sentence? Create a flow chart to show the possible outcomes of such a law change. Give your opinion on this issue and explain with reference to your research, to your ethical beliefs and supporting argument.

What might Affective Thinking look like in your subject area?

Active thinking is acting upon what we value. It is action to support a cause or belief with a focus on what individuals may do about a circumstance or situation. It is interventionist. It involves responding in an effective, productive way to things that affect us. It is closely linked to normative, valuational thinking, and affective thinking.

Thinking is easy, acting is difficult,
and to put one's thoughts into action is the most difficult thing in the world
- Johann Wolfgang von Goethe.

Active Thinking asks Big Questions such as:

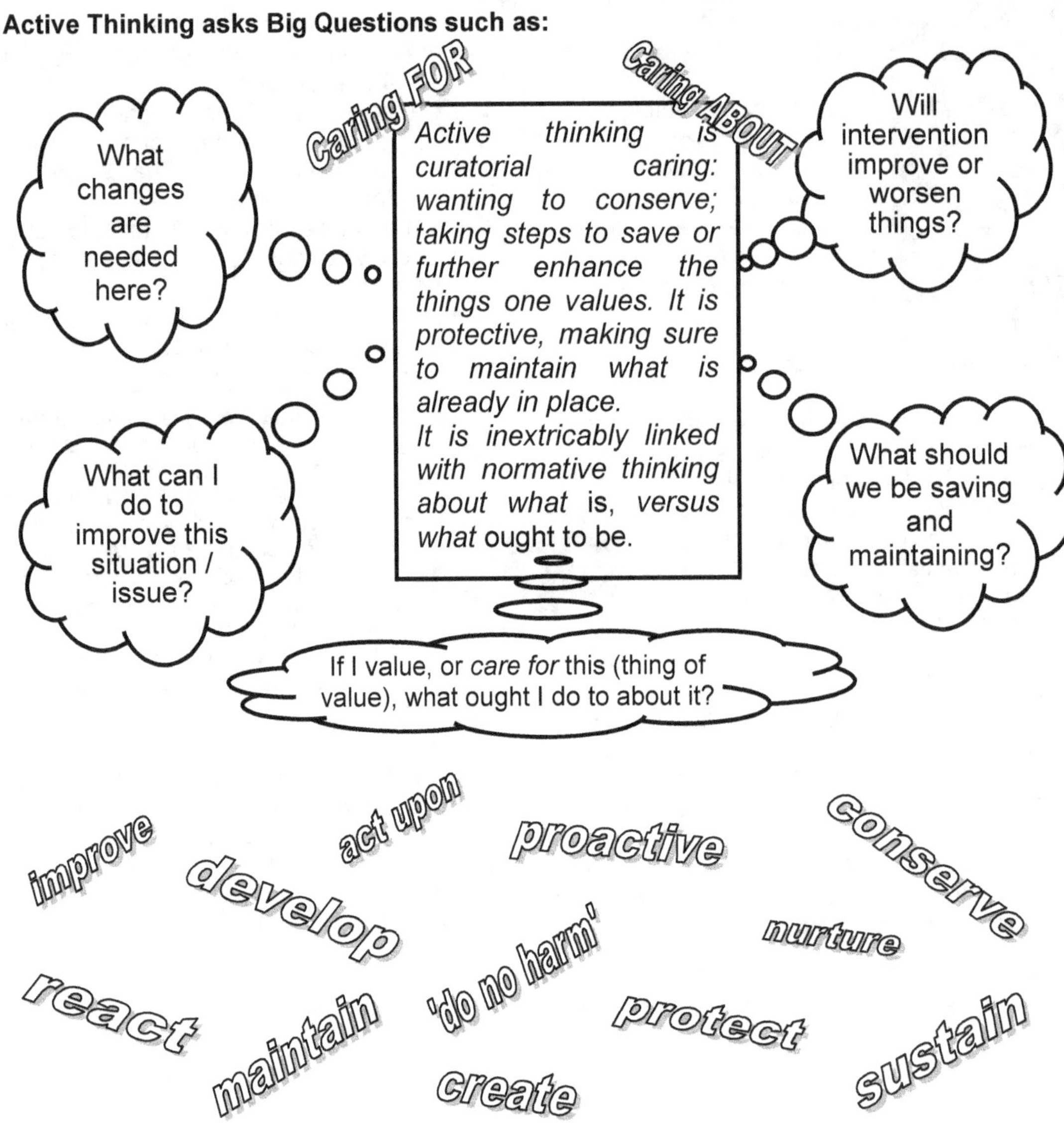

     Designing Defensible Programs for Gifted Secondary School Learners © Sonia White 2011

ACTIVE THINKING (acting upon what we value)

THINKING SKILLS	THINKING STRATEGIES	PLANNING IDEAS & STARTERS
Discussing Deciding Acting upon Intervening Conserving Protecting Generating Proactive Reactive Improving Apply Elaborating Represent Motivational Creational	Blue Hat; APC; community groups; community service; international orgs; Community Problem Solving; Examples of Habit* Evaluative situations* Class meetings Class / group responsibilities Peer mentoring Peer mediation Authentic learning (real issues); Intuitive expression*	Write a letter to the editor /community leaders about… Make suggestions about positive changes that could be made to…; Lead a discussion on… and gain a group consensus on appropriate action. Plan a campaign to reduce the negative effects of…; convince others to join you. Present to person(s) who has the authority to follow-up on your recommendations. Create and present a play/work of art / video / film which highlights an issue /concern and offers a feasible potential solution to the issue. - Consider ways that X situation/problem might be improved – generate a range of possible alternatives; select the best alternative and develop a plan of action to implement this. Implement your plan. - Evaluate X course of action a friend/ a character is considering making, and write a persuasive argument for or against.

EXAMPLES

If you had all the resources you needed, how would you deal with a major issue in your community? Brainstorm as many ideas as you can think of and show them in a chart. Select 3 or 4 of the ones you most value, and develop them further. Decide upon the criteria you will need to help you decide upon the best action to take.

What is the value of a school uniform? What, if any, changes would you recommend to the current situation In your school? Prepare a case to present your view to your school council. Give good reasons and evidence to support your view.

(Groups) As the leaders of a group of 100 people settled on the banks of the Euphrates River in 2,500 B.C., create 10 laws which will promote community wellbeing. Write rules on a chart and present to class. Evaluate all groups' laws. Consider your criteria for 'good' laws. Do the laws protect lives and property? Are these laws the most important laws? Have any important laws been missed out?

Group (3): A takeaway food chain sells "healthy meals" of salads, yoghurt 'smoothies' and low fat burgers. The packaging is large, non-recyclable plastic containers. List ethical considerations. Prepare a panel discussion which gives the points of view of the organization, a charitable trust which relies heavily upon donations from the food chain, and an individual concerned about pollution.

✍ What might Active Thinking look like in your subject area?

Normative thinking is thinking about what *is*, and what *ought to be*. It is the norm versus the ideal. In examining big issues or problems, it pushes us to think about what we desire, and what *ought to be* desired. It helps us to reflect upon actual current or proposed practice, examine what *is* done, and generate ideas, plans, an overview or blueprint for what *ought* to be done.
Normative thinking should be integrated with active thinking.

Normative Thinking asks Big Questions such as:

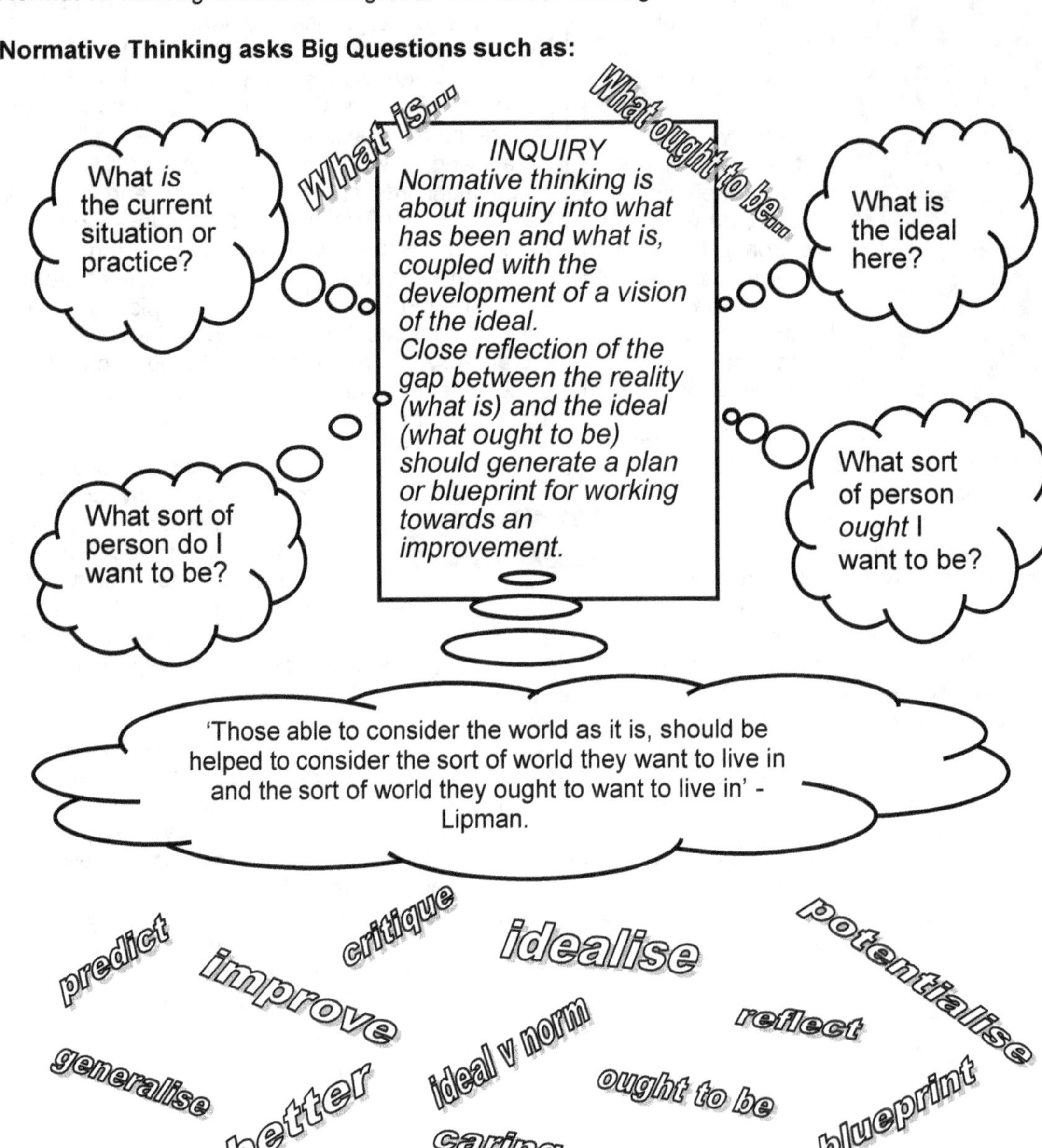

     Designing Defensible Programs for Gifted Secondary School Learners © Sonia White 2011

NORMATIVE THINKING (Ideal versus Norm)

THINKING SKILLS	THINKING STRATEGIES
Idealise Reflect Compare ideal to norm Potentialise Improve Plan Predict Forecast Critique Question Analyse Generalise	'Big ideas' / themes Community Problem Solving Tolerance for Ambiguities* Environmental studies Philosophy Provocative questions* Discrepancies* Examples of Change* Examples of Habit* Adjustment to Development*

PLANNING IDEAS & STARTERS

What is the ideal in this situation? Is it achievable? Why / why not? Develop a strategy / strategies that would achieve some improvement to the situation.

Explain why a constant state of peace is unachievable.

Defend a decision to ban (X). Anticipate the problems arising from this and attempt to circumvent them.

Describe how (X event) in history irrevocably changed the development of mankind

Examine the impact (X person) has had upon a specific area. List the key actions that caused this impact, and consider what might have occurred if that person had not acted.

Write a biographical sketch / cartoon of an historical figure who faced vilification because of their ideas.

Defend (unpopular idea) and show why it could have benefits

EXAMPLES

What is an ideal Government? Investigate a system of government and examine the degree to which that system meets your ideal. From that, create a list of "principles of ideal government" and invent a symbol to represent each

What are the key ideals expressed in "To Kill a Mocking Bird" and to what extent does the characters' reality differ from their personal ideal? Discuss the inner conflict caused by one of the main characters when they are unable to live up to their ideals.

In a real life environmental issue, what is the 'ideal' situation versus the 'reality'? How achievable is the ideal? What would some of the outcomes be if that 'ideal' situation existed? What can be realistically done to improve the situation? Write a letter to significant people in the community explaining your view of the situation and making recommendations for change. Defend your stance.

Do you agree with the statement "Fairy tales are filled with violence"? Are children able to distinguish from 'real' and imaginary? What place do fairy tales have in developing a healthy psyche in children?
Research differing opinions on these questions and formulate an ideal situation with regard to children's literature in the form of a Mission Statement for a children's book Publisher. Write to a publisher and ask them for comment.

✍ What might Normative Thinking look like in your subject area?

LIPMAN'S CARING THINKING

VALUATIONAL THINKING (what we value, prize, admire & appreciate; concrete & abstract)

THINKING SKILLS	THINKING STRATEGIES	PLANNING IDEAS & STARTERS
Value Prize Perspectives Qualify Quantify Debate Aesthetic View Questioning Paradoxical Define Clarify Bias Visualise Infer Critique Identify Analogise	Values clarification Metaphor Debating skills Analogies*; Tolerance for Ambiguities* Cultural perspectives Religious perspectives Philosophical enquiry Moral dilemmas Literary critiquing Provocative questions* Paradoxes* Visualisation* Kohlberg's Theory Moral Development Creative writing & reading*	So what? (Why is this important?) Discuss the value of…? Qualify / quantify the value of… (concrete or abstract) What would someone who disagreed with this idea think / say? Develop a metaphor that explains how you feel about… Explain how (X) is a / is like a (metaphor or analogy). What is the cultural bias of this idea? Investigate the advantages and disadvantages of … and decide upon the most important factors that should be considered… Write an analogy that demonstrates the value of…

 Designing Defensible Programs for Gifted Secondary School Learners © Sonia White 2011

AFFECTIVE THINKING (responding to how we feel; developing values & ethics)

THINKING SKILLS	THINKING STRATEGIES	PLANNING IDEAS & STARTERS
Feels right/ wrong Judge Evaluate Responding Legislating prioritising objecting Paradoxical 'best fit' Moral / immoral Ethical / unethical Conclude Verify Integrate	Black, Yellow, Red Hat Social/ moral issues Moral dilemmas Current events CAF; PMI; OPV; Philosophy; Paradoxes*; Tolerance for Ambiguities* Evaluative situations* Poetry / creative writing in response to issues; Authentic learning (real issues); Environmental studies Role play/ drama to reflect emotional responses to issues* Provocative questions* Discrepancies* Intuitive expression*	How do you feel about...? (ethical situation)? Why? Explain. Defend your position. What is morally defensible here? Against which measures? What would someone who disagreed with this idea think and feel? Give an alternative course of action / consequence / punishment which would be fairer ... Who benefits /suffers from this? Generate ethical ways of resolving the conflict of this situation. Write a story that justifies the choices made by... / that shows the decisions that would have to be made when.../ that shows the conflicts that arise when... Research other points of view on X topic; Argue convincingly from another person's viewpoint; Gather a range of differing views on this topic and analyse the biases.

ACTIVE THINKING (acting upon what we value)

THINKING SKILLS	THINKING STRATEGIES	PLANNING IDEAS & STARTERS
Discussing Deciding Acting upon Intervening Conserving Protecting Generating Proactive Reactive Improving Apply Elaborating Represent Motivational Creational	Blue Hat; APC; community groups; community service; international orgs; Community Problem Solving; Examples of Habit* Evaluative situations* Class meetings Class / group responsibilities Peer mentoring Peer mediation Authentic learning (real issues); Intuitive expression*	Write a letter to the editor /community leaders about… Make suggestions about positive changes that could be made to…; Lead a discussion on… and gain a group consensus on appropriate action. Plan a campaign to reduce the negative effects of…; convince others to join you. Present to person(s) who has the authority to follow-up on your recommendations. Create and present a play/work of art / video / film which highlights an issue /concern and offers a feasible potential solution to the issue. - Consider ways that X situation/problem might be improved – generate a range of possible alternatives; select the best alternative and develop a plan of action to implement this. Implement your plan. - Evaluate X course of action a friend/ a character is considering making, and write a persuasive argument for or against.

✍ (Note: Have students consider Normative thinking (what is & what ought to be) as a preface to planning action or before they are too far down the 'Active Thinking' implementation path.)

NORMATIVE THINKING (Ideal versus Norm)

THINKING SKILLS	THINKING STRATEGIES	PLANNING IDEAS & STARTERS
Idealise Reflect Compare ideal to norm Potentialise Improve Plan Predict Forecast Critique Question Analyse Generalise	'Big ideas' / themes Community Problem Solving Tolerance for Ambiguities* Environmental studies Philosophy Provocative questions* Discrepancies* Examples of Change* Examples of Habit* Adjustment to Development*	What is the ideal in this situation? Is it achievable? Why / why not? Develop a strategy / strategies that would achieve some improvement to the situation. Explain why a constant state of peace is unachievable. Defend a decision to ban (X). Anticipate the problems arising from this and attempt to circumvent them. Describe how (X event) in history irrevocably changed the development of mankind Examine the impact (X person) has had upon a specific area. List the key actions that caused this impact, and consider what might have occurred if that person had not acted. Write a biographical sketch / cartoon of an historical figure who faced vilification because of their ideas. Defend (unpopular idea) and show why it could have benefits

Reflection

| TEACHER LEARNING MAP: Caring Thinking -
Principles and Strategies |

What I know	What I thought I didn't know BUT I do!
What I thought I knew BUT I don't	What I didn't know I didn't know!

What I would now like to know more about

What I deny or refuse to look at:

Figure 71 Teacher Learning Map: Caring Thinking

Fill in first box before beginning the section, and the remaining boxes subsequent to reading and discussion.

7.3 Strategies that support Caring Thinking

Almost every school curriculum area has rich material to which caring thinking can be applied. Where an authentic inquiry approach can be made into serious issues, opportunities abound for students to consider values, ideals, norms, actions and choices.

Moral Dilemmas

Maker's Model for Moral Reasoning[19] is a practical method of conducting reasoned discourse around moral or ethical dilemmas

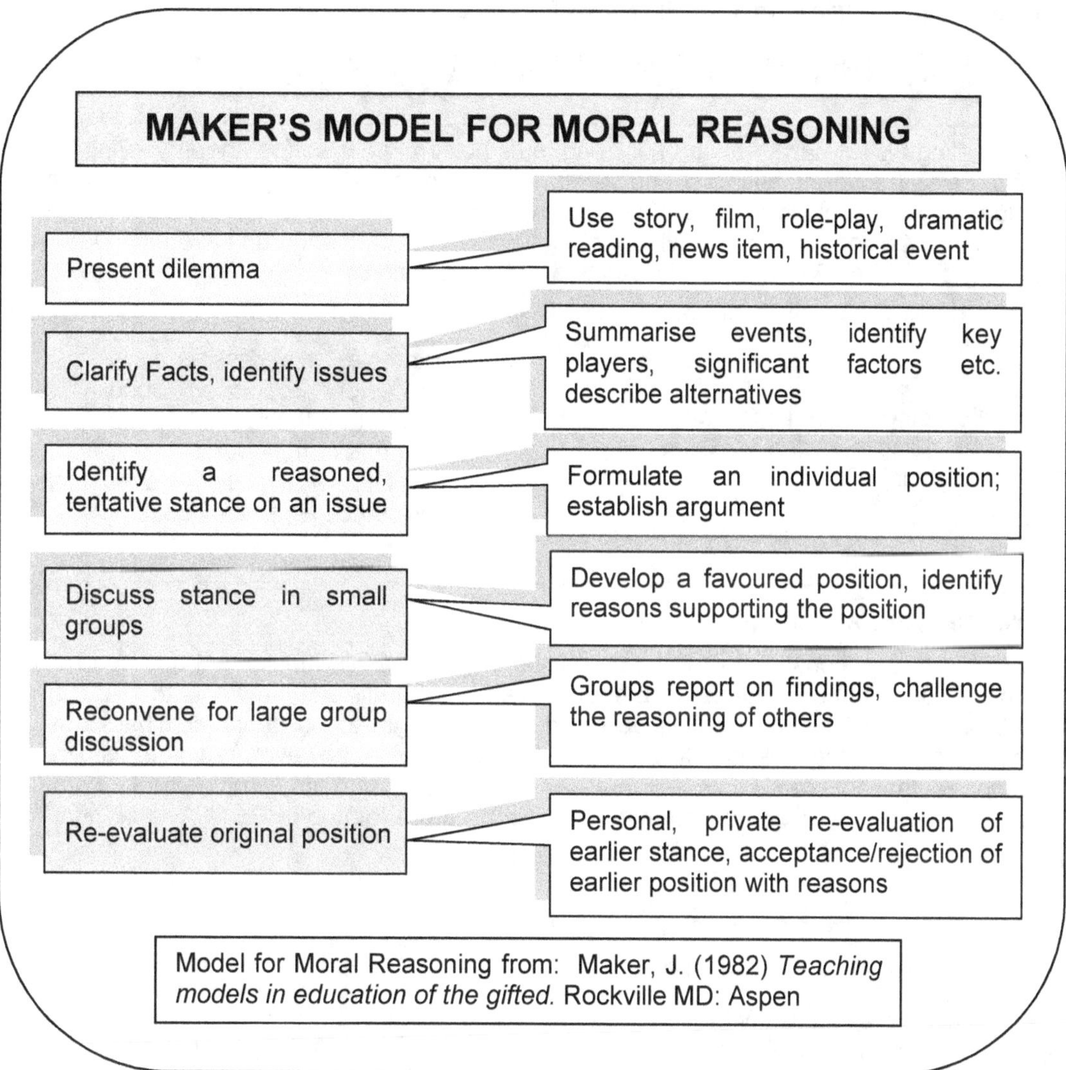

Figure 72 Makers Model for Moral reasoning

---

[19] Maker, 1982.

Students often expect that there is a 'right' or 'wrong' answer in a dilemma situation, but often there *is* no solution, and decisions must be based upon what the individual feels is morally or ethically 'right' or just.

Often the dilemma is presented when doing *right* results in some bad happening, and doing *wrong* brings about a desirable consequence.

The point in having these conversations is not to persuade someone that doing right is a bad thing; it is to clarify values, and what is really important.

The following examples are from http://www.friesian.com/valley/dilemmas.htm#8

Examples of Moral and Ethical Dilemmas

Tom, hating his wife and wanting her dead, puts poison in her coffee, thereby killing her. Debbie also hates her husband and would like him dead. One day, Debbie's husband accidentally puts poison in his coffee, thinking it is cream. Debbie has the antidote, but she does not give it to him. Knowing that she is the only one who can save him, Debbie lets him die. Is Debbie's failure to act as bad as Tom's action?

Is doing nothing the same as doing no harm? When might it be?

Examples: the passers-by in the story of the Good Samaritan; those like Debbie in the example above, and those who did offer assistance when they could.

The Partiality of Friendship

Jim has the responsibility of filling a position in his firm. His friend Paul has applied and is qualified, but someone else seems even more qualified. Jim wants to give the job to Paul, but he feels guilty, believing that he ought to be impartial. That's the essence of morality, he initially tells himself. This belief is, however, rejected, as Jim resolves that friendship has a moral importance that permits, and perhaps even requires, partiality in some circumstances. So he gives the job to Paul. Was he right to do so?

Does the end justify the means? Always? Sometimes? Ever?

Example: In order to develop a free society, where there is even distribution of wealth, like in Communist Russia, or Maoist China, tens of millions of people had to die.

Other examples of moral dilemmas can be found from the following websites:

www.friesian.com/valley/dilemmas.htm

www.haverford.edu/psych/ddavis/p109g/kohlberg.dilemmas.html

There are almost daily incidences of moral dilemmas in current events and media reports. Authentic moral dilemmas from real life events are ideal. There is an inexhaustible source of moral and ethical dilemmas in the media, in history and in the arts. Examine the moral dilemmas and subsequent choices made by historical figures, or by fictional characters (your choice, or encourage student selection).

7.4 Programs that support Caring Thinking

Programs that include / address global or community issues, and encourage inquiry such as the Community of Inquiry approach to learning are invaluable in promoting caring thinking. Subjects with topics that involve environmental sustainability, law and justice, or community / global social issues can promote valuational, affective, normative and active thinking. Cultural language or cultural dance groups, where they exist in a school, often foster active thinking through their efforts to conserve and maintain language and customs. Others include:

> *Many cultures (for example, Māori and Tongan cultures) place high importance upon their gifted and talented giving back to the community. There is an expectation that their gifted will serve the community through their gifts and talents. Whilst there may be a cultural 'shyness' of putting oneself forward, there is no such reluctance to serve.*

Philosophy for Children (P4C) Developed more than twenty years ago by Dr. Matthew Lipman, a philosophy professor at Montclair State College in New Jersey, Philosophy for Children is an international educational programme taught widely in many countries. At last count, Philosophy for Children was represented in some thirty countries around the world - ranging from Austria to Iceland, Bulgaria to Brazil and Canada to Taiwan - with philosophical conversations among children taking place in sixteen languages.

Community Problem Solving

Students work in teams to identify a school or community problem, write a scenario to describe the problem, then apply the steps of the Future Problem Solving process which they see as being appropriate for their particular problem, so that they can develop a plan of action. They then implement the plan of action to solve their problem. This is a year-long component of the FPSP program which has seen some students have profound impacts on their local community. http://www.fpspi.org/

Future Problem Solving

This is a year long programme where students, working in teams, learn and apply a six-step problem solving process which provides them with the tools to tackle problems which they will meet throughout their life. Throughout the year, students apply the process to consider the challenges and issues contained within complex social and scientific problems to be faced in the future or tackle existing problems in their own communities. The programme encourages students to carry out in-depth research, to think creatively and critically, to apply ethical thinking skills and to work as part of a team. http://www.fpspi.org/

M.U.N.A. (Model United Nations Assembly)

This program for high school or middle school students uses teams from different schools to represent a pre-determined country's perspective in a set topic for discussion and debate during a weekend long model United Nations Assembly. More information about MUNA can be found at http://www.unausa.org/modelun

Other Essential Opportunities

Schools who value and foster student community activities beyond the classroom reap the benefits in immeasurable ways. Those that deliberately incorporate caring thinking into meaningful contexts can enhance the personal moral development of their students in a non-paternalistic, facilitatory manner that is respectful of all cultures and beliefs. Students benefit from involvement in (and staff support of) volunteer programs such as:

CanTeen A Youth Organisation in New Zealand and Australia which supports teens with cancer and their families. Students hold major fundraising events to donate to this organisation. Most countries have similar agencies that students may choose to actively support.

Students Against Drunk Driving (SADD) A student led education program on drug and alcohol abuse. Information and resources available from www.sadd.org

World Vision - 40 Hour Famine The 40 Hour famine is an event held in 21 countries to raise money for countries suffering from famine. www.worldvision.com

Amnesty International An international human rights group that raises awareness of individuals suffering in countries abusing human rights and offers practical, peaceful ways of taking action. www.amnesty.org

Community Volunteer groups, e.g.:

Rest Homes, Disabled Children, church volunteer groups such as Caritas
Restorative Justice
Peer mentoring; in-school, or beyond (Mentoring a younger gifted student with a similar interest / area of passion
Reading to students in primary school
Coaching younger students in e.g. Maths, Science, Sport.

> Gifted learners often worry intensely about global issues.
> Providing them with opportunities where they take action with others
> to make a difference in their world
> goes a long way towards alleviating those concerns.
>
> *Let our advance worrying become advance thinking and planning.*
> *Winston Churchill*

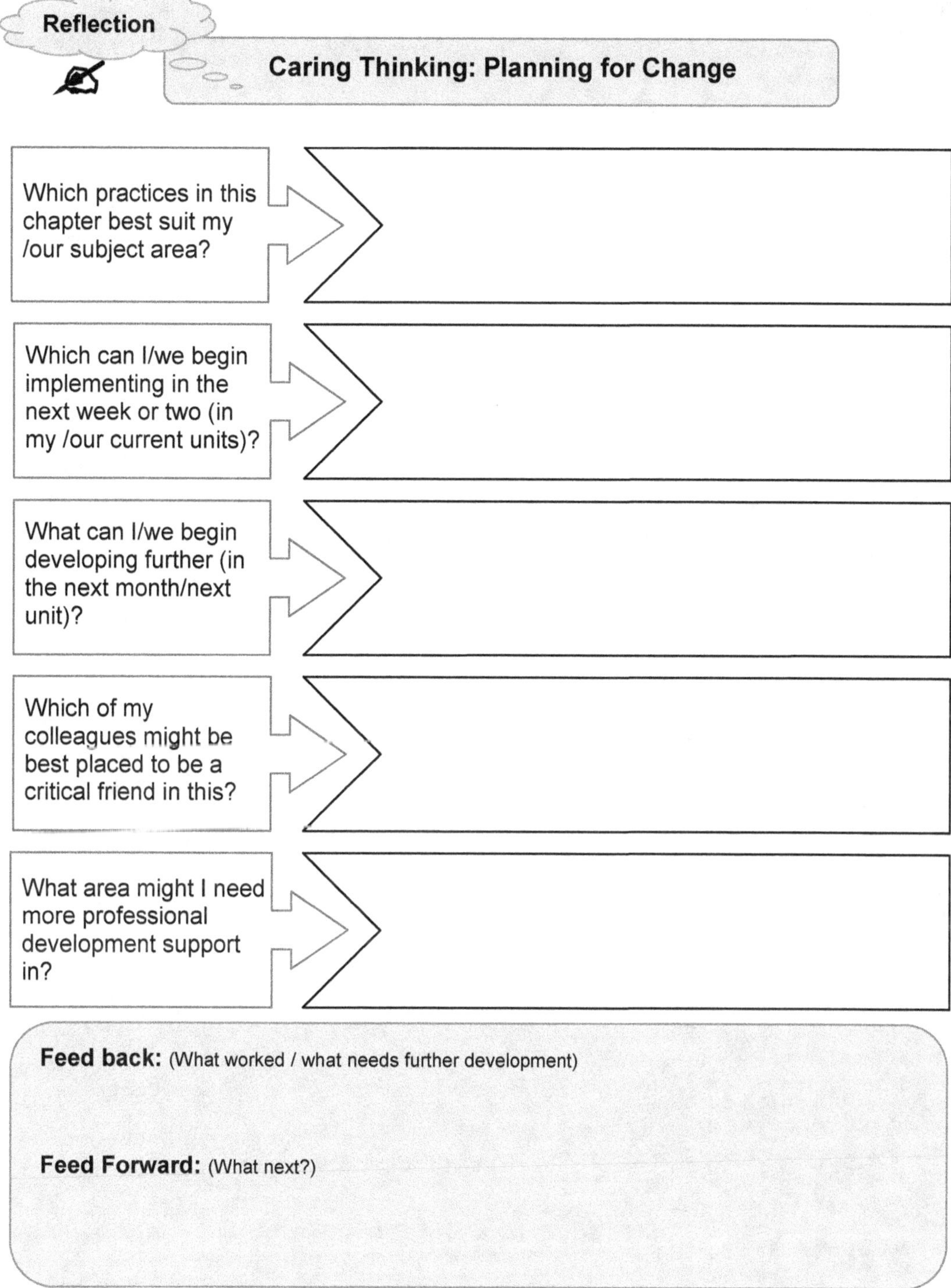

Figure 73 Caring Thinking:Planning for Change Template

NOTES:

Further Reading on Caring Thinking & Social Emotional Curriculum:

Brunt, J. (2000). *Caring thinking: The new intelligence.*
Accessed 4 Jan 2004. http://www.nexus.edu.au/teachstud/gat/brunt.htm

Department for Education and Children's Services, S. A. (1997). *Thinking, feeling and learning.* South Australia: Department for Education and Children's Services.

Franklin Smutny, J. (2001). Spiritual intelligence: Developing higher consciousness. *Roeper Review, 24,* 40-41.

Fraser, D. (2004). Some educational implications for spiritual giftedness. *Gifted Education International, 18*(3), 255-265.

Fraser, D. (2003). From the playful to the profound: What metaphors tell us about gifted children. *Roeper Review, 25*(4), 180-184.

Goleman, D. (1999). *Working with emotional intelligence.* Great Britain: Bloomsbury.

Greenspon, T. S. (2000, Apr). The self experience of the gifted person: Theory and definitions. *Roeper Review.*

Gross, M., Macleod, B., & Pretorius, M. (2001). *Gifted students in secondary schools: differentiating the curriculum* (2nd ed.). Sydney: Gifted Education Research, Resource and information Centre (GERRIC), UNSW.

Gust-Brey, K., & Cross, T. (1999). An examination of the literature base on the suicidal behaviors of gifted students. *Roeper Review, 22*(1), 28.

Hague, W. J. (1998). Is there moral giftedness? *Gifted Education International, 12*(3), 170-174.

Hebert, T. P. (2001). "If I had a new notebook, I know things would change": Bright underachieving young men in urban classrooms. *Gifted Child Quarterly, 45*(3), 174-194.

Henderson, L. (2003, 1-5 August). *Combining moral philosophy and moral reasoning: The P.A.V.E. Moral Reasoning Strategy.* Paper presented at the 15th Biennial World Conference, Gifted 2003: A Celebration Down-under, Adelaide, Australia.

Jacob-Ryan, J. (1999, Sep/Oct). Behind the mask: Exploring the need for specialized counseling for gifted females. *Gifted Child Today Magazine.*

Kaplan, S. N., Henderson, C. E., Henderson, J., & Fleming, D. L. (2002). Socio-emotional factors contributing to adjustment among early-entrance College students. *Gifted Child Quarterly, 46*(2), 124-134.

Kline, B. E., & Short, E. B. (1991). Changes in emotional resilience: gifted adolescent boys. *Roeper Review, 13*(4), 184 -187.

Kline, B. E., & Short, E. B. (1991). Changes in emotional resilience: gifted adolescent females. *Roeper Review, 13*(3), 118 -121.

Kohlberg, L. (1971). Stages of moral development as the basis for moral education. In C. M. Beck, B. S. Crittenden & E. V. Sullivan (Eds.), *Moral education: Interdisciplinary approaches* (pp. 23-92). New York: Newman Press.

Lipman, M. (1991). *Thinking in education*. Cambridge: Cambridge University Press.

Lipman, M. (1995). Caring as Thinking. Retrieved 21 May 2006, from http://www.chss.montclair.edu/inquiry/fall95/lipman.html

Lovecky, D. (1998). Spiritual sensitivity in gifted children. *Roeper Review, 20*(3), 178.

Maker, C. J. (1982). *Teaching Models in education for the gifted*. Rockville, MD: Aspen.

Piirto, J. (2000, Nov/Dec). The Piirto Pyramid of talent development. *Gifted Child Today*.

Piirto, J. (1999). *Talented children and adults: their development and education* (2nd ed.). Upper Saddle River, New Jersey: Prentice-Hall.

Piechowski, M. (2006). *"Mellow out" They say. If only I could: Intensities and sensitivities of the young and bright.* Madison WI: Yunasa Books.

Pohl, M. (2000). *Teaching complex thinking: critical, creative, caring*. Victoria: Hawker Brownlow Education.

Rimm, S. B. (2008). *Why bright kids get poor grades and what you can do about it.* (3rd ed.). Scottsdale, AZ: Great Potential Press.

Schmitz, C. C., & Galbraith, J. (1985). *Managing the social and emotional needs of the gifted: A teacher's survival guide.* Melbourne: Hawker Brownlow Education.

Sisk, D. A. (2009). *Making great kids greater: easing the burden of being gifted.* Thousand Oaks, CA: Corwin Press Inc.

Sisk, D., & Torrance, E. P. (2001). *Spiritual intelligence: developing higher consciousness.* Buffalo, NY: The Creative Education Foundation Press.

Tieso, C. (1999, May/Jun). Meeting the socio-emotional needs of talented teens. *Gifted Child Today Magazine.*

VanTassel-Baska, J. L., Cross, T. L., & Olenchak, R. F. (Eds.). (2009). *Social-emotional curriculum with gifted and talented students.* Waco TX: Prufrock Press.

White, S. (2010). Practical illustrations of global awareness activities in New Zealand schools. *Gifted Education International, 27* pp 34-38.

Chapter 8. Beyond Blooms: Williams Taxonomy

At the heart of science is an essential balance between
two seemingly contradictory attitudes –
an openness to new ideas, no matter how bizarre or counterintuitive,
and the most ruthlessly sceptical scrutiny of all ideas,
old and new
-   Carl Sagan in 'The Demon-Haunted World'.

Williams Dimension II Strategies as described in Williams Model is an extraordinarily rich source of higher order thinking tools that is often under-utilised by teachers[20].   This section briefly describes Williams Taxonomy tools and strategies, and elaborates on some with examples of how these might be applied in various subject areas.

8.1 Williams Model

This model integrates well within other models, (e.g. the DPI model, Renzulli's SEM, Kaplan's Grid, Maker's Model, etc.).

Williams Model has three dimensions all of which intersect.

Dimension I represents all the areas of the Curriculum.

Dimension II contains 18 teaching strategies for teachers to use to develop student thinking and creativity. These are elaborated upon in this section in some depth.

Dimension III represents the ideal student behaviours that result when Dimensions I and II are applied.

---

[20] Williams, F.E. (1993). The cognitive-affective interaction model for enriching gifted programs. In J.S. Renzulli (Ed.), *Systems and models for developing programs for the gifted and talented* (pp. 461-484). Highett, Vic.: Hawker Brownlow.

Dimension II: William's 18 teaching strategies

The 18 teaching Strategies in William's Taxonomy which develop cognitive and affective behaviours are:

1. Paradox: Common idea not necessarily true; self-contradictory statement or observation. A statement or proposition which seems to be contradictory, but may express a truth.

2. Attribute Listing: Unpacking inherent properties or qualities of things, concepts, situations, models, persons; (Analysis).

3. Analogy: Comparing one thing to another. Finding similarities between things or situations that may in other ways be different.

4. Discrepancy: Finding the gaps of limitations in knowledge; what's missing; what is not known; the exploration of deficiencies in opinions, or ideas.

5. Provocative Statements: Statements or questions that provoke thought and require careful consideration before responding. They may demand clarification or develop new knowledge.

6. Examples of Change: Understanding the dynamic nature of things and how things change over time. Provide opportunities for making alterations, modifications or substitutions.

7. Examples of Habit: Effects of habit-bound thinking. Build sensitivity about rigidity in ideas and habitual behaviours, methods, traditions or systems.

8. Organized Random Search: Investigate a body of knowledge, situation, structure or method and explore what other options there may be.

9. Skills of Search: Research the ways something has been done before, or is currently done. Examine cause and effect, analyze results, and draw conclusions. Research: trial and error on new ways.

       Designing Defensible Programs for Gifted Secondary School Learners © Sonia White 2011

10. Tolerance for Ambiguity: Situations, events, comments or ideas that may mean one thing or another thing entirely. These puzzle, intrigue, or challenge thinking, are open-ended and do not force closure.

11. Intuitive Expression: Using intuition and being sensitive to inner hunches or nudges.

12. Adjustment to Development: Learning from mistakes and failures; explore how mistakes and failures have led to significant discoveries; develop from, rather than adjust to something; develop many options or possibilities.

13. Study Creative Process: Analyze the traits and characteristics of eminently creative people through biographies; analyze creative processes such as problem finding and solving, invention, incubation, and insight.

14. Evaluate Situations: Consider the implications and potential consequences, outcomes or possibilities of situations.

15. Creative Reading Skills: Generating as many ideas as possible after reading a text.

16. Creative Listening Skills: Generating as many ideas as possible after listening to story /music/ speech etc.

17. Creative Writing Skills: generating and communicating creative ideas in writing

18. Visualization: Opportunities for students to perceive or visualize themselves in many contexts; express ideas or concepts in a visual format; illustrate thoughts and feelings.

TIP: Most of these strategies are particularly suited to more able learners and the remaining, which are suitable for all learners, can be differentiated through modifying the content, process, or product.

Dimension III

When students are working on Williams Taxonomy strategies in Dimension II, they should be demonstrating, or learning to demonstrate 8 key behaviours described in **Dimension III**:

<table>
<tr><td rowspan="4">COGNITIVE BEHAVIOURS</td><td>FLUENCY – generation of a quantity of relevant responses</td></tr>
<tr><td>FLEXIBILITY – variety of ideas or a shift in categories and directions of thought</td></tr>
<tr><td>ELABORATION – embellishment or improvement of ideas; addition of details</td></tr>
<tr><td>ORIGINALITY – unusual and /or unique ideas and responses, movement away from the obvious</td></tr>
<tr><td rowspan="4">AFFECTIVE BEHAVIOURS</td><td>RISK-TAKING – expose oneself to failure; take a guess; function in unstructured conditions</td></tr>
<tr><td>CURIOSITY – be inquisitive; toy with ideas; follow hunches; be open to puzzlement</td></tr>
<tr><td>COMPLEXITY – delve into intricate problems willingly; seek alternatives; see gaps</td></tr>
<tr><td>IMAGINATION – visualise; build mental images; feel intuitively; reach beyond reality</td></tr>
</table>

Figure 74. Williams Taxonomy Dimension II

The classroom environment impacts upon the degree to which students exhibit these behaviours. The cognitive behaviours described are those that can be enhanced by teaching strategies that demand fluency, flexibility, elaboration and originality.

Teacher expectations, flexibility, tolerance of ambiguity, and encouragement of 'ideas risk-taking' will all affect students' affective behaviours. A learning environment where it is safe to take risks by offering ideas that are different or may be 'wrong', and where the joy of exploration, curiosity and puzzlement is celebrated, fosters the desirable risk-taking and curiosity behaviours. Similarly, the classroom where critical reasoning and critique of concepts and ideas is valued and creativity and lateral thinking is appreciated will also foster complexity and imagination. (See Chapter 6, Creativity p125 - 130 where Dimension II is elaborated upon further.)

Teachers can plan activities that promote these 8 affective behaviours. Regrettably, sometimes Dimension III is the only aspect of William's Model that some teachers use. They appear to be unaware that Dimension II is a rich source of inspiration for developing all of the above behaviours, and is a fundamental part of Williams Taxonomy.

8.2 Exploring Williams' Taxonomy Dimension II Activities

It is worthwhile investing time in exploring and sharing these activities amongst your colleagues. To that end, examples of many of the strategies are given on pages 184 - 190.

The following approach is recommended for professional learning groups:

Work in pairs or threes.

TASK 1
A. **Choose 1 of the first 4 Strategies examples:** Paradox, Provocative Statements, Discrepancies, and Examples of Habit (pages 184 - 187). (Different strategies each pair).

Your Goals:
- to be able to explain to others what the strategy is
- to design an extension activity for a group of your own students

B. Read and discuss.
Take your time! If you don't understand it yourself, you will have difficulty explaining it to others.

C. Design an activity that is appropriate for your more able students, which you can trial in the next week or so.
When designing your own activity to match the Teaching Strategy, use the **Template** on page 191 (figure 76).
Consider:
- instructions that will accompany it, regarding expected process and possible end product.
- What the learning outcome will be for the students who do this activity. (The 'so what?' factor).
- The type of thinking required (lower order / higher order / complex/ abstract)
- Whether *all* students in the class could do the activity, and if so,
- How the activity could be made more challenging for gifted learners.
- What the success criteria are for successful completion of this complex task.

NOTE: While it is not expected that teachers would fill in this template every time they design a learning activity, following this process helps teachers analyse the actual strategy and the value of its inclusion in their teacher's toolkit.

D. Share: Explain the strategy to others. Discuss. Listen to others explain their strategies. Take notes about the other strategies that are being explained.

TASK 2. Choose another strategy each, and repeat the process.

Figure 75 Williams Taxonomy: Teacher Learning Tasks

PARADOXES

A statement or proposition which seems to be contradictory, but may express a truth. Present students with paradoxes to analyse and test. Paradoxes can be used to evaluate ideas & to challenge students to reason and find proof.

"Sometimes one has to be cruel to be kind". Explore this paradox through considering which music may best confirm or contradict this paradox. Collect short excerpts as examples to put together a taped musical illustration of this paradox. Be prepared to present an explanation of how these excerpts either contradict or confirm the paradox.

Diluted nitric acid will corrode steel, while concentrated nitric acid doesn't.

You are an Israeli who is against concentration camps. Defend the need for American concentration camps for Al Quada terrorists.

"Less is more, Lucretia" – Robert Browning. Examine the work of two significant artists and consider ways that this paradox could be considered true of their work. Prepare a talk to explain your views to the group.

Increasing the food available to an ecosystem may lead to instability, and even to extinction.

Why is bottled water more expensive than soda, when humans need water to survive, not soda? How does this paradox relate to your current area of study? Discuss the parallels that can be drawn, and draw a conclusion.

Prepare a short argument on 'Integrity gets in the way of a good story'.

"Paradoxically though it may seem, it is none the less true that life imitates art far more than art imitates life" Oscar Wilde

"And the greatest paradox of them all is 'civilized warfare'" – source unknown.

"Only one thing is certain – that is, nothing is certain. If this statement is true, it is also false." - Ancient Paradox.

"There is nothing in the world more soft than water, yet for attacking things that are hard and strong, there is nothing that surpasses it; nothing can take its place. – Lao-Tzu

"The more we know, the more we know we don't know" – anonymous.

 "Man learns from history that Man learns nothing from history".

"Can an irresistible force move an immovable object?"

Your Turn: ✍

A rich source of Paradoxes in all subjects: http://en.wikipedia.org/wiki/List_of_paradoxes
Mathematics specific: http://en.wikipedia.org/wiki/Category:Mathematics_paradoxes
More paradoxes (Eschler, Maths, Logic,) on http://www.paradoxes.co.uk

Examine one of Michael Moore's documentaries (or a similar political documentary)

What discrepancies can you find?

Why have introduced animals or plants such as possums and gorse become a problem in some countries, but not in their native environment?

DISCREPANCIES

Gaps of limitations in knowledge
Missing links in information
What is not known?

Williams is referring to the exploration of deficiencies in a person's understandings. Allow students to think about discrepancies in what is known, and be challenged to discuss what is not known or understood.

Investigate the differences between fact and perceptions e.g. select an issue in the news where perspective is clouded by propaganda.

SOME DISCREPANCY DISCOVERY QUESTIONS:
- What information is being disregarded or left out here?
- Whose conflicting opinions are not stated?
- What bias does the author have?
- What conclusion would the author have me draw?
- What will be the result in my believing this?
- How valid are the claims made here? What if…?
- How many other reliable sources confirm this?

Investigate discrepancies between findings of related science research – (take from current research reported in newspapers).

Select a book / article / letter to the editor about (a current social issue under debate). Whose opinions are not being voiced? Make a list, and describe the key opinions that others would hold. Choose one opinion to voice and make a case.

Take a persuasive, convincing argument for an historical scientific belief (e.g. flat earth) and prepare to argue an opposing viewpoint given only the evidence that would have been available at the time.

Are there obvious discrepancies between what is said and what is done by the main character? What appears to be the motivation for these discrepancies?

You have been given an article on (X topic) which supports (e.g. smoking, marijuana, other high risk activities). What information has been left out? What will be the result of my believing this?

Take two different methods of solving a problem and compare them. What is left out in one that is in the other? Which method is more effective in your opinion, and why?

Your Turn: ✍

PROVOCATIVE STATEMENTS
Inquiry to incite exploration and curiosity

These are STATEMENTS or QUESTIONS that give pause for thought and require careful consideration before responding. They may demand clarification or develop new knowledge. Many types of challenging questions can be posed to elicit higher-order thinking using Bloom's Taxonomy, e.g. questions that require analysis, synthesis and evaluation.

Ask provocative questions *and allow time for inquiry.*

Provocative questions or statements are structured by both teacher and students to elicit higher-order thinking, e.g. a class dialogue on the topic *"In what instances can portraying human frailties be justified by the media?"*

Does music / art Television / sport reflect a culture or shape it? Consider, then take a stance and defend it.

What is the relationship between greed and peace?

How would the world appear different if humans could only perceive the colour green? What might change? Examine how this would impact upon the media you are currently exploring.

A cube is like a sphere. Explain, giving as many similarities as possible.

Take a favoured attitude or opinion and ask a question that promotes a differing view.

Does Science matter? Should we improve our genome? Can robots become conscious? Are men necessary? …are women necessary? Could we live forever? What happened before the Big Bang? How much of the body is replaceable? What is gravity, really? Will we ever find Atlantis? Is war our biological destiny? (Source: see below)

Why do people fear things that are new or people who are different?

Did (villain in film /novel) feel he had a moral right to do what s/he did? What might have led him/her to this belief?

A non-conformist is conforming to non-conformity. Discuss this in relation to (X) character /historical figure.

Science: more from http://www.nytimes.com/indexes/2003/11/10/science/text/index.html

Your Turn: ✍

 Designing Defensible Programs for Gifted Secondary School Learners © Sonia White 2011

EXAMPLES OF HABIT

Effects of habit-bound thinking
Building sensitivity against rigidity in ideas and well-tried ways

Use examples of habit and the results of habit-bound thinking. Teach about rigidity, fixations and habitual thinking.

Examine examples that demonstrate rigidity and inflexibility. E.g. stereotypical portrayal of people, places and ideas in the media, such as politicians or cultures

Any activity which examines stereotypical portrayals of people, places, ideas, and causes students to challenge them

Consider architecture and locations that create an illusion of defying gravity. Explain the phenomenon.

What types of habit-bound thinking led to events such as the Holocaust? How was such thinking popularised? Compare and contrast this with an aspect of current habit-bound thinking.

How does habit-bound thinking impact upon health in our community? What positives can we take from this? What myths or misinformation need to be 'debunked'?

There is a limit to what the human body can achieve. Or is there? Consider / research outstanding physical feats of the past that have been exceeded today. Investigate the reasons for this and consider future trends.

Art is a slavish follower of fashion. Consider this statement with reference to an historical art movement, and consider the 'habitual' thinking that had to be discarded for a new art movement to be formed.

Examine a character in (film/play/book) whose rigidity of thinking impeded his / her fortunes, or his / her personal growth. What circumstances or character traits do you believe created this rigidity of thinking? Give examples to support your conclusions.

Is rigidity of thinking synonymous with holding on to one's ethics and morals? Why / why not?

Choose a traditional idea /method /approach and consider its strengths as well as the problems that might arise by continuing to follow it. Devise a fresh approach that embraces the best of the 'old'. Convince others of your improvements.

Your Turn: ✍

<table>
<tr><td>**ANALOGIES**</td><td>Comparing one thing to another. Finding similarities between things or situations that may in other ways be different.
Tip: Use unusual combinations to force considered thinking.</td></tr>
</table>

How are electricity and water similar? Consider current, voltage, resistance, capacity and flow and any other attribute you consider significant.

Create a presentation that answers the question: "How was the Maoist revolution like a clock?"

How was Nazi Propaganda like a popular television show? Develop this analogy to demonstrate the complexities of political spin.

How is the work of Picasso similar to the work of Michelangelo? (or a specific art movement with a different art movement; one art medium with another). Consider which is more effective against criteria appropriate for the subjects being compared.

How is King Lear (or another Shakespearean character) like Nelson Mandela (or: another world leader / well-known personality/ cartoon character / film character.

Your Turn: ✍

<table>
<tr><td>**EXAMPLES OF CHANGE**</td><td>Understanding the dynamic nature of things and how things change over time. Provide opportunities for making alterations, modifications or substitutions.</td></tr>
</table>

How has technology impacted upon personal privacy? Consider viable solutions to some of the issues.

What issues has genetic engineering raised that may need to be addressed through legislation or ethics committees?

Track the significant changes in (x) music or art movement as it developed. Consider the value of the alterations.

Investigate a key law change in your country that has changed the way people deal with a specific issue.

Knowledge about (x topic) has developed over the last 100 years. Compare and discuss a recent development with reference to earlier beliefs.

How has high performance athlete training changed over the last 50 years? What impact has this had upon sports injuries?

Your Turn: ✍

INTUITIVE EXPRESSION	Using intuition and being sensitive to inner hunches or nudges. • Consider the role of intuition in decision making and investigation. • The arts are our natural expression of intuitive response. Consider activities in your subject area that students can use to better understand concepts or issues, (e.g. through poetry, art, dance, rap, photo essay, political cartoon, role play).

Role play a mock trial of Christopher Columbus

Research a scientist in (X) field who has had success through investigating a hunch. Consider the barriers to be overcome and the emotions involved

Consider the role of intuition and the importance of senses to medical professionals when making a diagnosis.

Music in film provides important auditory clues to the audience. Examine examples of this in (X) movie, and evaluate how effectively this has been done. Give evidence to support your opinions.

Your Turn: ✍

TOLERANCE FOR AMBIGUITY	Situations, events, comments or ideas that may mean one thing or another thing entirely. These should puzzle, intrigue, or challenge thinking. They should be open-ended and not force closure, (e.g. moral dilemmas (pp 171-173), scientific conundrums).

Investigate a topical current issue. Interview a broad range of ages to research varying opinions. Consider the validity of individual perspectives.

Design a recreational room for a blind person. Consider aspects that sighted people take for granted, and find solutions to possible barriers to use of equipment or technology.

Investigate conflicting human migratory theories e.g. the populating of South America, or the Pacific Islands & New Zealand. Defend an opinion.

Investigate products that have been designed to answer a need that doesn't really exist. How have they been advertised?

Characters in books often demand one thing of others, yet do the opposite. Consider examples where this ambiguity exists, and discuss. Give thought to the complexities of the character and the situation. What similar examples occur in real life?

Your Turn: ✍

Investigate a body of knowledge, situation, structure or method and explore what other options there may be.

Examine the methods used for tooth extraction /medical intervention / scientific experiment 100 years ago. Choose ONE modern invention and explore the difference in methodology and possible varying outcomes. Justify the conclusions you draw.

Consider a specific law that is currently under discussion in your country. Investigate how this same issue is dealt with in other countries, and what changes you might recommend and why.

Consider a decision made by an historical figure (X), given the situation, personal beliefs and the information at the time. Assemble factual information that is now available about that situation, and decide how X may have responded 'with hindsight'. Justify your conclusions with reference to the individual's thinking, character and beliefs.

Consider ways of adapting a specific genre (film /writing / art medium) by including elements of a different genre.

Your Turn: ✍

Research the ways something has been done before, or is currently done. Examine cause and effect, analyze results, and draw conclusions. Research on something done before: trial and error on new ways.

Examine the link between bullying and use of cell phones by teenagers. Consider other research in this area, claims made, conclusions drawn, and potential solutions. Trial a solution to this problem; analyse the results/ make adjustments and recommendations (See Caring Thinking Chapter – Active & Normative Thinking).

Research the differences in the modern manufacture of (X) and methodology used in earlier times. Consider both the positive and negative differences & the short, medium and long term effects of change.

Research the benefits of having a control group in experiments and investigate faulty application and consequent misinterpretation of data.

Your Turn: ✍

WILLIAMS TAXONOMY Activity /Assessment Task Planner

Curriculum Area: _________________________   **Level:** _____

Activity:

Learning Outcomes:

Type of thinking required:

Is this activity more challenging than many of the class could manage successfully? (Could, Would, Should Rule)

YES

NO

Figure

What activities could this activity <u>replace</u>, so students choosing to do this activity wouldn't have to do extra?
(Quality, not quantity, of work)

Ideas for alternative (more complex) adaptations:

What criteria would indicate successful completion of this task?
Students can:

Figure 76 Williams Taxonomy Dimension II Planning Template 1

Williams Taxonomy Dimension II Planning Template	
Paradox	Common idea not necessarily true; self-contradictory statement or observation. A statement or proposition which seems to be contradictory, but may express a truth.	
Attribute Listing	Unpacking inherent properties or qualities of things, concepts, situations, models, persons; (Analysis).	
Analogy	Comparing one thing to another. Finding similarities between things or situations that may in other ways be different.	
Discrepancy	Comparing one thing to another. Finding similarities between things or situations that may in other ways be different.	
Provocative Statements	Statements or questions that provoke thought and require careful consideration before responding. They may demand clarification or develop new knowledge.	
Examples of Change	Understanding the dynamic nature of things and how things change over time. Provide opportunities for making alterations, modifications or substitutions.	
Examples of Habit	Effects of habit-bound thinking. Build sensitivity about rigidity in ideas and habitual behaviours, methods, traditions or systems.	
Organised Random Search	Investigate a body of knowledge, situation, structure or method and explore what other options there may be.	
Skills of Search	Research how something has been done before, or is currently done. Examine cause & effect, analyze results, & draw conclusions. Research: trial & error on new ways.	

Figure 77 Williams Taxonomy Dimension II Planning Template 2a

   Designing Defensible Programs for Gifted Secondary School Learners © Sonia White 2011

Tolerance for Ambiguity	Situations or ideas that may mean one thing or another thing entirely. These puzzle, intrigue, or challenge, are open-ended and do not force closure.	
Intuitive Expression	Using intuition and being sensitive to inner hunches or nudges.	
Adjustment to Development	Learning from mistakes and failures; explore mistakes & failures that led to significant discoveries; develop from, rather than adjust to something; develop many options or possibilities.	
Study Creative Process	Analyze traits & characteristics of eminently creative people through biographies; analyze creative processes e.g. problem finding & solving, invention, incubation, & insight.	
Evaluate Situations	Consider the implications and potential consequences, outcomes or possibilities of situations.	
Creative Reading Skills	Generating as many ideas as possible after reading a text.	
Creative Listening Skills	Generating as many ideas as possible after listening to story /music/ speech etc.	
Creative Writing Skills	Generating and communicating creative ideas in writing	
Visualisation	Opportunities for students to perceive or visualize themselves in many contexts; express ideas or concepts in a visual format; illustrate thoughts and feelings.	

Figure 78 Williams Taxonomy Dimension II Planning Template 2b

NOTES:

Readings

Davis, G. A., & Rimm, S. B. (2003). *Education of the Gifted and Talented* (5th ed.). Needham Heights, MA: Allyn and Bacon, Inc.

Forte, I., & Schuur, S. (1997). *Tools, treasures and measures of Middle School success.* Australia: Hawker Brownlow Education.

Gross, M., Macleod, B., & Pretorius, M. (2001). *Gifted students in secondary schools: differentiating the curriculum* (2nd ed.). Sydney: Gifted Education Research, Resource and information Centre (GERRIC), UNSW.

Le Sueur, E. (2010). *Provocative Questions: expanding horizons for thinking.* Nelson, New Zealand: Thinkshop Thinking Resources Ltd.

Le Sueur, E. (2006). *Higher order thinking units for gifted readers: using sophisticated picture books.* Nelson, New Zealand: Thinkshop Thinking Resources Ltd.

MacLeod, B. (2004). *Gifted & Talented Education Professional Development Package for Teachers: Module 5.* From http://www.dest.gov.au/NR/rdonlyres/54063D73-3271-4AF1-84AF-10E601B26F38/5469/Module5_SECONDARY.pdf.

NSW Dept of Education & Training. (2004). The Williams Model: Extract from Support package: Curriculum differentiation. From http://www.curriculumsupport.education.nsw.gov.au/policies/gats/assets/pdf/uhsi3hstanzac.pdf

Phye, G. D. (1997). *Handbook of academic learning: construction of knowledge.* San Diego: Academic Press.

Pohl, M. (2002). *Infusing thinking into the middle years: a resource book for schools.* Victoria, Australia: Hawker Brownlow.

Riley, T. L. (2004). Curriculum models: the framework for educational programmes. In D. McAlpine & R. Moltzen (Eds.), *Gifted and talented: New Zealand perspectives* (2nd ed., pp. 309-344). Palmerston North, New Zealand: ERDC Press.

Williams, F. E. (1993). The cognitive-affective interaction model for enriching gifted programs. In J. S. Renzulli (Ed.), *Systems and models for developing programs for the gifted and talented* (pp. 461-484). Highett, Vic.: Hawker Brownlow.

Chapter 9. Pulling it all together

The beginning of wisdom is found in doubting;
by doubting we come to the question,
and by seeking we may come upon the truth.
- Pierre Abelard

This handbook has been designed so teachers can dip in and out of different sections during their ongoing drive to develop their units of work and classroom pedagogy. There will be times that one section holds far more significance than another, and time spent reflecting upon, and developing a specific area will be at the expense of others. This is a natural part of the learning process, which is not so much cyclical as needs-based, timely and meaningful in the context of each teacher's professional journey.

How to use strategies such as Williams Taxonomy, Thinkers Keys and Socratic Questions for Assessment, Teaching Practice and Thinking

This final chapter responds to a question teachers often ask when practicing teacher inquiry:

"All these teaching strategies are great – but how and where can we use them effectively?"

The answer is "in multiple ways" – and creative teachers will no doubt be able to add to the suggestions given over the next seven pages.

Figure 79 gives an overview showing the three major areas of Teaching Practice, Thinking, and Assessment in which the strategies can be used. The remaining pages elaborate on each of these, with suggestions and recommendations.

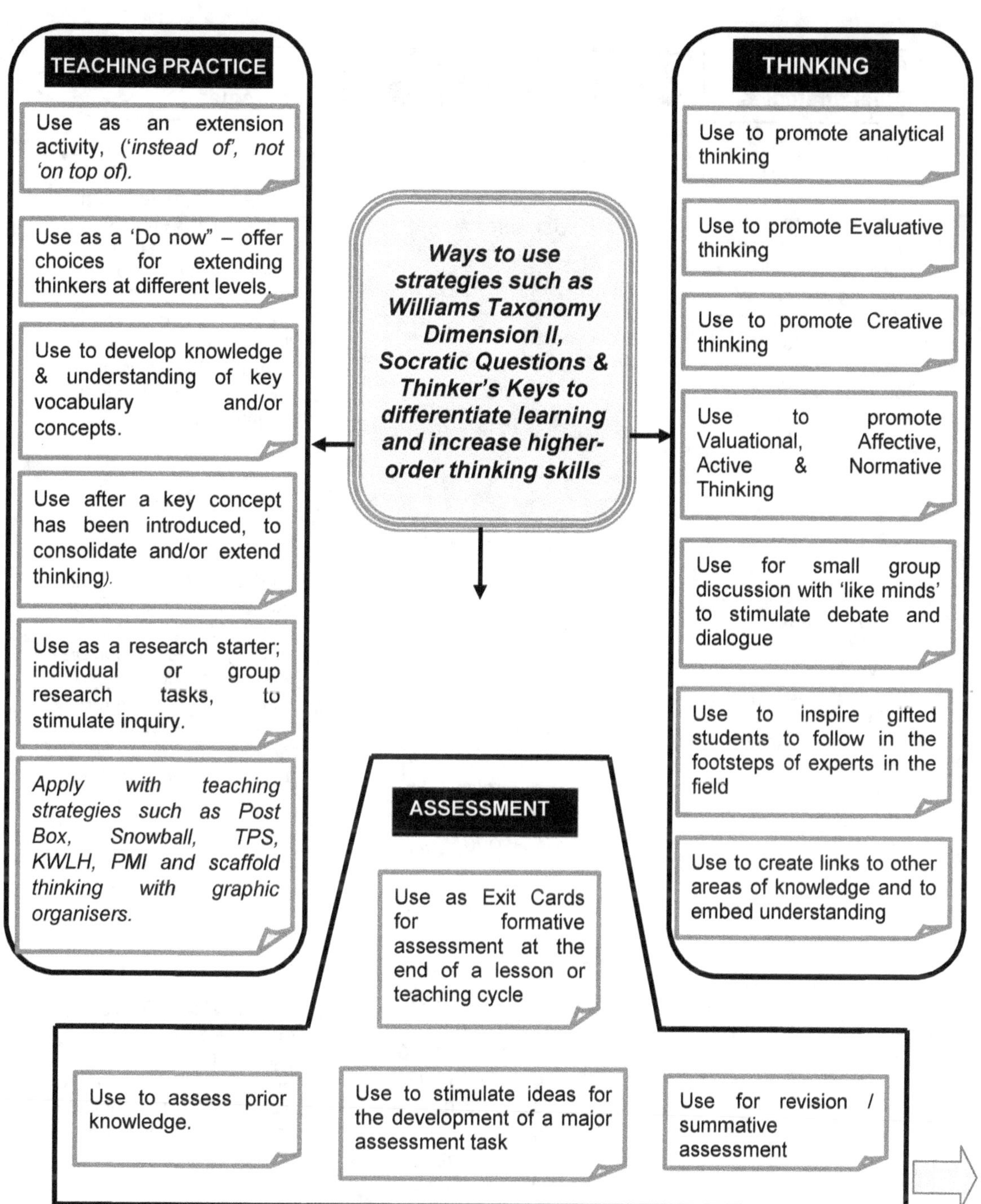

Figure 79 Overview of Use of Strategies & Tools for Learning

<table>
<tr>
<td>Thinker's Keys & Other strategies</td>
<td>TEACHING PRACTICE</td>
<td>William's Taxonomy Strategies</td>
</tr>
<tr>
<td>Thinkers Keys where complex instructions have been added to ensure depth of thinking (e.g. justify / evaluate/ consider medium and long term consequences of/ give the opposing point of view) Socratic Questions</td>
<td>Use after a key concept has been introduced, to consolidate and/or extend thinking – (differentiate difficulty level)</td>
<td>Paradox; Attribute listing; Analogy; Discrepancy; Provocative question; Examples of change; examples of habit; `organised random search; Skills of Search; Tolerance for Ambiguity; Adjustment to Development; Evaluate situations</td>
</tr>
<tr>
<td>Reverse Key; Alphabet Key; 'What if' Key; Disadvantages Key; Picture Key; Interpretation Key; S.C.A.M.P.E.R. Socratic Questions</td>
<td>Use as an extension activity, 'instead of, not on top of'. (Promote independent learning, while other groups revise / go over basics / do easier, consolidating work)</td>
<td>Attribute Listing; Organised Random search; skills of search; (most William's strategies are too complex to be done quickly if they are done well – however, one could be used to cover several days as an option to choosing other "Do Now's").</td>
</tr>
<tr>
<td>Any of the Thinker's Keys; CoRT thinking skills; Six Hats; Socratic Questions;</td>
<td>Use as a 'Do now" – offer differentiated choices for extending thinkers at different levels. Use of Flow charts, T Charts, Venn Diagrams, Fishbone, and similar will help students structure their thoughts cohesively.</td>
<td>Any of Williams Tools /Strategies (Note – the William's Strategies could be for the hardest level, the Thinker's Keys for moderate and easier level)

Continued next page</td>
</tr>
</table>

 Designing Defensible Programs for Gifted Secondary School Learners © Sonia White 2011

<table>
<tr><th>Thinker's Keys & Other strategies</th><th>TEACHING PRACTICE
Continued</th><th>William's Taxonomy Strategies</th></tr>
<tr><td>Prediction; Interpretation; Construction, Brick Wall, What if? (married with short, medium & long term consequences or other CoRT Thinking tools) In some cases: the Reverse Key.</td><td>Use as a research starter; individual or group research tasks, to stimulate inquiry. *Use Flow charts, T Charts, Venn Diagrams, Fishbone, so students can structure their thoughts cohesively.*</td><td>Provocative Question; Paradox; Analogy; Discrepancies; Examples of Change; Examples of Habit; Organised random search; Skills of Search; Tolerance for Ambiguity;</td></tr>
<tr><td>Question Key; Attributes Key; Commonality Key;</td><td>Use to develop knowledge and understanding of key vocabulary and/or concepts</td><td>Attribute listing; Organised Random Search; Visualisation</td></tr>
<tr><td>Socratic Questions, all Thinkers Keys, providing the instructions match the learner-readiness level of the group – *(levels based on complexity of thinking required &/or prior knowledge and skills)*</td><td>Use for small group discussion with 'like minds' *(allow higher ability groups to work together at times)* with "Bus Stop" style dialogue; Think, Pair Share; Snowball, or similar dialogue strategies;</td><td>Analogy, Paradox, Examples of Habit; Examples of Change; Provocative Question; Discrepancy; Tolerance for Ambiguity; Evaluate situations; Adjustment to development</td></tr>
</table>

Thinker's Keys & Other strategies	THINKING	William's Taxonomy Strategies
Attributes Key; Commonality Key; CoRT thinking: P.M.I; C.A.F; OPV; C & S; A.G.O; F.I.P; Socratic Questions	Use to promote **analytical thinking** *(Add instructions /questions to ensure depth of thought)* *Use Flow charts, T Charts, Venn Diagrams, Fishbone, and similar*	Paradox, Analogy, Attribute listing; Discrepancy; Provocative Question; Examples of Change; Examples of Habit; Organised Random Search; Skills of Search;
Disadvantages Key; Ridiculous Key; Skills in development of criteria & ranking; Associated CoRT thinking tools: P.M.I; C.A.F; OPV; C & S;	Use to promote **evaluative thinking** *(Add instructions /questions to ensure depth of thought) Use of graphic organisers, matrices criteria, rank ordering and similar techniques will help students evaluate effectively.*	Evaluate Situations; Attribute Listing; Discrepancy; Examples of habit; Adjustment to Development; Provocative Questions; Examples of Change; Examples of Habit; Organised random search; Skills of Search; Tolerance for Ambiguity;
Thinkers Keys: Reverse; 'What if?'; BAR; Variations; Picture; Combination; Forced Relationship; Alternative;	Use to promote **creative thinking** *(Add instructions /questions to ensure depth of thought, especially to promote critical thinking after the creative idea has surfaced. The creative process requires critical thinking as well)*	Paradox; Analogy; Provocative Question; Examples of Change; Adjustment to Development; Study creative people and process; Intuitive expression; Creative reading skill; Creative Listening Skill; Creative Writing Skill; Visualisation;

Continued next page

Thinker's Keys & Other strategies

THINKING
Continued

William's Taxonomy Strategies

Ethical questions & moral dilemmas;
Any activity which requires students to reflect on: what they value, the ethics of a situation, ideals versus norms, and proactive ways in which situations can be improved.
Associated CoRT thinking tools: P.M.I; C.A.F; OPV; C & S;

Use to promote **Valuational, Affective, Active and Normative Thinking** *(ethics, values, citizenship) – (add instructions /questions to ensure depth of thought and follow-through).*

Evaluate situations; Paradox; Analogy; Study creative people and process; Tolerance for Ambiguity; Adjustment to Development; Provocative Questions; Examples of change; Examples of habit; Skills of search; study creative people and process;

Use to inspire gifted students to follow in the footsteps of experts in the field.

Study creative people and process; *(biographies of eminent in field: achievements: barriers they faced; processes which led to problem-finding and solving, invention, incubation and insight. How they were as people);*

Adjustment to development; Examples of Habit; Examples of Change; *(linked to the life and work of an eminent person in the field)*

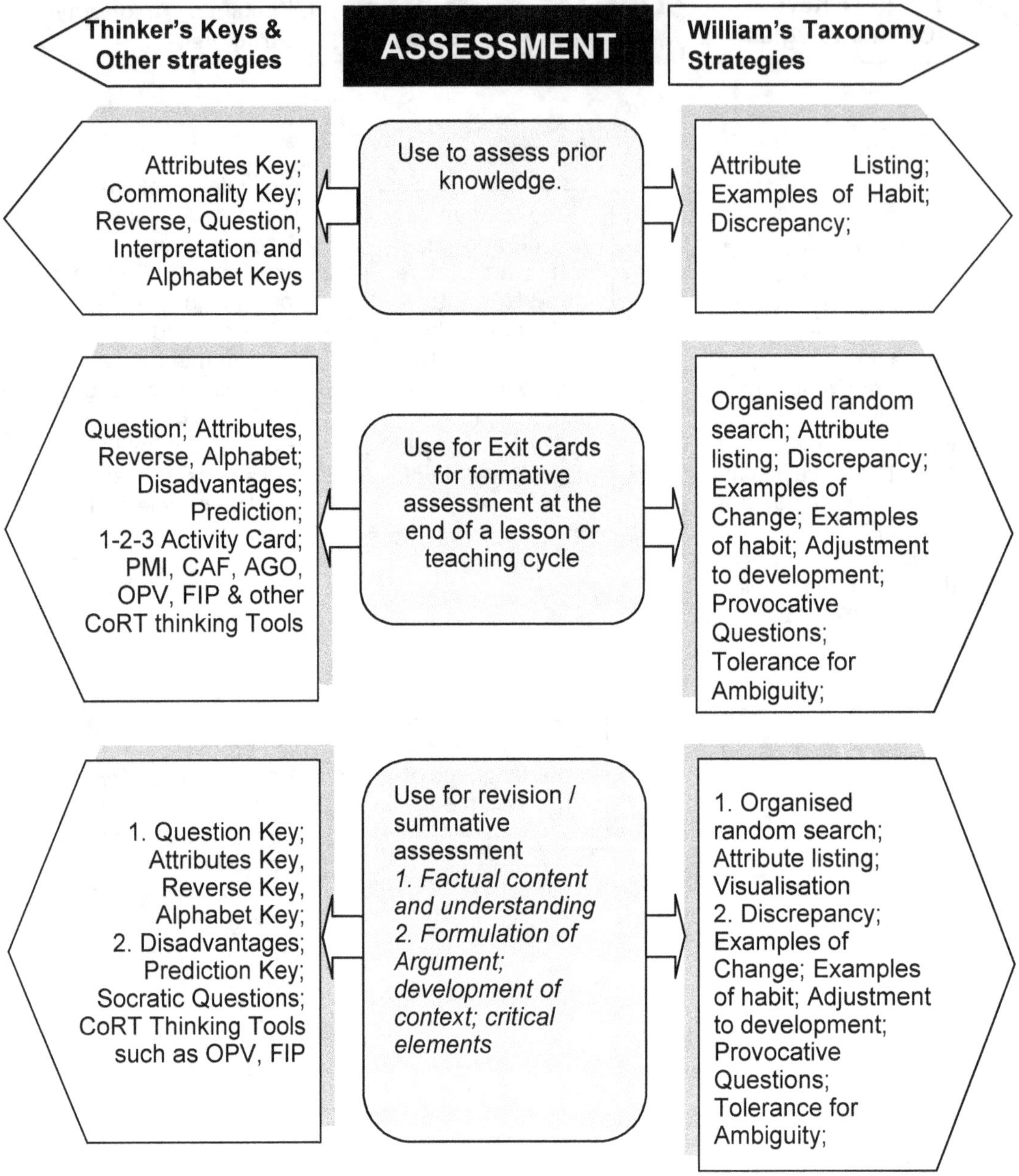

Continued next page

    Designing Defensible Programs for Gifted Secondary School Learners © Sonia White 2011

The more complex Thinkers Keys such as Prediction; Interpretation; Construction, Brick Wall, What if? (married with short, medium & long term consequences or other CoRT Thinking tools) In some cases, the Reverse Key.

Use to stimulate ideas for the development of a major assessment task (include in instructions) / summative assessment. *Use of Flow charts, T Charts, Venn Diagrams, Fishbone, and similar will help students assemble their thoughts coherently.*

Tolerance for Ambiguity; Paradox; Analogy; Discrepancy; Provocative Question; Examples of Change; Examples of habit; Organised Random Search; Skills of Search; Adjustment to Development; Study Creative People &/ or Process; Evaluate situations;

Any Thinker's Keys, CoRT Thinking Tools, Socratic Questions, or other tools where you have required analytical, evaluative or creative thinking (preferably a blend of these) and/or valuational, affective, active and normative thinking.

Use to promote achievement at EXCELLENCE or SCHOLARSHIP level

Williams Taxonomy Strategies, especially first eleven. *See below.*

Williams Taxonomy Dimension II Strategies:

Paradox; Analogy; Attribute Listing; Discrepancies; Provocative questions/ statements; Examples of Change; Examples of Habit; Organised Random Search; Skills of search; Tolerance for ambiguity; Adjustment to development; Intuitive expression; Study creative people and process; Evaluate situations; Creative Reading skill; Creative listening skill; Creative writing skill; Visualisation. (See Chapter 8 for descriptors)

NOTES:

Afterword

So how far has your journey brought you? Sometimes in taking many small steps we do not have the sense of achievement we should have, so it is worthwhile taking the time to reflect on where we've been and discover just how far we have travelled.

Return to your original Graduate Profile, your vision for your gifted learners, and your starting place.

Celebrate each small step you have taken along the way and the point you have reached today.

Know that this process is just that: *a process*, not an end point.

Remember that one of the key reasons you value being in the teaching profession is the stimulus of the continual professional growth it demands.

Your vision becomes a reality over time.
Time.
Change takes time.
Lots of it.
Give it the time,
and the enormous amount of unfailing energy and commitment it deserves.

Surround yourselves with others who are prepared to embark on this journey,
Believe in it;
take those small steps one at a time,
and before long you will witness your students taking flight
and say

"This is right, this is what I should be doing, this is why I teach".